PHILIPPE LACOUE-L
(UN)TIMELY MEDI

LEGENDA

LEGENDA, founded in 1995 by the European Humanities Research Centre of the University of Oxford, is now a joint imprint of the Modern Humanities Research Association and Routledge. Titles range from medieval texts to contemporary cinema and form a widely comparative view of the modern humanities, including works on Arabic, Catalan, English, French, German, Greek, Italian, Portuguese, Russian, Spanish, and Yiddish literature. An Editorial Board of distinguished academic specialists works in collaboration with leading scholarly bodies such as the Society for French Studies, the British Comparative Literature Association and the Association of Hispanists of Great Britain & Ireland.

MHRA

The Modern Humanities Research Association (MHRA) encourages and promotes advanced study and research in the field of the modern humanities, especially modern European languages and literature, including English, and also cinema. It also aims to break down the barriers between scholars working in different disciplines and to maintain the unity of humanistic scholarship in the face of increasing specialization. The Association fulfils this purpose primarily through the publication of journals, bibliographies, monographs and other aids to research.

LONDON AND NEW YORK

Routledge is a global publisher of academic books, journals and online resources in the humanities and social sciences. Founded in 1836, it has published many of the greatest thinkers and scholars of the last hundred years, including adorno, einstein, Russell, Popper, Wittgenstein, Jung, Bohm, Hayek, Mcluhan, Marcuse and Sartre. Today Routledge is one of the world's leading academic publishers in the Humanities and Social Sciences. It publishes thousands of books and journals each year, serving scholars, instructors, and professional communities worldwide.

www.routledge.com

Many have tried, but in vain, with joy to say the most joyful;
Here at last I find it said fully, but in grave sadness.

HÖLDERLIN, 'Sophocles'

Philippe Lacoue-Labarthe

(Un)timely Meditations

John McKeane

Routledge
Taylor & Francis Group

LONDON AND NEW YORK

2015

First published 2015 by Modern Humanities Research Association and Routledge

2 Park Square, Milton Park, Abingdon, Oxfordshire OX14 4RN
52 Vanderbilt Avenue, New York, NY 10017

Routledge is an imprint of the Taylor & Francis Group, an informa business

First issued in paperback 2020

ISBN 13: 978-1-909662-42-1 (hbk)
ISBN 13: 978-0-367-60118-8 (pbk)

CONTENTS

Acknowledgements   ix

Abbreviations   x

Introduction   1

PART I: TIMELY MEDITATIONS

1   Avant-garde   11

2   Philosophy and the Political   33

3   L'Écriture   53

PART II: UNTIMELY MEDITATIONS

4a   The Stage (Introduction)   81

4b   The Stage (Tragedy)   87

4c   The Stage (Opera)   109

5   Phrase   129

Conclusion: Mimesis   151

Primary Bibliography   159

Secondary Bibliography   164

Bibliography of Translations into English   170

Index   173

ACKNOWLEDGEMENTS

I wish to thank first of all Claire — Nancy? Lacoue-Labarthe? —, who never failed to be generous and clear-eyed in her discussions with me.

Jean-Luc Nancy and Lucien Braun not only made time for my questions, but demonstrated their unwilting strength and commitment to thought. George Steiner, Jean-Christophe Bailly, and David and Maryse Burns were also supportive in various ways. Those associated with Lacoue-Labarthe's archive also deserve thanks, from Léonid Kharmalov and Aristide Bianchi to the staff of IMEC at the Abbaye d'Ardenne in Caen. I am also grateful to The Queen's College, Oxford, whose Laming Junior Fellowship allowed me to work on the project, and to the University of Warwick. Anna Davies did an excellent job in copy-editing the work, and I am indebted to her for this reason.

Much of the research was done in Paris, and to those who made life there possible, I am deeply indebted: Pascal, Beatrice, Ayalet, Silvia, Cristina, Chloé and Adrian, and the runners of Montrouge. Back across the channel, the generosity of Mary Burns assisted with the final stages of writing up. Hannes Opelz should also be thanked for our discussions over Lacoue-Labarthe and for reading sections of the work.

My deepest gratitude is reserved, as ever, for Lucy.

J.McK., London, August 2014

ABBREVIATIONS

Works in French

AL	*L'Absolu littéraire: Théorie de la littérature du romantisme allemand*
AN	*L'Animal*
AdS	*Antigone de Sophocle*
ALEG	*L''Allégorie'*
ATAI	*Agonie terminée, agonie interminable*
FH	*Les Fins de l'homme: à partir du travail de Jacques Derrida*
FP	*La Fiction du politique: Heidegger, l'art et la politique*
IM	*L'Imitation des modernes (Typographies I)*
PE	*La Poésie comme expérience*
PH	*Phrase*
SP	*Le Sujet de la philosophie (Typographies II)*

Translations into English

HAP	*Heidegger, Art and Politics: the Fiction of the Political*
LA	*The Literary Absolute: the Theory of Literature in German Romanticism*
PE2	*Poetry as Experience*
SP2	*The Subject of Philosophy*
TYP	*Typography: Mimesis, Philosophy, Politics*

INTRODUCTION

There is no right time, Nietzsche tells us, to die: one either goes too early or too late.[1] It is certainly a thought that we can consider following the death in 2007 of Philippe Lacoue-Labarthe. On the one hand, his death at the age of 66 deprives readers and students of his guidance concerning modern writing and thought. This study, for instance, is based on Lacoue-Labarthe's writing and published interviews, as well as on my correspondence and interviews with those who knew him: the project began too late for me to have met the man known as 'Philippe' or 'Lacoue'. On the other hand, perhaps death did not come too soon for someone who had written that 'je n'ai jamais pu ne pas penser à l'injustice qui nous fait naître [...]. [D]evant cette injustice-là, je n'ai jamais pu retenir ma colère' ['I have never been able not to think of the injustice that causes us to be born [...] [F]aced with this injustice, I have never been able to contain my anger'].[2] It would be wrongheaded and selfish to wish that this existential anger had been longer lived. In any case, it is an eerie phenomenon that since his death his frequency of publication has increased, with six posthumous publications to date and more on the way.

The question of timeliness or untimeliness, when applied to Lacoue-Labarthe's work, governs my approach in this study. No biography of him has yet appeared, and whilst I provide some indications of this nature, my aim is not to write a solely historical account, presenting his work as necessary, timely, and perhaps also — such is the pressure exerted by the critical gaze — inevitable. Such a study would doubtless have its uses, given the important role Lacoue-Labarthe played in French thought after 1968, both institutionally (he was president of the *Collège international de philosophie*) and in its dissemination in the wider world (he was visiting professor at UC Berkeley from 1981–93). Nonetheless, whilst my study engages in dialogue with Lacoue-Labarthe's contemporaries and their accounts of his thought, it also analyses his work as present and future readers might encounter it, which is to say not entirely as the remainder of a lived presence, but as a collection of texts readable in their own right. I do not claim that this approach is utterly radical; indeed Jacques Derrida, writing about his close relation to Lacoue-Labarthe and Jean-Luc Nancy, states that '[l]e plus urgent, j'essaierai de m'y employer, ce serait de rompre ici avec les airs de famille, d'éviter les tentations généalogiques, projections, assimilations ou identifications' ['the most urgent thing — I'll try to work on this — would be to break with the family atmosphere, to avoid genealogical temptations, projections, assimilations, or identifications'].[3] This approach is in accordance with Lacoue-Labarthe's own work, emerging as he does from a group of sophisticated thinkers of language who insist upon the power of writing to transform rather than simply represent our experiences. Yet this is not to say that he thinks in a detached or bloodless way: I draw on the various short texts in which his personal itinerary is explored, from 'Biographie' (1969; ['Biography']) to 'Bye bye farewell' (1983; [title originally in English]), and from 'La Fiction du biographique' (1987; ['The Fiction of the Biographical']) to various interviews given by himself, Nancy, and others.[4]

Whether this itinerary can be said to be personal in any rigorous sense, however, is a matter for debate. For Lacoue-Labarthe's signature often appeared alongside others, most often that of Jean-Luc Nancy (with whom he lived, lectured, and wrote for two decades), but also as a part of at least three separate collectives. Here is a writer who responded in a concrete way to his epoch's theoretical and political objections to the figure of the author, preferring collaboration and multiplicity. And similarly, even in his solo writings, there is no straightforward way of prising Lacoue-Labarthe's signature apart from numerous others. This is the case in his deconstructive readings of philosophy, where Heidegger is a constant presence; in his many translations, commentaries on translation, and translations of translations; and it is the case in his writing on literature, in which he constantly circles around others' work, for instance that of Friedrich Hölderlin, Paul Celan, and Maurice Blanchot. Rather than presenting a single thinker's work in glorious isolation, this study therefore aims to give full voice to the importance Lacoue-Labarthe placed upon these various collaborations, both concretely in terms of writing alongside others, and in terms of responding to the others always already present in writing.

★   ★   ★   ★   ★

Lacoue-Labarthe is both a diligent guide and a remorseless pace-setter, accompanying us over vastly divergent areas of modern writing and thought. This does not stem from any detached eclecticism on his part, but from a real commitment to thinking comparatively. Attempting to account for his work reveals that he advances into some of the most crucial terrain of late twentieth-century thought. For instance, for two decades Lacoue-Labarthe co-habited and worked in near symbiosis with Nancy — they lived, taught at the university, and published together in Strasbourg.[5] Given that Nancy's landmark work *La Communauté désœuvrée* [*The Inoperative Community*] was published during this period, Lacoue-Labarthe's thought is important for those interested in his writing partner — something underplayed by the account given in Marie-Ève Morin's recent work named *Jean-Luc Nancy* —, and particularly so where the intersections of writing and community are at issue. What's more, Lacoue-Labarthe contributes both practically and theoretically to research into translation, which he sees as a first-rank mode of enquiry into philosophical debates over foreignness and naturalization. In a different key, he devotes extensive attention to the relationship between philosophy, art, and politics, at the time of the late-1980s 'affair' which concerned Martin Heidegger's relationship with Nazism. And as he addresses these and other questions, he is influenced by and influences the work of major contemporary figures of French thought since May '68: Nancy and Derrida in the first instance, but also those such as Jean-François Lyotard, Sarah Kofman, Avital Ronell, Alain Badiou, and Jean-Christophe Bailly.

The œuvre across which this study ranges is thus large and varied, and certain short, uncollected or unpublished texts are shown to be more important than their status suggests. Nonetheless, an aerial reconnaissance of the published œuvre's peaks, as it were, can be helpful before we begin a more detailed approach. The central massif of Lacoue-Labarthe's work on philosophy is probably *La Fiction du politique: Heidegger, l'art et la politique* (1987; [*Heidegger, Art, and Politics: the Fiction of the Political*]), the thesis submitted for his *doctorat d'état* and the one dealing most definitively with his lifelong engagement with Heidegger.[6] Other major works include a critical anthology co-authored with Nancy, *L'Absolu littéraire: Théorie de la littérature du romantisme allemand* (1978; [*The Literary Absolute: the Theory of Literature in German Romanticism*]);[7] and two volumes of collected essays, *Le Sujet de la philosophie: Typographies I* (1979; [*The Subject of Philosophy: Typographies I*]) and *L'Imitation des modernes: Typographies II* (1986; [*The Imitation of the Moderns: Typographies II*]).[8] Selected essays from these two volumes are collected together with a piece by Derrida and an early text named 'Typographie' in the English-language volume *Typography: Mimesis, Philosophy, Politics*. The later of the original, French collections contains several key texts setting out a thinking of the stage, as it was developed by his French translation and then staging of Friedrich Hölderlin's German translation of Sophocles (*Antigone de Sophocle*, 1978–79; [*Antigone by Sophocles*]).[9] Another distinct strand in his work consists in a relationship to literature, poetry, or writing, which was developed throughout his career but only revealed latterly by the publication of *Phrase* (2000; *Phrase*) and *L'Allégorie'* (2006).[10] However, signalling the major reference points in this way excludes much work, for instance numerous collaborations with Nancy, Derrida, and others, as well as a good deal of unpublished seminars and projects. It is problematic to present Lacoue-Labarthe's work in any systematic manner, or to arrange it around central concepts or theses.

Nonetheless, certain patterns and tendencies do feature repeatedly, providing ways of passage between areas of his thought that might otherwise appear to be distinct. One such motif that we can reliably locate in almost any aspect of his work is that of the comparison and tension between different discourses, most often those of philosophy and literature. For this thinker, the slippage between discourses is of greater importance than the notion of inhabiting any particular one: and indeed, his work is rigorous in explaining its reticence for discursive labels ranging from 'philosophy' to 'theory' and from 'literature' to 'poetry'. On the rare occasions that any positive designation is accepted, it is most likely to be either that of 'thought' or of 'deconstruction'. To this extent, Lacoue-Labarthe can be said to be a more resolutely comparative thinker than his long-time co-author Nancy; writing a philosophically-oriented companion volume to Ian James's clear-sighted and helpful *The Fragmentary Demand: an Introduction to the Philosophy of Jean-Luc Nancy* (2006) would therefore be misplaced.[11] Instead, presenting this study as an overview of his work poses the challenge of addressing the relationship between the divergent strands of his thinking, for instance those on the stage and on poetry.[12] With this thinker, such a challenge is particularly apt, given that he has done (even) more than his contemporaries to take on board the principles of comparative thought and to engage with modes of expression that at first sight seem to be alien to philosophy. In short, the difficulty of reading Lacoue-Labarthe as a comparative thinker, working across and between several domains, is none other than the difficulty of reading his work full stop. And whilst John Martis's study *Philippe Lacoue-Labarthe: Representation and the Loss of the Subject* (2005) has a pioneering role as the first in English, it makes some strange choices on this question.[13] For instance, it refers unproblematically to Lacoue-Labarthe as a 'philosopher', despite his significant reservations over the term. The work's title issue of representation is addressed wholly legitimately in terms of the philosophical texts Lacoue-Labarthe discusses — but one wonders why the question of art, literature, and the stage, i.e. the laboratories in which representation is put to the test, are almost completely omitted from the discussion. By couching itself as an overview of his work and thereby including the multiple strands of his activity, the present study aims to ensure that these discussions are had and these questions asked.

★　★　★　★　★

Bearing in mind his comparative approach, it is worthwhile reading Lacoue-Labarthe on his relationship to the discourses to which he is often taken to belong. For instance, given that a majority of the writers and thinkers he studies and translates are German — from Hölderlin to the early Romantics Schlegel, Novalis et al., from Hegel to Nietzsche, from Heidegger to Celan —, one might be tempted to see his work as that of a Germanist. Responding to an American colleague's letter in which a similar assertion is made regarding his 'germanophilie' ['Germanophilia'], he writes that 'je ne trouve pas le mot très juste,' (AN 127; ['I do not find the word very fitting']) and rejects the scholarly or philological horizons it suggests. He goes on to admit that there is some truth in the assertion, but that his attention to German thought sees it as the archetype of modern, Western thinking, rather than as one national tradition amongst others. His approach to German thinkers is therefore a comparative one, as is indeed the case when he discusses passages across the boundaries of national traditions, such as Hölderlin's voyage to Bordeaux, Baudelaire and Mallarmé's reactions to Wagner, or Nietzsche and Heidegger's views of Greek philosophy.

Beyond the area of literary scholarship based on national or linguistic identity, there is the possibility of Lacoue-Labarthe forming part of a literary community beyond the university world. One role in such a community is that of a reviewer or critic; however, despite the fact that much of his œuvre performs readings of one or more writers, there is always the sense that he does so according to the notion of deconstruction as a practice of reading, rather than out of respect for the role itself. On a rare occasion when he adopts the role of a critic, writing a review of his collaborator Mathieu Bénézet's *Dits et récits du mortel: Ménipée* (1977; [*Sayings and Tales of the Mortal: a Menipean*]), the resultant piece opens with palpable unease: 'J'ai accepté le rôle, je ne m'y déroberai pas. J'accompagne, donc, ou "critique" — en connaissance de cause. Et sans plus de fioritures, j'irai droit, pour commencer, à ce qui m'intéresse dans ce livre [...]' ['I have accepted the role, I will not shy away from it. I am therefore accompany, or 'critique' — fully consciously. And without further ado, I shall begin by going straight onto what interests me in this book [...]'].[14] It goes without saying that this opening does something more than to proceed 'straight' into the main discussion: the form of a book review sits too uneasily with

Lacoue-Labarthe to pass without comment (perhaps being too closely associated with Blanchot, a critic he admired). A second possibility in the literary domain is that of he himself being a writer or poet: an issue that provokes contrasting approaches. On the one hand, we are told that 'j'exècre ce qu'on range de manière emphatique sous le nom de "poésie"' (PH 19; ['I loathe what is emphatically classed under the name of "poetry"']); but on the other, this 'loathing' seems to stem from a deep-seated dedication to poetry, and a consequent dislike for poetic practices not conforming to his understanding. Although even in the volumes published late in his career he will not adopt the term 'poet', in an autobiographical text he has written that '[i]l a fallu m'admetttre après coup — la loi de ce retard est effrayante — né pour la littérature. "Écrivain" était un mot magique. Un livre, la chose au monde la plus bouleversante' ['I had to admit, after the fact — the law of this delay is frightening — that I was born for literature. "Writer" was a magical word. A book was the most overwhelming thing in the world'].[15] And this is backed up by the written record insofar as his first published texts were poems which led during the 1960s and 70s to numerous fragmentary, explicitly non-philosophical texts, some of which appear in *Phrase*, *L'Allégorie'*, and a text he was reworking during his last days, *Préface à 'La Disparition'* ([*Preface to 'Disappearance'/'Death'*]).[16]

The conflicted nature of Lacoue-Labarthe's relationship with poetry is equalled only by that with philosophy.[17] One understanding of this term is of course as 'theory' — a prevalent term for his generation, but one he that he rejected both in conceptual terms (as too associated with the dominant gaze, the Greek *theorein* meaning to view or contemplate) and in more contingent, timely ones (the work in *L'Absolu littéraire* on Jena Romanticism and its *Theory of Literature* provides a way of distancing himself from an avant-garde group which he sees as reproducing Romantic discourse, *Tel Quel*). Beyond this, we should recall that Lacoue-Labarthe's career was spent teaching philosophy — specifically, aesthetics — at the University of Strasbourg. Nonetheless, he exercises considerable caution when addressing his relationship to the discipline, and tends to avoid describing himself as a philosopher. For instance, describing his reaction to being taught by Gérard Granel in his *khâgne* or *classe préparatoire*, Lacoue-Labarthe states that: 'cela m'a totalement illuminé et je suis "entré en philosophie"' ['it totally illuminated me and I "entered philosophy"'].[18] We can note that this entry into the discipline is closely marshalled by inverted commas which serve to problematize it; elsewhere he states that '[l]es propos que je tiens ne sont pas ceux d'un philosophe: pour de multiples raisons je ne prétends pas à ce titre, au reste à mon sens irréversiblement et définitivement périmé' ['[t]he statements I make are not those of a philosopher: there are many reasons that I do not pretend to this title, which in any case is irreversibly and definitively wrecked in my eyes'].[19] Informing this resistance to calling himself a philosopher is Lacoue-Labarthe's adherence to the thesis whereby the Western philosophical tradition — whether it is qualified as dialectical, speculative, or metaphysical — has reached a point of qualitative closure, despite the fact that it continues to function. This dauntingly large thesis is that Western philosophy can and should be referred to as a unitary tradition, and what's more, as one requiring deconstruction: i.e. requiring that we unpack the various stages of its construction and bring to light the various Others that have been excluded during this process. According to this strand of thinking, which proceeds from Heidegger to Derrida and then to Lacoue-Labarthe and Nancy, deconstruction cannot be said to belong fully to philosophy, but instead to a practice of reading that looks at philosophical texts, stripping them of any privileged status, and also without affording privileged status to their concepts, as opposed to the repetitions and rhythms though and by which they are written.

★   ★   ★   ★   ★

Lacoue-Labarthe's writing does not fall into any clear chronological phases that could be used to organize the chapters of this study. A sense of multiple, distinct explorations being conducted in parallel always accompanies what milestones do exist, for instance the *Antigone* theatre project (1978–79), the breakup of the community with Jean-Luc Nancy (late 1980s), or the publication of *Phrase* (2000). Therefore instead of adopting an artificially chronological framework, the chapters of this study form interweaving strands discussing the major areas of Lacoue-Labarthe's thinking.

These chapters take as their path through the oeuvre in question the interface between the timely (i.e. this thinker's contributions to French thought of his period) and the untimely (what is unexpected or delayed, happening either too early or too late). Part I looks at his work within a *timely* framework, i.e. insofar as it took a direct part in the debates of his time. Thus chapter 1 examines his engagement with the avant-garde as the predominant model for collaboration and innovation in writing and thought; in his collective endeavours with Nancy, and especially their work on Jena Romanticism (in *L'Absolu littéraire*), which they see as the first modern avant-garde, Lacoue-Labarthe questions the assumptions of this model. Chapter 2 shows how this thinking of the group develops into an extensive engagement with notions of community and the political, centring on Heidegger's relation with politics; the latter is shown to be more than a simply biographical affair, instead calling into question philosophical discourse itself. Chapter 3 then examines the relationship between Lacoue-Labarthe and Derrida, ten years his senior and a first-rank figure in French thought. It explores their interaction as it is mediated by first Nietzsche and then Heidegger, always in relation to the radically destabilizing notion of *l'écriture*. Although the tension between the timely and the untimely is — as it were — granular in Lacoue-Labarthe's thought, present at whichever level of detail one chooses to examine, part I is organized in order to foreground his relation to timely concerns: some of the major figures (Nancy, Derrida) and notions (the avant-garde, the political, *l'écriture*) of French thought following 1968.

Part II provides the counterpoint to this, being organized around areas of Lacoue-Labarthe's œuvre that appear to be untimely in their relation to narratives of the period. The first of these is the theatrical stage, which he explored so richly that I devote two chapters to it. The first, chapter 4b, looks at his engagement with tragedy, and particularly two Sophocles plays as they had been translated and commented on by Hölderlin. Lacoue-Labarthe himself translated these translations and then staged the two productions, and I examine these diverse areas of his practice before drawing out the motif of 'antagonism' that caused him to do so. Chapter 4c deals with a different area of his interest in theatre, namely opera. This art-form is seen as both the culmination and the overcoming of philosophy, and I explore how Lacoue-Labarthe treats this situation both discursively (in *Musica ficta: Figures de Wagner*) and via fictional or allegorical texts depicting an opera singer collapsing on stage.[20] Chapter 5 follows on to explore his writing in the form of fragments or poems; by engaging with writers Celan and Blanchot, Lacoue-Labarthe moves towards a practice of what he names 'phrase', and in doing so towards a 'clarification' that he had been unable to situate in philosophical discourse. It seems fair to say that tragedy, opera, and poetry are not the discourses for which the period in question in France is best known. However, in engaging with these untimely demands Lacoue-Labarthe demonstrates the unusual adaptability of his thinking, and makes key contributions to wider debates on the interaction between philosophy and literature.

Notes to the Introduction

1. Cf. *Thus Spoke Zarathustra*, trans. by R. J. Hollingdale (Harmondsworth: Penguin, 1961), p. 97.
2. In 'Hommage', *Rue Descartes*, 48 (2005), 74–78 (p. 77). Unless indicated otherwise, all translations are my own.
3. Derrida, 'Désistance', in *Psyché: Inventions de l'autre* (Paris: Galilée, 1987), pp. 597–638 (pp. 602–03); 'Desistance', in *Typography: Mimesis, Philosophy, Politics*, ed. by Christopher Fynsk (1989; Stanford: Stanford University Press, 1998), pp. 1–42 (p. 7); references to this volume are henceforth abbreviated to TYP.
4. 'Biographie', in *L'Allégorie* (['*Allegory*']; Paris: Galilée, 2006), pp. 115–18, henceforth abbreviated to ALEG; 'Bye bye farewell', in *L'Animal*, 19–20 (Winter 2008), 191–98 (references to this volume are henceforth abbreviated to AN); 'La Fiction du biographique', in *Lignes*, 22 (May 2007), 195–204.
5. The two often taught as a pair, running large and popular seminars at the University of Strasbourg. Previously, Lacoue-Labarthe had taught the *terminale* class in French (rather than philosophy) in Bordeaux: one of his students, Jean-Michel Rabaté, recounts this in 'Bordeaux 1965: pour Philippe Lacoue-Labarthe' ['Bordeaux 1965: for Philippe Lacoue-Labarthe'], in *Lignes*, 37–41.
6. *La Fiction du politique: Heidegger, l'art et la politique* (Paris: Bourgois, 1987), henceforth abbreviated to FP; *Heidegger, Art, and Politics: the Fiction of the Political*, trans. by Chris Turner (Oxford: Blackwell, 1990), henceforth abbreviated to HAP.
7. *L'Absolu littéraire: Théorie de la littérature du romantisme allemand* (Paris: Seuil, 1978), henceforth abbreviated to AL; *The Literary Absolute: the Theory of Literature in German Romanticism*, trans. by Philippe Barnard and Cheryl Lester (Albany: SUNY Press, 1988), henceforth abbreviated to LA.
8. *Le Sujet de la philosophie (Typographies I)* (Paris: Aubier-Flammarion, 1979), henceforth abbreviated to SP; *L'Imitation des modernes (Typographies II)* (Paris: Galilée, 1986), henceforth abbreviated to IM. The first volume has been translated by Thomas Tresize as *The Subject of Philosophy* (Minneapolis: University of Minnesota Press, 1993), henceforth abbreviated to SP2.
9. Hölderlin, *Antigone de Sophocle*, trans. into French by Lacoue-Labarthe (Paris: Bourgois, 1998), henceforth abbreviated to AdS.
10. *Phrase* (Paris: Bourgois, 2000), henceforth abbreviated to PH.
11. *The Fragmentary Demand: an Introduction to the Philosophy of Jean-Luc Nancy* (Stanford: Stanford U. P., 2006).
12. I have had to largely ignore his writing on art in *La Vraie semblance* (Paris: Galilée, 2008) — the title means both '(the) true semblance' and is a homophone for *la vraisemblance*, verisimilitude — and *Écrits sur l'art* (['*Writings on Art*']; Genève: Réel, 2009).

13. *Philippe Lacoue-Labarthe: Representation and Loss of the Subject* (New York: Fordham U. P., 2005).
14. In 'Précis: Compte-rendu de Mathieu Bénézet, *Dits et récits du mortel: Ménipée*' ['Précis: Review of Mathieu Bénézet, *Sayings and Tales of the Mortal: a Menipean*'] in *Critique*, 357 (February 1977), 146–53.
15. In 'La Fiction du biographique', *Lignes*, p. 197.
16. *Préface à 'La Disparition'* (Paris: Bourgois, 2009).
17. André Hirt argues that Lacoue-Labarthe should be considered a philosopher: 'Dans Lacoue, il y avait quelque chose non seulement de rigoureux, mais d'implacable. C'est pourquoi, envers et contre tout, contre lui-même, je tiens Lacoue pour un philosophe', in *Un Homme littéral: Philippe Lacoue-Labarthe* [*A Literal Man: Philippe Lacoue-Labarthe*]; Paris: Kimé, 2009), p. 12 ['[i]n Lacoue, there was something not simply rigorous, but remorseless. This is why, over and against everything, against himself, I take Lacoue to be a philosopher'].
18. In Dominique Janicaud, *Heidegger en France*, vol. II: *Entretiens* ([*Heidegger in France*, vol. II: *Interviews*]; Paris: Albin Michel, 2001), p. 199. There is certainly more to be written on Lacoue-Labarthe's relationship to his teachers Gérard Genette, Gérard Granel, and art critic Jean-Marie Pontévia. An account of the latter relationship can be found in Lacoue-Labarthe's preface in Pontévia, *La Peinture, masque et miroir*, 2nd ed. ([*Painting: Mask and Mirror*]; Bordeaux: William Blake & Co., 1993), pp. vii–xvii.
19. In 'La Philosophie fantôme' ['Philosophy as Ghost'], *Lignes*, 205–14 (p. 213).
20. *Musica ficta: Figures de Wagner* (Paris: Bourgois, 1991); *Musica Ficta: Figures of Wagner*, trans. by Felicia McCarren (Stanford: Stanford University Press, 1994).

PART I

Timely Meditations

CHAPTER 1

Avant-garde

On an initial reading of the thinkers to whom Lacoue-Labarthe is most dedicated, it appears that he is drawn to solitary figures: Hölderlin and his four decades of confinement, Heidegger and his Black Forest hut, Blanchot and his decade as a recluse in Èze. But on looking more closely at Lacoue-Labarthe's trajectory, it soon becomes apparent that much of it was spent working in close collaboration with other writers and thinkers. These range from the Situationist and *soixante-huitard* groupings of his early years in Strasbourg to numerous theatre projects with the director Michel Deutsch, and from his philosophical collaborations with Derrida, Kofman, Nancy and others in the mid-1970s to those with Mathieu Bénézet in a literary arena at the end of that decade. And providing as it were a constant base note to all of these enterprises was his relationship with Jean-Luc Nancy, which is important and complex in equal measure.

This chapter sets out to measure the importance of these various contemporary collaborations — or engagements with 'the timely', to use to Nietzsche's term — in Lacoue-Labarthe's thinking. It does not do so simply via a historicized account, but links on the one hand Lacoue-Labarthe's dedication to contemporaneity, and on the other the underlying reflections that drove it. This is to say that the notion of collaboration or community was not simply a reality in Lacoue-Labarthe's career, but part of his discourse on modern thought and on the relations between philosophy, literature, and politics. Beyond the groupings he was part of, others inform his horizons in significant ways. For instance, in an interview, Nancy spoke to me of role-plays that he and Lacoue-Labarthe would perform: each would adopt the role of a historical thinker, with Lacoue-Labarthe adopting the role of Schelling or Hölderlin to Nancy's Hegel.[1] The three German figures were of course friends at the Tübingen seminary in the early 1790s, suggesting that this represented a model for the community Lacoue-Labarthe and Nancy formed in Strasbourg. The early German Romantic group at Jena and the contemporary 1970s group *Tel Quel* provide other models and counter-models in this same vein. As Lacoue-Labarthe later stated, '1976 était encore une époque où nous cherchions à nous déprendre des mouvements d'avant-garde, *Tel Quel* et tous ses succédanés — tout ce qui avait occupé la scène pendant les dix ou quinze dernières années' ['1976 was still an era when we were trying to free ourselves of the avant-garde movements, *Tel Quel* and all the imitations of it — everything that had occupied centre-stage for the previous ten or fifteen years'].[2] In short, these groups are taken to represent the modern avant-garde: Jena Romanticism as its first and definitive appearance, and *Tel Quel* as the major contemporary example of the genre. The metaphor employed when calling a group of writers or thinkers an 'avant-garde' is of course a military one: they are presented as the advance troops of a larger armed force. Lacoue-Labarthe repeatedly distanced himself from this metaphor and from the notion of a small, closed group. For instance, in 1979 he and Bénézet wrote that:

> [L']avant-garde ne nous intéresse pas. Ladite avant-garde, ou du moins ce qui en reste: parce que le mouvement s'essouffle, c'est certain [...]. Pourquoi, cela dit, l'avant-garde ne nous intéresse-t-elle pas ? Tout simplement parce que nous en avons assez de 'théorie' [...]. Nous ne voulons pas dire par là: trop de théorie étouffe la littérature. C'est le vieil argument, mettons 'poujadiste'; il n'a aucune pertinence.[3]

> [[T]he avant-garde does not interest us. This so-called avant-garde, or at least what remains of it: because the movement is running out of steam, that much is certain [...]. Why then does the avant-garde not interest us? Quite simply because we have had enough of 'theory' [...]. By this we do not mean that too much theory smothers literature. That is the old, 'poujadist' argument; it is not relevant at all].

Thus the resistance to the rhetoric of the avant-gardes was not based in a conservative return to 'literature' at the expense of 'theory', here labelled as 'poujadist' i.e. parochial, bourgeois, and reactionary. Instead, in discussing such avant-garde groups, Lacoue-Labarthe attempts to glimpse an alternative way of interacting with his contemporaries: one that remains undetermined, open to the what is to come, without presenting that *à-venir* as a predetermined future heralded by marching jackboots.

Community is a fraught term, meaning very different things in contemporary Anglo-Saxon and French discourse; and Nancy's interest in the term is in a *communauté désœuvrée*, i.e. a community based around our most irreducible existence, rather than on particular values or identities. But these observations notwithstanding, it is the term that he and others use to refer to his relationship with Lacoue-Labarthe. We can note that in French one connotation of *communauté* is the small-scale alternative societies that were in vogue in the 1970s. In English these are referred to less often as 'communities' than as 'communes', and we should remain open to this resonance when thinking Lacoue-Labarthe and Nancy's project for a *communauté*. In any case, the two figures often refer to this project as one influenced by the counter-cultural atmosphere of May '68 and following years, and in time it will perhaps come to be seen as an important after-effect of the *événements* within French thought; certainly it places them closer to the student revolts than major contemporary figures such as Derrida, Barthes, Foucault, Lacan, or Levinas, who all adopted a certain distance. Indeed, the first of these figures, who would go on to collaborate on many occasions with Lacoue-Labarthe and Nancy, expressed his reservations regarding their mode of community. He wrote that:

> Cette écriture ou cette pensée à deux, trois ou quatre mains a toujours été pour moi une apparition fascinante, admirable, énigmatique, mais aussi impensable et impossible aujourd'hui encore. Rien ne me paraît aussi inimaginable, et je le ressens comme ma propre limite, aussi inimaginable que, dans la vie privée

qui fut indissociable des expériences publiques dont je parle, leurs liens de communauté familiale.[4]

[This two-, three-, or four-handed writing or thought has always been a fascinating apparition for me, one that is admirable, enigmatic, but also unthinkable and impossible, even today. Nothing seems to me quite so unimaginable, and I feel that this is my own limit, just as unimaginable as, in the private lives which were indissociable from the public experiences I am talking about, their links in a family community].

By referring to these 'links in a family community', Derrida nods to the shared living arrangements of the pair and their families (these arrangements are the subject of many anecdotes, which it is not my role to repeat). More generally, this seems an important statement: the figure often taken to be amongst the major representatives of French thought in the late 1960s and 70s is distancing himself from Lacoue-Labarthe and Nancy's mode of writing almost as responding too fully or too promptly to the demands of the age: namely what in 1968 Blanchot had called 'un communisme d'écriture' ['a communism of writing'].[5] It is worth noting that Lacoue-Labarthe (here with Nancy) had the capacity to be disruptively contemporary and timely, just as elsewhere — for instance with his work on Hölderlin's theatre or on poetry — he could be radically untimely.

This chapter is concerned primarily with this version of timeliness as it drove his work within collaborations and communities of thought. I thus begin by looking at the mode of his relationship with Jean-Luc Nancy and the various forms this dialogue takes, whether explicit or implicit, playful or serious. We then move on to *L'Absolu littéraire*, their jointly prepared critical anthology of Jena Romanticism: this work is examined both in itself and in light of its contemporary targets, namely the discourse of a theoretical avant-garde which was greatly prominent in the 1970s — Peter Bürger's *Theory of the Avant-Garde* was published in German in 1974 —, and especially in a French context with the group *Tel Quel*. The chapter then closes by examining Lacoue-Labarthe's displacement of the modern, which forms the impulse behind his rejection of a certain version of Wagnerian opera (see chapter 4c) and of Blanchot's post-romantic fragmentary writing (see chapter 5), both of which he sees as too intricated within a modernist aesthetic.

Community in Strasbourg

The collaboration between Philippe Lacoue-Labarthe and Jean-Luc Nancy, which Derrida refers to as 'unthinkable' and 'unimaginable', occupies a place in the work of each that is both fundamental and strangely under-emphasized. The dozens of books, articles, translations, conferences, research seminars and teaching projects they undertook as a pair make only rare references to the fact that these collaborations are the product of two minds. And yet throughout these same projects there is a striking insistence on thematics of the group, of the communal and the political. We shall come to see that these two facts are not unrelated.

Their joint work originated in 1967 when Lacoue-Labarthe and Nancy were introduced to each other at the University of Strasbourg by Lucien Braun. The experimental community they went on to share for many years then fed their written production, they and their families living together (from 1970 to the late 1980s) at a time of aspiration towards political, intellectual, and sexual freedom. They lectured on philosophy as a pair, as well as leading numerous research seminars and conferences, for instance *Les Fins de l'homme: à partir du travail de Jacques Derrida* (1980; [*The Ends of Man: Beginning from the Work of Jacques Derrida*]) at Cerisy-la-Salle, and the *Centre de recherches philosophiques sur le politique* (1980–84; [*Centre for Philosophical Research into the Political*]).[6] The cross-fertilization between their thought also gave rise to many publications: from *Le Titre de la lettre: une lecture de Lacan* (1973; [*The Title of the Letter: a Reading of Lacan*]) to *L'Absolu littéraire* (1978), from texts in the collective volume *Mimesis: des articulations* (1975; [*Mimesis: (Dis) Articulations*]) to those recently re-edited as *La Panique politique* (1979–80 / 2013; [*Political Panic*]) and *Scène suivi de Dialogue sur le dialogue* (1995, 2002 / 2013; [*Stage/Scene* followed by *Dialogue on Dialogue*]). A wide range of topics and of modalities of thought is thus present in their work, meaning that it cannot be defined as predominantly literary or philosophical, for instance, but instead as resolutely installing itself in the zones of slippage between such disciplines.

The relationship between the two thinkers is so symbolically charged that it is sometimes hard to remember that it originated in reality. This symbolic charge can be seen in various areas: for instance, their work together was largely carried out in Strasbourg, a town on the edge of France whose university has strong German roots. More than this, much of the thinkers' careers was dedicated to German literature and philosophy, from Hegel to Nietzsche, but most of all Heidegger, who was professor just across the border at Freiburg (he died in 1976).[7] The notion of comparative thought was therefore a lived reality for Lacoue-Labarthe and Nancy, and Strasbourg's de-centered situation proved a spur for them to address the notion of Europe beyond fixed national identities. Nonetheless, the pair do not play equal roles in acting as *passeurs* between national discourses: theirs is not a community of sameness facing the foreign. For, whilst both atheists, culturally-speaking they come from different religious backgrounds, Nancy's Catholic and Lacoue-Labarthe's, via his mother, Calvinist. Since Lacoue-Labarthe's death, Nancy has addressed this situation — 'd'un côté, le protestant, de l'autre, le catholique' ['on one side the Protestant, on the other the Catholic'] —, arguing that the distinction counts for more than 'du biographisme' ['mere biographism'].[8] Another axis of difference exists concerning the modes of thought privileged by one or the other thinker. In other recent texts, Nancy has identified Lacoue-Labarthe as leaning more towards literature, indeed as someone whom he initially understood to be primarily a poet or a writer. We read: 'Pour Philippe, le rapport à la littérature — c'est-à-dire à la mimesis — était prégnant, tandis que pour moi c'était le mode, disons, de l'abord métaphysique, la "question de l'être" d'un côté et de l'autre la "différance" comme transformation de la différence ontologique' (AN 107; ['For Philippe, the relation to literature — which is to say to mimesis — was a pregnant one, whereas for me it was more a question of the metaphysical approach, the "question of being" on one hand and on the other, that of "differance" as a transformation of the ontological difference']).[9] We are even treated to the revelation that Nancy had to teach Lacoue-Labarthe how to use a typewriter, which is pushed beyond the realm of the anecdotal: 'Lui l'écriture et le poème, moi le concept et la machine' (AN 109; ['Him writing and the poem, me the concept and the machine']). The attractive simplicity of such a relationship between the two should be cause for some hesitation, however, particularly when placed in the context of their work's extensive investigation into the relations between philosophy and literature. This investigation demonstrates an aversion on the one hand to identifying themselves as philosophers (philosophy being too closely associated with metaphysics), and on the other hand, to champion literature in and of itself, given that such a literature would be merely the reverse side of philosophy, a reversal of Plato's hierarchy without displacement of it. And indeed, these important nuances are addressed by Nancy when he discusses his collaboration with Lacoue-Labarthe in terms of a role-play: 'Quels rôles? En un sens, peu importe. De toute évidence les protagonistes ont été l'Écrivain et le Philosophe. Mais il importe de remarquer ce trait décisif: s'il est manifeste que je dois jouer le Philosophe, il ne l'est pas moins que Philippe tient à endosser les deux masques tour à tour ou superposés' ['What roles? In a sense, it doesn't matter. Quite clearly the protagonists were the Writer and the Philosopher. But it is important to underline this decisive feature: whilst it is obvious that I had to play the Philosopher, it is no less obvious that Philippe thought it important to wear the two masks in turn or superimposed on one another'].[10]

In terms of their working practices, Nancy on being interviewed suggests that an initial phase of joint reading or study preceded the writing, rather than each thinker individually reading the texts in question.[11] The writing phase was then constituted by Nancy pushing his collaborator to both begin and finish discrete pieces of work, Lacoue-Labarthe for his part locating the avenues to be pursued in the first place. Of the resultant texts, the vast majority are signed with a single, composite name: 'Lacoue-Labarthe and Nancy'. It is possible to find in their joint work passages largely similar to those published individually by either writer; but given the greater relevance of what takes place *between* these thinkers, rather than the particular elements of a text that can be attributed to either one of them, such a work of reconstitution would be of limited interest (Nancy has noted that 'plus d'un a joué à deviner de qui était tel chapitre de tel livre ou telle partie de tel article. Mais certains parfois se sont trompés...' (AN, 108; ['more than one has played the game of guessing who wrote a given chapter of a book or a given part of an article. But sometimes they have got it wrong...']). A minority of texts do adopt the dialogue format, however: for instance the two collected in *Scène*, 'Monogrammes X' ['X Monograms'], 'Noli me frangere', and an interview of Lacoue-Labarthe by Nancy where *vouvoiement* is ironically — given their close, informal friendship — used.[12] There is a sense on these occasions that such collaborations are deviating from the main thrust of the two thinkers' work: this comes across via a notable playfulness. For instance, to make a point about the interaction between the name of theatrical interlocutors and the interventions they make, one text contains an intervention written in alexandrines (and which I have attempted to translate using iambic pentameter):

PHILIPPE
Arrêtons un moment, cette présentation,
Je le vois bien, Jean-Luc, manque de précision...[13]

[PHILIPPE
Let us stop now this here presentation,
I see it clear, Jean-Luc full lacks rigour...]

The article 'Noli me frangere', on the other hand, is a short, three-part study in deconstructive experimentation. Beginning with co-authored fragments, a second section then moves into a dialogue between two anonymous voices. This section ends with the proposal to establish a more formal dialogue — which then features in part three. Rather than bearing Lacoue-Labarthe and Nancy's signatures, however, the interlocutors of this final section are named Lothario and Ludovico, aping and ironizing the style of Schlegel's 'Dialogue on Poetry', which featured the interlocutors Ludoviko and Lothario, and is translated in *L'Absolu littéraire*.[14]

We shall shortly begin looking at this text and its approach to the experimental literary, philosophical, and sexual community formed at Jena. Before doing so, it is worth noting the circumstances of Lacoue-Labarthe and Nancy's meeting at Strasbourg in 1967. Both place and date are important. For the importance of Situationism in the town established ambitious parameters for political debate as well as strongly influencing Lacoue-Labarthe.[15] The importance of this ferment of thinking meant that May '68, when it arrived, was more of a continuation than a shock (although the contrary is sometimes said of the events in Paris); it nonetheless gave added impetus to Lacoue-Labarthe and Nancy's activities and reflections both within and beyond the institution. That these factors determined the *Grundstimmung* of their collaboration is crucial in understanding that it cannot be analysed separately from their reflections on the common and the political (which of course include Nancy's seminal *Communauté désœuvrée*, 1983–86), and vice-versa. Lacoue-Labarthe provides confirmation of the link between his and Nancy's writerly practice and the motifs discussed within that writing:

> Sans Jean-Luc Nancy, sans son exemple et son soutien, sans l'amitié, tout simplement, ou la fraternité, je sais très bien que je ne me serais pas risqué dans l'écriture 'philosophique'. Sans ce 'communisme des esprits', comme dit Hölderlin, 'la *psuchè* entre amis', sans cet 'entretien infini', comme dit Blanchot, je sais que je n'aurais pas pu élaborer ce qu'il m'a été donné d'élaborer, à ma mesure. C'est là probablement ce qu'a réinscrit, autobiographiquement, notre travail sur le romantisme, s'il est vrai qu'il y a dans notre projet commun une volonté de répétition, et de déplacement, de l'expérience d'Iéna. Cela ne veut nullement dire que nous avons joué aux 'romantiques', mais que nous était commun le désir de nous inscrire sous un certain horizon historique et spirituel, non pour renouer le fil d'une tradition perdue (ce fil a été définitivement tranché, et c'est le nazisme qui l'a tranché), mais pour, depuis une mémoire forcément lacunaire, tenter de sauver ce qu'il était possible de sauver pour notre à-venir sans futur.[16]

[Without Jean-Luc Nancy, without his example and his support, without the friendship, quite simply, or the brotherliness, I know full well that I would never have ventured into 'philosophical' writing. Without this 'communism of spirits', as Hölderlin says, 'the *psuchè* between friends', without this 'infinite conversation', as Blanchot says, I know that I would never have been able to produce what I have produced, in my own way. This is probably what was reinscribed, autobiographically, by our work on Romanticism, if it is true that our joint project contained a will to repeat, and to displace, the experience of Jena. This does not at all mean that we played at being 'Romantics', but that we shared the desire to write ourselves into a given historical and spiritual horizon; not in order to reforge the chain of a lost tradition (this chain was broken definitively, and it was Nazism that broke it), but, faced with necessarily patchy reconstructions, to attempt to save what it was possible to save for our futureless *to-come* [*à-venir*]].

There is a sense here that whatever relation existed between the two thinkers, it is still looking for the language in which it can be best expressed, leading to subtle — some would say awkward — formulations such as 'our futureless *to-come* [*à-venir*]'. We can further explore this search for a language and a model by looking at *L'Absolu littéraire* and its reflection on Romanticism. It seems crucial that this passage establishes Lacoue-Labarthe and Nancy's relation to this Romantic model under the sign of a hesitation, or an instantaneous, automatic displacement, between a 'will to repeat' and a 'will to displace'.

L'Absolu littéraire

Contemporary resonances

The critical anthology *L'Absolu littéraire: Théorie de la littérature du romantisme allemand* (1978) is certainly one of the works, and perhaps *the* work, for which Lacoue-Labarthe is best-known. It is sometimes said that its publication came as a surprise on the French scene, presenting as it did texts by relatively unknown and exclusively German authors (Friedrich and August Wilhelm Schlegel, Novalis, Schleiermacher), as well as a considerable philological apparatus including a chronology, bibliography, summaries of issues of the *Athenaeum* (the group's journal), a glossary, two indexes, as well as essays introducing each section.[17] Susan Bernstein rightly laments the decision to omit the anthologized Romantic works presented from the English translation, *The Literary Absolute*, a decision which 'adamantly alters the figure of this book, making it a centre where it began as a translation and commentary'.[18] In any case, the volume combines this scholarly side with undeniable philosophical ambition and breadth of reference, arguing that the group of Jena Romantics sought out a new mythology that touches on the essence of modern thought by bringing together philosophical, literary, political, and other elements (in the words of Friedrich Schlegel, '[w]e have no mythology, but we are close to getting one, or rather, it is high time we set to work together to produce one').[19] Whilst such a mythology might nowadays go by the name of interdisciplinarity, and with the emphasis on slippages between disciplines rather than on fusion, Lacoue-Labarthe and Nancy's argument is that something about the Romantic's thinking remains unchanged. For his part, Derrida saluted the volume's contribution to contemporary reflections on genre, which after all consisted in situating *l'écriture* between philosophy and literature, but as reducible to neither; his text 'La Loi du genre' states that '*L'Absolu littéraire* aura fait événement [...] et tout ce que je risquerai ici se situera dans les marges de ce *grand livre* dont je suppose constamment la lecture' ['*The Literary Absolute* has already created quite a stir [...], and everything that I shall risk here should perhaps resolve itself in a modest annotation on the margins of this *magistral work* which I assume some of you have already read'].[20] For their part, Lacoue-Labarthe and Nancy set out as follows their case for the relevance of Jena Romanticism to contemporary thinking: 'Il y a aujourd'hui, décelable dans la plupart des grands motifs de notre "modernité", un véritable *inconscient* romantique.' (AL 26, emphasis original; ['A veritable romantic *unconscious* is discernable today, in most of the central motifs of our "modernity"', LA 15, emphasis original]) Or put more simply, 'le romantisme est notre *naïveté*' (AL 27, emphasis original; ['Romanticism is our *naïveté*', LA 17, emphasis original]). This is to say that when we do not analyse but simply or naïvely think about art, we belong to Romanticism. Translating these texts into French for the first time therefore aimed to create a more informed understanding of this hitherto unthought or unexamined Romantic legacy.

We have already seen Lacoue-Labarthe evoking his and Nancy's 'joint project' as 'a will to repeat, and to displace, the experience of Jena'. Beyond this, there are further resonances with French thought of the 1970s that are worth exploring as we seek to understand the two authors' notions of the political and the community, and therefore also what — if anything — they shared with other contemporary thinkers and groups. Lacoue-Labarthe spoke revealingly of *L'Absolu littéraire* in an interview:

> très vite nous est apparu que la plupart des motifs dominants en France depuis une quinzaine d'années [...] pouvaient être fédérés de manière assez précise au romantisme [...]. D'où pouvait-on parler, par exemple, d'une autosuffisance ou d'un autofonctionnement, voire d'une auto-production, du texte, si ce n'est à partir d'une conception de l'œuvre-sujet qui provenait en droite ligne du romantisme ? C'est-à-dire de l'Idéalisme allemand ? D'un moment très déterminé de la métaphysique moderne ? (AN 151–52)

> [it soon became clear to us that most of the motifs that had been dominant in France for around fifteen years [...] could be traced back fairly precisely to Romanticism [...]. On what basis was it possible to speak, for instance, of a self-sufficiency or a self-functioning, even of a self-production, of the text, if not beginning from a conception of the work as subject which originated directly in Romanticism? Which is to say in German idealism? In a very determinate moment of modern metaphysics?].

What is interesting there is that he does not present *L'Absolu littéraire* as having aimed to demonstrate the relevance of Jena Romanticism, to French thought in the 1970s: after all, this would have been to reduce the past to the present. Instead, the present is seen as merely an new iteration of a pre-existing paradigm (that of the avant-garde group). Whether willingly or not, this is *imitatio* in its least imaginative form, and therefore calls for the radical rhetoric surrounding the newness of the avant-garde to be called into question.

In this light, the sub-title of *L'Absolu littéraire* is highly useful in situating Lacoue-Labarthe and Nancy's gesture vis-à-vis their contemporary context. By couching their discussion in terms of a *Théorie de la littérature du romantisme allemand*, they were making a very deliberate statement. For 'theory' had begun to emerge as a term designating an alternative space for reflection, one not entirely reducible to literary criticism or scholarship, or to political ideology or canonical philosophy.[21] In other words, the gesture interpreting Jena Romanticism as 'theory' allowed Lacoue-Labarthe and Nancy to create a margin for thinking that is autonomous from both Romanticism and the dominant trends in contemporary French thought. Such a gesture would therefore help us to explain the fact that, whilst closely following Derrida's thinking, Lacoue-Labarthe and Nancy reserve very little space anywhere in their wider work for some of the main representatives of 'theory': the *Tel Quel* group, Barthes, Lévi-Strauss, structural anthropology and linguistics, even the umbrella term 'post-structuralism'. Whilst psychoanalysis does feature to an extent, the tradition most commonly evoked is Heideggerian thought, with its overcoming of metaphysics and deconstruction of 'philosophy'; this involves looking at thinkers such as Nietzsche and at more recent readers such as Derrida.[22] In short, the work subtitled *Théorie de la littérature du romantisme allemand* performs a clear distancing from the 'theory' it presents; the latter is not a privileged discourse by which other discourses might be measured, or which can be applied unproblematically to others.[23] Instead, the authors state that:

> le romantisme n'est ni 'de la littérature' ([les romantiques] en inventent le concept) ni même, simplement, une 'théorie de la littérature' (ancienne et moderne), mais *la théorie elle-même comme littérature* ou, cela revient au même, la littérature se produisant en produisant sa propre théorie. L'absolu littéraire, c'est aussi, et peut-être avant tout, cette absolue *opération littéraire* (AL 22, emphases original).

> [Romanticism is neither mere 'literature' ([the Romantics] invent the concept) nor simply a 'theory of literature' (ancient and modern). Rather, it is *theory itself as literature* or, in other words, literature producing itself as it produces its own theory. The literary absolute is also, and perhaps above all, this absolute *literary operation* (LA 12, emphases original)].

Here neither position in the binary opposition of 'literature' and 'theory' is seen as satisfactory. This is because each always already relies on the other, a reading suggested when Lacoue-Labarthe and Nancy recall that both terms came into being in the late 18th century, and found their major early expression thanks to the Jena group. One therefore cannot have literature without theory as its horizon, and vice-versa. And it is the association or intrication of each with the other that constitutes the Romantic 'operation', i.e. what Romantic thought carries out, the gesture that it performs. It is of course also a gesture characteristic of deconstruction to move away from binaries, yet to do so without proposing any solution to the tension between them, or any new, third term which could provide a resolution. Lacoue-Labarthe and Nancy hold themselves in that tension, where literature and theory come into existence always already intricated with or inflected by the other.

Repetition or displacement?

L'Absolu littéraire consists in seven critical essays interjected between and presenting various key texts by Friedrich and A. W. Schlegel, Schelling, Novalis, as well as unattributed or collective ones, all translated into French for the first time (by Lacoue-Labarthe, Nancy, and Anne-Marie Lang). Nancy has recently downplayed his involvement in the volume, discussing 'L'Être abandonné' ['Being abandonded'], an early-1980s text, as the first to be truly his.[24] He states: 'ce texte représentait pour moi une prise d'indépendance par rapport à Philippe. Jusque là, je m'étais plutôt développé dans ses parages: *L'Absolu littéraire*, en particulier [...] se référai[t] d'abord à ses intérêts' (AN 109; ['this text represented for me a declaration of independence in relation to Philippe. Until then, I had mostly developed in his slipstream: *The Literary Absolute*, in particular [...] referred mainly to his interests']). However, Nancy's solo work of the 1970s on Kant and Hegel means that his contribution can certainly be felt in the volume's account of the relations between philosophy and literature — which is after all a crucial point, given the two authors' express desire to write deconstructively rather from within philosophical discourse, which they saw as having reached its point of closure.[25] Regarding their collaboration, it is too schematic vis-à-vis each author to argue that Nancy provides the philosophical contribution and Lacoue-Labarthe the literary one.[26] And as for their general desire to escape the dualism of philosophy/literature, it is clear that this implies a mistrust of the view that would champion literature as able to resist philosophical systematization owing to its radical singularity: such a vision of 'literature' does little more than to set it up as the other of philosophy, thus falling into a trap set by Plato in his exclusion of poets from the city; in place of a literature distinct from philosophy, one instead needed to explore a writing that retained the capacity to think.

The volume was written over a single summer and a critical voice might argue that it shows: the authors make extensive use of underlinings, scare quotes, and self-corrections; we are a world away from Lacoue-Labarthe's later clipped and lapidary style. In terms of the motifs employed in the approach to Jena Romanticism, a large number of disparate topics jostle together in a restricted space: Blanchot and fragmentation, *imitatio* of the ancients as a defining mode of European culture, Nietzsche's distinction between Apollo and Dionysos, and so on. The work's heterogeneity in style and in argument, although factors of only local relevance in themselves, are nonetheless revelatory of the deeper split at the heart of Lacoue-Labarthe and Nancy's thinking here. For in the volume there is ample evidence to confirm Lacoue-Labarthe's later hesitation over whether it represented a desire to 'repeat' Romanticism on the one hand, or to 'displace' it on the other. Thus on a first reading (we shall return to a second, alternative one), the Romantics' project of founding a new mythology based around art is seen as a way of installing the Subject. The latter is understood as a self-same, essentially unchanging presence, a first mover that is itself immobile, untouched by variation or difference. In his work on Lacoue-Labarthe, John Martis provides some useful philosophical background for the term 'Subject':

> [Aristotle] says that some beings 'are called substance because they are not predicated of a subject but everything else is predicated of them'. But here Aristotle uses a single word for subject and substance — *hupokeimenon*, 'that which lies under'; it is subsequent Latin translation of the word as *subiectum* and *substantia* that more clearly makes the point of this sentence.[27]

In other words, tracing the term 'Subject' back to its philosophical origins means that whenever it is broached we ought simultaneously to hear 'substance', understood literally as a sub-stance, something standing below. This substance or Subject would therefore be an essence standing at a remove from worldly contingency, and as such the ultimate horizon of meta-physical discourse, given its attempts to locate unchanging essences. But this is not the whole picture painted by the first reading present in *L'Absolu littéraire*, as it leaves no room for the Romantics' project of founding a new art form. The aim of the latter, on this view, was to use art as a means of installing the Subject, giving it the expression it had hitherto been denied (i.e. by Kant).[28] Thus, art's role would be simply to carry out the operation of philosophy, doing its work or indeed *being* that Work: this is what permitted Lacoue-Labarthe and Nancy to propose *L'Opération littéraire* (*The Literary Operation*) as the volume's title (*L'Absolu littéraire* was eventually adopted on the suggestion of the series editor at Seuil, Tzvetan Todorov).[29] Such is the suggestion made by the relation sketched out in *L'Absolu littéraire* between Kantian philosophy and Romanticism: 'La philosophie [...] commande le romantisme,' ['philosophy [...] drives romanticism'] which is glossed as follows: 'Kant ouvre la possibilité du romantisme' (AL 42; ['Kant opens up the possibility of romanticism', LA 29]). The Romantics would therefore not only be engaged in metaphysics, but in a metaphysics of presence: giving concrete form and expression to what is withdrawn from the world. It is notable that Lacoue-Labarthe and Nancy tie this first plank of their reading of Romanticism to the notion of reflexivity between 'literature' and 'theory': the apparent difference between these two discourses only serves to make the Subject's return to itself all the more powerful. As they write,

> dans tout ce qui commande à la fois la littérature comme auto-critique et la critique comme littérature, c'est bien nous qui sommes impliqués, c'est notre image — au miroir de l'absolu littéraire — qui nous est renvoyée. Et cette vérité massive qui nous est assénée: nous ne sommes pas sortis de l'époque du Sujet (AL 27).

> [we ourselves are implicated in all that determines both literature as auto-critique and criticism as literature. Our own image comes back to us from the mirror of the literary absolute. And the massive truth flung back at us is that we have not left the era of the Subject (LA 16)].

Such is the first reading of Romanticism that emerges from *L'Absolu littéraire*, one where the role the Romantics afford to art — to the literary absolute, namely the merging of literature and theory — serves as a new mode of expression for the unchanging essence named 'the Subject'. This new art-form was painted as being not just one amongst others, but a super-genre uniting all others within it, living up to the totalizing dimensions of *the* Subject, i.e. the Subject in general terms.

In order to see how the second plank of Lacoue-Labarthe and Nancy's reading complements and supplements this first one based around the Subject, it is necessary to look more closely at the detail of this Romantic project for an absolute, fusional artwork. We can do this by noting that a key chapter in the volume recycles an expression used by Blanchot, 'l'exigence fragmentaire' ['the fragmentary demand'], before using a discussion of conceptions of the artwork to look at the fragment both as 'le genre romantique par excellence' (AL 58; ['the romantic genre par excellence', LA 40]) and as that which confirms the Jena group's modern credentials.[30] It is worthwhile pausing over the attention given to fragmentation here, and considering that one way of articulating the difference between a fragmentary and a non-fragmentary text is that the former is composed largely of beginnings, endings, and edges, with only minimal middle. In other words, a fragmentary text has a large surface area in comparison to its mass. The argument that *L'Absolu littéraire* makes in relation to the Jena Romantics' fragmentary work is that this large surface area, as it were, allows a work of this type to comment relatively more on its own form and make-up, and relatively less on its supposed subject-matter. On this reading, fragmentation is not just one form amongst several, but is a way of allowing a particular work to have *more* form(s), and to be always distancing itself from any single iteration of form.

Such a principle informs Lacoue-Labarthe and Nancy's volume insofar as its conclusion in fact refuses to conclude, stating instead that they have been driven by a desire to question the validity of conclusions, given that the Romantics' thinking arises from the tension between resolution and dispersion, between the absolute and dissolution. And indeed, throughout the course of the work — although in conjunction with their first, Subject-oriented reading — Lacoue-Labarthe and Nancy discuss a striking variety of proposals made by the Jena Romantics in the course of their reflection on new forms for thinking. In their words,

> le romantisme implique quelque chose d'inédit, — la *production* de quelque chose d'inédit. Ce quelque chose, à vrai dire, les Romantiques en ignorent le nom: ils parlent tantôt de poésie, tantôt d'œuvre, tantôt de roman, tantôt de... romantisme. Ils finiront quand même par l'appeler — bon an, mal an — *littérature* (AL 21, emphases original).

> [romanticism implies something entirely new, the *production* of something entirely new. The Romantics never really succeed in naming this something: they speak of poetry, of the work, of the novel, or... of romanticism. In the end, they decide to call it — all things considered — *literature* (LA 11, emphases original)].

This variety of forms being considered for a privileged role is testament to the inventive energies of the Romantic group; but it also demonstrates that the question of form, or more properly *Darstellung* (presentation), remains without resolution. Perhaps the best-known expression of this iterability or transferability of form can be found in Friedrich Schlegel's statement that modernity has come about in a triple form: in politics with the French Revolution, in philosophy with Fichte's *Wissenschaftlehre* [*Epistemology*], and in art with Goethe's *Wilhelm Meisters Lehrjahre* [*Wihelm Meister's Apprenticeship*; AL 127]. We can relate the second plank of Lacoue-Labarthe and Nancy's reading to this statement as follows: the Romantic 'operation' comes about in the fusional interplay of different forms and genres, and the task remaining for deconstruction is to mark and re-mark upon the slippages between them, without falling back into any single, absolute genre, be it philosophy, literature, or politics.

Looking back over the two readings jostling within Lacoue-Labarthe and Nancy's account of Jena Romanticism, we can see that there is no resolution to the considerable divergences between them — Jena telling us on the one hand that 'we have not left the era of the Subject', but on the other signalling the possibility of 'something entirely new'. What both readings share is the sense that the relation between philosophy and literature is crucial, being understood either as a relation of self-reflexivity and mutual reinforcement underlining the domination of the Subject, or as one of mutual erosion with each discourse clashing with the other, leading to the interruption of the Subject. In any case, this major early work sets the terms of debate that will reverberate throughout many aspects of Lacoue-Labarthe's thinking, from his approach to *l'écriture* as something escaping the dualism between philosophy and literature (see chapter 3) to the reading of Blanchot's fragments (see chapter 5), and from opera and the Wagnerian *Gesamtkunstwerk* to Hölderlin's translations of theatre, the latter being seen as interrupting philosophical interpretations of tragedy (see chapters 4b and 4c).

The question of whether Jena Romanticism represents a centripetal movement in which an underlying Subject is always being shored up, or something more centrifugal and fragmentary, is also explored by *L'Absolu littéraire* in terms of community and the political. This critical anthology was in part a gesture concerning the limitations of the contemporary, theoretical scene, albeit one made in and through the exposition of a group of Romantic thinkers that was largely new to French thought. But beyond this, it also had something to say about the privilege afforded to avant-garde groups as the intellectual unit charged with advancing thought. And it made this intervention both via its discussion of Jena Romanticism, and methodologically, via Lacoue-Labarthe and Nancy's practice of writing as a pair. We can grasp this better by looking at the relationship between the forms of community attempted at Jena, and the similarly experimental community existing in Strasbourg. In other words, in looking at the account given of the Jena group we make discoveries about how Lacoue-Labarthe and Nancy conceived of their own collaboration, as well as how — and whether — it fitted in to the French intellectual scene of the 1970s. In this light, the following passage is significant:

> [le romantisme d'Iéna] est en fait, il n'est pas du tout exagéré de le dire, le premier groupe d'"avant-garde' de l'histoire. Nulle part en tout cas, dans ce qui s'intitule à notre époque 'avant-garde' [...], on ne peut constater le moindre écart par rapport à cette forme inaugurée il y a aura bientôt deux cents ans. L'*Athenæum* est notre lieu de naissance. (AL 17)

> [In fact, and without any exaggeration, [Jena romanticism] is the first 'avant-garde' group in history. At no point, in any case, can one discern the slightest departure from this nearly two-hundred-year-old form on the part of what calls itself 'avant-garde' today [...]. The *Athenæum* is our birthplace (LA 8, trans. mod.)].

Here the link that above we saw being drawn between Jena and the (then) present day is clear; but the element concerning the avant-garde is new. The reference to 'what calls itself "avant-garde" today' is explicit, and the relation with Jena is couched in wholly unambiguous language: 'at *no* point can one discern the *slightest* departure' (emphases added). What is missing is an explicit reference to which 1970s avant-garde groups are being referred to; but the statements seen above give us cause to see this as a reference to *Tel Quel*, with that group's insistence on textuality, self-reflexivity, and *l'écriture*. If this is the case, then Lacoue-Labarthe, whilst exploring the question of *l'écriture* in depth and holding a deep respect for Derrida, for instance, sees his own avowedly deconstructive practice as sitting uneasily with the dominant contemporary 'avant-garde'. But this does not prevent the fact that an avant-garde of this same type is said to be 'our birthplace'. This is to say that despite Lacoue-Labarthe and Nancy's unease as to the self-justifying practices prevalent amongst avant-garde groups, they nonetheless form a phenomenon that must be engaged with. Even if one does not endorse the model of the avant-garde, preferring to question rather than assume its ultimate validity, it is nonetheless a question that the contingencies of modern thought force one to ask. Indeed, such an engagement is a pre-requisite for any investigation into the assumptions and preconditions informing our common existence alongside each other, which is to say into who — and how — 'we' might be.

Displacing the Modern

At stake in the identification with and ultimate rejection of the avant-garde model represented by Jena Romanticism and by *Tel Quel* is Lacoue-Labarthe's understanding of the modern. For, as we have seen, he sees this model as being present not only at Jena but as having become a constitutive part of the way we approach writing and thinking. And it is indeed true that the language of the group and the movement inflects modern production, from Romanticism and surrealism to post-1960 thinkers who are labelled as 'post-structuralists' or 'theorists'. However, whilst Lacoue-Labarthe recognizes the dominance of this model — he and Nancy after all wrote that the avant-garde Jena review the *Athenæum* was 'our birthplace' —, he also seeks to displace it. This is because he sees it as unrealistic for a modern movement to detach itself totally from what made it possible, i.e. to provide an auto-foundation. In place of such an assertive modernity, he pursues a more deconstructive line of thinking, i.e. one that presents itself as a practice of reading rather than as assertion or creation. In Lacoue-Labarthe's view, much of the most radical writing proceeds from this bracketing or suspension of possibility. Indeed, often this writing both fails to fit into avant-garde, programmatic horizons (such as those of Jena) and at the same time narrates this very failure. As he puts it, '[l]a littérature [...] n'est jamais née. Ce n'est pas faute d'avoir *répété*, inlassablement, interminablement, son effort à naître' ['[l]iterature [...] has never been born. This is not because it did not rehearse, untiringly, unceasingly, its attempts to be born'].[31] In other words, the type of writing in question can be defined as resisting any mythology being built around it, even mythologies based on the power and the special role of art, and can instead be defined as the resistance to such mythologization.

The concept of birth that we have seen being used on various occasions will be a recurrent motif as Lacoue-Labarthe seeks to distance himself from Romantics both past and present. In this vein, he writes that:

> Dans son concept — je ne parle ni du mot ni, encore moins, de la chose —, la littérature a vu le jour dans les brèves (et fulgurantes) années du romantisme d'Iéna [...]. Le concept de littérature a vu le jour entre 1798 et 1800.
>
> [...] le concept de littérature est contemporain — en tant qu'il le suppose et l'exige — du concept philosophique de naissance.[32]

> [In its concept — I am not speaking about the word nor, even less, about the thing itself—, literature saw the light of day in the brief (and dazzling) years of Jena Romanticism [...]. The concept of literature saw the light of day between 1798 and 1800.
>
> [...] the concept of literature is contemporary to — insofar as it assumes and demands it — the philosophical concept of birth.]

In other words, by becoming aware of the contemporaneous emergence of 'literature' as a term, of early German Romanticism, and of the concept of birth, we can free ourselves of some of the clichés of critical language. And one of those clichés, that of birth, appears particularly problematic insofar as it collapses historical difference, replacing it with a bloodline, filiation, or genealogy linking — for instance — Jena and Strasbourg, the location of Lacoue-Labarthe and Nancy's community. This is to say that the metaphor of birth posits an underlying Subject, which is simply renewed and reconfirmed by birth, rather than altered in any fundamental way. Lacoue-Labarthe reacts against this with a line of thinking alluded to by the title *L'Avortement de la littérature* — first proposed for the second volume of *Typographies* (which instead appeared as *L'Imitation des modernes*), and eventually used for a conference paper published in 1992.

The paper discusses the novel *Lucinde: Confessions of a Blunderer* (1799) by the Jena Romantic Friedrich Schlegel, and chimes with the feminist aims of the conference at which it was given by studying what Lacoue-Labarthe calls 'ce moment où ont été pensées ensemble, en effet, "femme, écriture, société"' ['this moment when, indeed, "woman, writing, society" were thought together'].[33] One sense of *avortement* that Lacoue-Labarthe brings out of the novel concerns the latter's incomplete nature: Schlegel presents it as 'Part I', but part II never appeared. The Romantic propensity for fragmentation therefore prevails in this case over that for completion. And there also seems to be an argument applicable beyond the Romantics: not so much that 'abortion' is a good thing in itself, but that it might be an important element of an approach to literature that focuses exclusively on birth, privileging the new and therefore failing to learn from past writers. Another second sense of *avortement* that Lacoue-Labarthe underlines relates to choice, freedom, and the thematic of an experimental sexual community. This recalls his discussion of Hegel's reading of *Lucinde*, which consists not in lengthy exposition but simply by writing the title of the novel in the margin of a text discussing marriage as the raising of biological sexual difference into social law. Representing dissolute experimentation, even from the marginal space afforded to it by Hegel, the novel provides a threatening counter-example. As Lacoue-Labarthe remarks,

'*Lucinde*, en (re)présentant l'insoumission au mariage, [est] un [...] scandale pour le spéculatif' ['*Lucinde*, by representing insubordination to marriage, [is] a [...] scandal for the speculative'].[34] In seeking to move away from Hegel's speculative reading, the French thinker's reading nonetheless employs Hegelian categories, according to which the interaction between man and woman ultimately stems from that between *physis* and *technè*, nature and technology. In the text, the twist is provided by the man's fumbling and clumsy *modus operandi* — these are, after all, the *Confessions of a Blunderer*. Despite the couple having sex, and despite the woman previously having previously been a mother (the child has since died), no child is born. Lacoue-Labarthe writes:

> [il n'y a] aucune sorte d'enfantement. Le génie, accouplé à la *technè*, n'est capable d'aucun enfant. Il révèle et élucide — il se révèle et s'élucide —, ce qui est déjà beaucoup. Et la littérature peut être, en effet, cette révélation, cette élucidation. Que porte par exemple, jusque dans son titre, la *Lucinde*. Cela ne veut pas dire qu'elle puisse naître, ni qu'elle soit née. — Peut-être parce que c'est la littérature, notre naissance.[35]

> [[there is] no childbirth at all. Genius, coupled with *technè*, is incapable of producing any children. It reveals and elucidates — it reveals and elucidates itself —, which is already a lot. And literature can indeed be this revelation, this elucidation. Which *Lucinde*, for example, carries even in its title. This does not mean that it can be born, nor that it has been born. — Perhaps because literature is our birth].

On this account, the true drama of the novel would be the possibility of art, arising — or failing to arise, arising in the form of failure — from an interaction between nature and technology; despite its claims to be morally experimental, Schlegel's novel on this reading repeats Hegel's gender bias whereby woman represents the natural world, waiting to be transformed and rendered whole by technology in the guise of man. In any case, the art in question is never born, existing rather in a state of suspension or impossibility, making demands upon us without laying foundations for the future, or making these demands precisely because it does not lay such foundations. Lacoue-Labarthe's final twist, on which the article ends — 'literature is our birth' — brings out the significance of this state of affairs. Whereas previously Jena Romanticism represented 'our birthplace', as Lacoue-Labarthe and Nancy wrote in *L'Absolu littéraire* (1978), now in 1992 'our birth' is to be found via a novel written by the leading Jena Romantic. But there is a crucial difference to be found in the fact that this novel gives us to think 'the abortion of literature'. This change is a telling one: the coherent 'we' is still being used as a cipher for our common existence, for the community which is at the base of any political reflection. 'We' are still reading and writing literature, but these actions no longer need to be placed under the sign of birth. There is no obvious genealogy, nor foundation laid for the future.

The underlying line of thinking here can be named as that of mimesis: instead of creating something new starting from nothing, this is the idea of always responding to an other, to what has gone before. Nancy has discussed the question of Lacoue-Labarthe's self-distancing from the notion of modernity in terms of this mimesis:

Philippe ne voudrait pas entendre parler de sa 'modernité'. Il dirait en effet que le Moderne se spécifie par une protension vers l'avenir qui implique une volonté d'autoproduction, ou d'autoengendrement, dont le ressort inavoué est un refus, ou plutôt une dénégation de la mimesis originaire qui aura été, au bout du compte, son maître-concept ou son leitmotiv obsédant (AN 110).

[Philippe would not like to hear discussion of his 'modernity'. Indeed he would say that the Modern is characterized by a protension towards the future which involves a will to self-production, or to self-generation, which unavowedly refuses or denies the originary mimesis which will have been, ultimately, his master-concept or the leitmotiv that obsessed him].

Interestingly, although the conception of the group of writers or thinkers as an avant-garde is rejected by Lacoue-Labarthe, this statement by Nancy clarifies an important strand in his collaborator's thought. For if this rejection is made in the name of an 'originary mimesis', i.e. a sense of being always already exposed to what lies outside oneself, then the issue of community continues to be pertinent. In other words, it is precisely by such collaborations as these two thinkers pursued that an individual thinker can be taken out of his own 'self-production', i.e. taken away from any act of self-founding as a distinct subjectivity. Instead, collaboration can represent an originary exposure to others. Perhaps counter-intuitively, it is therefore by their acute sensitivity to the demands of the age, namely the contemporary or the 'timely', that Lacoue-Labarthe and Nancy move beyond the modern, which thereby comes to be seen as a particular cultural form and one representing a closed tradition.

In this light, the modern can be seen as a cultural form with certain defined characteristics: avant-garde groups, narratives of self-foundation, a tendency towards totalization. If this view is adopted, then the modern can no longer be assumed to be the category obtaining to late twentieth-century thinkers (and Lacoue-Labarthe and Nancy collaborated on several occasions with Lyotard, author of *La Condition postmoderne*, 1979). In Lacoue-Labarthe's case, this opens up possibilities within his thought that we might not intuitively expect to feature in it: for instance, Nancy has reported that his reading of nineteenth-century novels tended more towards the classicizing Stendhal than the more modern Balzac or Zola.[36] And indeed, he addresses at some length the question of Lacoue-Labarthe's interest in what lies outside the particular cultural form of the modern:

[L]e rapport de Philippe au moderne a toujours été un rapport de méfiance dans la mesure où le moderne était pour lui caractérisé en effet par la 'protension vers l'avenir' et plus encore par la forme la plus accusée de cette protension, l''avant-garde'. L'idée d''avant-garde' était très liée pour lui à la fois à la nature militaire de cette métaphore et à l'affirmation conquérante, anticipatrice, impérieuse qu'il y discernait [...]. Il a toujours été ironique et sévère pour les 'avant-gardes'. En même temps ce motif évoquait la volonté d'innover, de faire de l'inédit, de se montrer original alors que pour lui rien n'était plus dangereux et au fond plus faux qu'une telle volonté. Il fallait au contraire pour lui être sobre (la 'sobriété junonienne' de Hölderlin était un thème favori) et classique — pas tout à fait au sens du classicisme français (encore que Racine, bien sûr, était bien présent pour lui) mais au sens d'une sorte d'épure allant de Montaigne à Rousseau puis

Stendhal et peut-être pas ou peu au-delà. Je crois que même Proust l'intéressait moins, pour ne rien dire de Joyce qu'il détestait.

'Classique' voulait dire pour lui sans effets, sans ornements presque (je pense à [Adolf] Loos, 'l'ornement c'est le crime' mais je ne sais plus ce qu'il pensait de cette phrase), dans une retenue ascétique, pudique. Il reconnaissait pourtant qu'on pouvait aussi produire des 'effets' de retenue, d'ascèse et de pudeur. Mais il maintenait cette position, quitte à se méfier d'une retenue trop ostensible (c'était pour lui le cas de Blanchot) autant que d'une exubérance (par exemple celle de Derrida).[37]

[Philippe's relation to the modern was always a relation of mistrust insofar as the modern for him was indeed characterized by 'protension towards the future' and even more by the most advanced form of this protension, the 'avant-garde'. The idea of the 'avant-garde' for him was strongly linked both to the military nature of this metaphor and to the conquering, anticipatory, imperious statement he believed it to be making [...]. He was always full of irony and severity for 'avant-gardes'. This motif also evoked the will to innovate, to create something new, to show oneself to be original, whilst for him nothing was more dangerous and ultimately more false than this wish. For him, one instead had to be sober (Hölderlin's 'Junonian sobriety' was a favourite theme) and classical — not completely in the sense of French classicism (even though Racine, of course, was certainly present in his thinking) but in the sense of a sort of sketch running from Montaigne to Rousseau then Stendhal and perhaps not far, or only a little, beyond that. I believe that even Proust interested him less, to say nothing of Joyce, whom he hated.

'Classic' for him meant without effects, almost without decorations (I think of [Adolf] Loos, 'decoration is crime' but I do not know what he thought of this expression), remaining in an ascetic, modest reserve. He was aware, however, that it was also possible to produce 'effects' of reserve, askesis, and modesty. He nonetheless maintained this position, all the while remaining mistrusting of over-ostensible reserve (this was Blanchot's situation, for him) as well as of exuberance (Derrida's, for instance)].

This passage presents us with an entire range of ways of locating Lacoue-Labarthe's thinking, for instance suggesting that what Hölderlin named 'sobriety' was a key motif in the French thinker's devotion to him, or in the final part locating Lacoue-Labarthe between the reserve or asceticism of Blanchot's writing and the 'exuberance' of Derrida. These two important interlocutors for Lacoue-Labarthe are thus seen not simply as influences, but counter-influences or counter-models, to be read and then rejected rather than simply imitated.

But beyond the localized interest represented by the presence of these or the other names in Nancy's statement, what is important is the underlying thought causing Lacoue-Labarthe to adopt these positions (and there is no particular reason to doubt Nancy's account in this instance). Namely, this is the thought of mimesis, i.e. that of responding to something lying outside the individual subject. Such a response should not be confused with a conservative resistance to the assertion of any particular individuality that might invoke some underlying essence or impersonal Subject, thus evading difficult questions of class, gender, and so on (such is often the reading given of discourses of 'the classical'). Instead, here the motif of mimesis produces an aversion to 'the will to innovate, to create something new, to show oneself to be original' — and this scepticism regarding originality suggests that it is for necessary rather than contingent reasons that Lacoue-Labarthe's oeuvre so often takes the form of readings, just as it is for the same type of reasons that he so often collaborated with other thinkers and in doing so sought to leave institutional traces of his activity. Having looked at some of these collaborations and the thinking underpinning them, let us now turn to a related area of his work with Nancy: namely, their exploration of the thematics of mutual exposure and originary sociality in the domain of what they name 'le philosophico-politique' ['the philosophico-political'].[38]

Notes to Chapter 1

1. In interview of 27 July 2013. Another role-play of this nature was established between Lacoue-Labarthe as the Heidegger of the mid-1930s on (with his interest in *Dichtung*) versus Nancy's early Heidegger (with his interest in fundamental ontology).
2. In interview with Pascal Possoz, unpublished (early 2000s).
3. In *'Haine de la poésie'* (Paris: Bourgois, 1979), p. 164.
4. 'Le Lieu dit: Strasbourg', in Derrida, Lacoue-Labarthe, Nancy et al., *Penser à Strasbourg* ([*Thinking in/about Strasbourg*]; Paris/Strasbourg: Galilée/Ville de Strasbourg, 2004), pp. 31–59 (p. 46).
5. In *Écrits politiques 1953–1993* (Paris: Gallimard, 2008), p. 150; *Political Writings, 1953–1993*, trans. by Zakir Paul (New York: Fordham University Press, 2010), p. 85. Blanchot reportedly wrote to Nancy that he was amazed that Lacoue-Labarthe and Nancy's arrangement had not led them to destroy one another.
6. *Les Fins de l'homme: à partir du travail de Jacques Derrida* (1980; Paris: Hermann, 2013). Henceforth abbreviated to FH.
7. In 1975, Lacoue-Labarthe, Nancy, and Derrida had arranged a visit to Heidegger, but the philosopher was too ill for it to take place (see Janicaud, *Heidegger en France*, vol. II: *Entretiens*, p. 209). Lacoue-Labarthe also recounts that after the thinker's death the following year, he and Lucien Braun were invited to look over Heidegger's library, some of which was incorporated into the University of Strasbourg's collections. For his part, Nancy recounts a trip made with Lacoue-Labarthe to Heidegger's infamous hillside hut at Todtnauberg as 'une démarche un peu ironique' ['a slightly ironic enterprise'] — see the film *Voyage à Tübingen: un portrait de Philippe Lacoue-Labarthe* [*Voyage to Tübingen: a Portrait of Philippe Lacoue-Labarthe*].
8. 'Philippe', in *Philippe Lacoue-Labarthe: la césure et l'impossible* [*Philippe Lacoue-Labarthe: Cæsura and the Impossible*]; Paris: Lignes, 2010), pp. 409–33 (pp. 413–14).
9. See also 'Un Commencement' ['A Beginning'], in Lacoue-Labarthe, *L'Allégorie'*, pp. 123–66. Lacoue-Labarthe himself gives credence to this narrative in 'La Fiction du biographique'.
10. 'Un Commencement', p. 129.
11. In interview of 27 July 2013.
12. See 'Philippe Lacoue-Labarthe, *Le Sujet de la philosophie*', in *L'Actualité littéraire*, 18 (April 1979), 13.
13. *Scène suivi de Dialogue sur le dialogue* (Paris: Bourgois, 2013), p. 61.
14. A further text also features three different configurations of interlocutors: 'Entretien', in *Exercices de la patience*, 3–4 (Spring 1982), 219–31, has a first section containing named interventions by Lacoue-Labarthe, Nancy, Alain David, and Philippe Jandin. A second section then presents anonymous interlocutors, but is elaborated from the recording of discussions between the four men. Finally, Lacoue-Labarthe and Nancy seek to clarify their position (on Heidegger, the subject of the debate), which suggests that there was a limit to how far they were prepared to see their names being put to collective statements.
15. See Lacoue-Labarthe's 'Éloge: sur Guy Debord' ['Eulogy: on Guy Debord']; AN, 241–42) and Rodolphe Gasché, 'Situationniste pour une part?' ['A Situationist in Part?'], in *Lignes*, 22 (May 2007), 120–29. The important Situationist text, 'De la Misère en milieu étudiant' (['On Poverty in Student Life']; Strasbourg: A.F.G.E.S., 1966), contributed to his relationship with Strasbourg.

16. 'La Fiction du biographique', pp. 202–03.

17. The anthology was preceded by two others: Lacoue-Labarthe and Nancy's own, dedicated to 'Littérature et philosophie mêlées' ['Literature and Philosophy Intermingled'], in *Poétique*, 21 (1975), and Jean-Christophe Bailly's *La Légende dispersée: Anthologie du romantisme allemand* (1976; [*The Dispersed Legend: Anthology of German Romanticism*]. For an overview of the considerable number of critical reactions to *L'Absolu littéraire*, see Daniel J. Hooselma, 'The Echo of an Impossible Future in *The Literary Absolute*', in *Modern Language Notes*, 119:4 (September 2004), 845–68.

18. In 'Re-re-re-reading Jena', in *Modern Language Notes*, 110:4 (1995), 834–55 (p. 850).

19. In 'Rede über die Mythologie', in *Dialogue on Poetry*, trans. by Ernst Behler and Roman Struc (University Park: Pennsylvania State U. P., 1968), p. 81.

20. 'La Loi du genre' (1979), in *Parages*, rev. ed. (Paris: Galilée, 2003), pp. 231–66 (p. 238, emphasis added); trans. by Avital Ronell as 'The Law of Genre', in *Critical Inquiry*, 7:1 (Autumn 1980), 55–81 (p. 59, emphasis added).

21. See Tzvetan Todorov's anthology of Russian Formalist texts, *Théorie de la littérature* (*Theory of Literature*; Paris: Seuil, 1965) and the *Théorie d'ensemble* published by *Tel Quel* ([*Ensemble Theory*]; Paris: Seuil, 1968).

22. On psychoanalysis, see *Le Titre de la lettre: une lecture de Lacan* (1973), the two texts collected in *La Panique politique*, and 'La Scène est primitive' ['The Scene is Primal'] and 'L'Écho du sujet' ['The Echo of the Subject'], in *Le Sujet de la philosophie* (1979). We can also note that the title of *Agonie terminée, agonie interminable: sur Maurice Blanchot* ([*Agony Ended and Unending: on Maurice Blanchot*]; Paris: Galilée, 2011) — which is henceforth abbreviated to ATAI — is calked on a Freud text which in French is called *Analyse terminée, analyse interminable* and in English 'Analysis Terminable and Interminable' (1937). The essay itself affords great importance to the psychoanalytical notion of the *scène primitive* or primal scene.

23. Lacoue-Labarthe and Nancy's aversion to 'theory' is confirmed the following year when they discuss the figure of the Father in Freud as being a theory, i.e. something that allows itself to be seen, to fall within the power of the gaze (the etymology of the term being *theorein*, to view or contemplate). See *La Panique politique*, p. 73.

24. In *L'Impératif catégorique* ([*The Categorical Imperative*]; Paris: Aubier-Flammarion, 1992), pp. 139–53.

25. For instance, *La Remarque spéculative: un bon mot de Hegel* ([*The Speculative Remark: a Bon Mot by Hegel*]; Paris: Aubier-Flammarion, 1973) feeds into discussions of the Romantics' relationship with Hegelian dialectic; and *Le Discours de la syncope: I. Logodædalus* ([*The Discourse of Passing-Out/Syncopation: I. Logodædalus*]; Paris: Aubier-Flammarion, 1976), growing out of the article named 'Logodædalus (Kant écrivain)' ['Logodædalus (Kant as Writer)'], in *Poétique*, 21 (1975), 24–52, engages with one of the key questions addressed in *L'Absolu littéraire*: philosophy's reliance on a need for form, writing, or presentation (*Darstellung*).

26. As Ian James writes in his account of Nancy's *Logodaedalus*: 'in order to separate philosophy from literature in a clearly delimited and conceptually rigorous manner, philosophy must *already* be philosophy and this it cannot *yet* be', in *The Fragmentary Demand*, p. 42 (emphases added). See also the rest of his account of *Logodædalus*, pp. 26–48.

27. In *Philippe Lacoue-Labarthe*, p. 6.

28. Useful exposition of this point is found throughout Hooselma's article 'The Echo of an Impossible Future in *The Literary Absolute*'. For instance, he writes that '[a]lthough Kant insists that the presentation of this essential idea of the subject in art remains strictly analogical, the temptation to make the attempt proves to be too powerful for the Romantics to resist. They try to pick the forbidden fruit'. (p. 849)

29. In Nancy, 'Philippe', p. 427. Indeed, Nancy in an interview with the author (27 July 2013) stated that his and Lacoue-Labarthe's initial proposal to Todorov was for a translation of Jean Paul's *Vorschüle der Æsthetik* (*Introduction to Æsthetics*, 1804). This was refused, with Todorov instead suggesting an anthology of the Jena texts (on which he had already written two essays — see *La Notion de littérature et autres essais* ([*The Notion of Literature and Other* Essays]; Paris: Seuil, 1987), pp. 25–27.

30. Blanchot, *L'Entretien infini* (Paris: Gallimard, 1969), p. 206.

31. In 'Précis', p. 148, the original emphasis refers to the double meaning in French of *répéter*: to repeat and to rehearse.

32. In 'L'Avortement de la littérature' ['The Abortion of Literature'], in *Du Féminin* [*On the Feminine*] (Grenoble: Le Griffon d'argile and Presses Universitaires de Grenoble, 1992), pp. 3–19 (p. 3).

33. In 'L'Avortement de la littérature', p. 3.

34. In 'L'Imprésentable' ('The Unpresentable'), in *Poétique*, 21 (1975), 53–95 (p. 68).

35. 'L'Avortement de la littérature', p. 19.

36. Interview with the author of 19 September 2013.

37. Jean-Luc Nancy, correspondence with the author of 9 November 2011.

38. In *Rejouer le politique* (Paris: Galilée, 1981), p. 28; *Retreating the Political*, trans. by Simon Sparks (London: Routledge, 1997), p. 120.

CHAPTER 2

Philosophy and the Political

In the late 1970s and 1980s, Lacoue-Labarthe and Nancy undertook a reflection on discourses of shared existence, community, and politics. This was partly due to the circumstances of their early interactions (Strasbourg Situationism, May '68) and partly due to their interest in a mode of commonality distinct from that of closed, avant-garde groups. But although references to mainstream politics can be found in their work — for instance a shared desire not to 'nuire à la gauche' ['harm the left'] —, the political reflections in question go further than this.[1] For instance, Nancy has recently described as follows the differences between himself and Lacoue-Labarthe regarding the necessity of dismantling political figures or fictions: '[Philippe] voulait une réduction anarchisante de toute figure d'autorité, j'objectais à la fois l'irréalisme de l'anarchie et la nécessité d'une certaine "configuralité". Il me traitait de social-démocrate, je le traitais de rêveur conseilliste' (AN III; ['[Philippe] wanted an anarchist reduction of all figures of authority, I had objections based both on the unreality of anarchy and on the necessity of some kind of "configurality". He would call me a social-democrat, I would disparage him as a councilist dreamer').[2] As the terms of even this short statement begin to suggest, Lacoue-Labarthe and Nancy's discussions over politics play a full role in their wider thinking, a contribution underlined by the numerous moments which the two thinkers returned to this ensemble of questions.

These moments can be organized into two rough groups: the first consisted of collaborations between the two thinkers. This group includes the conference they organized (including a 'political seminar'), *Les Fins de l'homme* (1980), as well as shorter texts such as 'La Panique politique' (1979), 'Le Peuple juif ne rêve pas' (1980; ['The Jewish People does not Dream']), and *Le Mythe nazi* (1980; [*The Nazi Myth*]).[3] Beyond this, they established at the *École Normale Supérieure* in Paris a *Centre de recherches philosophiques sur le politique* [*Centre for Philosophical Research on the Political*], which gave rise to two collective volumes — *Rejouer le politique* (1981; [*Replaying the Political*]) and *Le Retrait du politique* (1983; [*(With)Drawing the Political*]) — and featured many prominent figures (Etienne Balibar, Derrida, Luc Ferry, Jean-François Lyotard, Jacques Rancière et al.).[4] Although scattered, these various texts form as it were the undergrowth from which will appear a series of reflections on what they name *le politique* or 'the political'. The second grouping of texts are those authored by each thinker working alone, and where this mature thinking of political discourse can be found: for Nancy, this means *La Communauté désœuvrée* (1983–1986), a text which has since become a landmark but which it seems necessary to place in the context of his work with Lacoue-Labarthe. For the latter, the text in question is *La Fiction du politique: Heidegger, l'art et la politique* (1987), one of the major pieces in his production. This chapter will be structured around this latter work, given that it is Lacoue-Labarthe's most developed approach to political discourse — although we will also refer back to the collaborations with Nancy from which several key concepts emerge.

Lacoue-Labarthe's thinking around politics and community therefore causes us to consider his collaborative writing in the light of his solo work, and vice-versa. What's more, his reflections on art, literature, and philosophy are also reconfigured by the works examined in this chapter. This is especially the case in terms of philosophy, which he comes to understand in the very particular, even idiosyncratic sense of Western metaphysics as a closed and limiting discourse. To this extent, we will see him adopting an increasingly hostile position towards Heidegger, who had been a formative influence on the early part of his career. As his thinking develops in these ways, Lacoue-Labarthe concentrates his efforts to demonstrate that both Heidegger's understanding of philosophy and that of political discourse constitute what he names a *fiction du politique* (fiction of the political). This notion, which we shall explore in due course, causes him to remain firmly opposed to what Nancy calls 'the necessity of a certain "configurality"', as is demonstrated by the attacks in *La Fiction du politique*, to which we now turn, on two notions that share the root *fingere*, and for him are synonymous: figure and fiction.

La Fiction du politique

La Fiction du politique: Heidegger, l'art et la politique (1987) makes a distinctive contribution to debates on Heidegger's relation to both philosophy and political discourse. As part of this undertaking, the work takes us through deconstruction's relation to 'philosophy' (metaphysics), art, and what it sees in Heidegger's work as *la fiction du politique*, a phenomenon encompassing — but not reducible to — his participation in Nazi politics. It therefore engages in a reading of Heidegger in parallel with Victor Farias's *Heidegger et le nazisme* [*Heidegger and Nazism*], a work Lacoue-Labarthe called 'pas juste' and 'malhonnête' (FP 178; ['unjust' and 'dishonest', HAP 127]) on the basis that it ignores vast, relevant swathes of Heidegger's work.[5] Strikingly, the books by Lacoue-Labarthe and Farias — as well as Derrida's *De l'Esprit: Heidegger et la question* (*Of Spirit: Heidegger and the Question*) addressing the same topic — all appeared the same year. This may have been down to the three authors' desire to react to Hugo Ott's biographical research on Heidegger that was being published in Germany from 1984–85 and culminated in his biography of 1988.[6] But I hope to show that Lacoue-Labarthe's thinking also draws on the category of 'the political' that he had been elaborating since at least the early 1980s. It is thus on the basis of these long-standing reflections that Lacoue-Labarthe is able to engage with Farias's assertions and to debate with Derrida.[7]

Before we look further at the argument of *La Fiction du politique*, namely that the political involves the production of fictions or figures, we can note the institutional conditions in which it arose. The slim but dense volume was presented as the centrepiece of Lacoue-Labarthe's dossier in application for a *doctorat d'État*, and as such raises the question of whether his work up to that point — much of it, of course, written in collaboration with Nancy — can be represented or summarized by a single and singly-authored volume. Indeed, it seems alien to deconstructive thought to suggest that one work can represent the essence of others, or indeed act as a centrepiece to them: Derrida, for example, refused to write such a centrepiece for his own doctoral examination in 1980.[8] However, Lacoue-Labarthe goes against Derrida's example here, and as such the work demonstrates a more confident, independent attitude than some of his earlier articles. The tension would have been clear given that alongside Jean-François Lyotard, George Steiner, Pierre Aubenque, Lucien Braun (supervisor of the thesis and the person who had introduced Lacoue-Labarthe and Nancy to one another), and Suzanne Saïd, Derrida featured amongst the examiners. However, *La Fiction du politique* does not necessarily show Lacoue-Labarthe casting off Derridean shackles and becoming a philosopher in the Anglo-American style. For instance, he does argue that '[j]e n'ai pas fait de thèse, l'ensemble que je présente ici est fragmenté. Cela ne fait pas un livre, sur un sujet ou un auteur déterminé. Ce sont, comme on dit aujourd'hui, des textes' ['I have not written a thesis, the collection that I am presenting here is fragmented. It does not make up a book on a given subject or author. They are, as people say nowadays, texts'].[9] But there is nonetheless a certain shift away from performativity — whilst fragmentation is still there, it is accompanied by the conviction that one can serve this fragmentation by holding a discourse upon it, rather than simply through performance or enactment of fragmentation.

The work's dense, compacted quality is another notable feature: in 175 pages we are taken on a fast-paced tour of Lacoue-Labarthe's thinking, ranging from readings of Hölderlin to Hans-Jürgen Syberberg's films, and from ancient Greek thought to the demand to respond to the concentration camps. The density of the work — Simon Critchley sees it as adopting 'an irritating and sub-Heideggerian grandeur of tone' — stems in part from the sense that it is a farewell to Lacoue-Labarthe's apprenticeship as a thinker.[10] In this vein, the appendix to the first printing of the thesis, which was excised from the work in its main published version and replaced by a text on Farias's *Heidegger et le nazisme*, is a text named 'La Fiction du biographique', which ventures beyond academic conventions in order to summarize its author's intellectual itinerary. It recounts his early fascination with literature, the subsequent draw of deconstructive thinking under Heidegger's influence, and conveys disappointment regarding the abandonment of both literature and, subsequently, Heideggerian philosophy.[11] To this double tone of disappointment we can add that concerning his collaboration with Jean-Luc Nancy: their collaboration is confined to isolated moments after the mid-1980s. In short, this first appendix reads like a self-written obituary, less autobiography than autothanatography. These considerations are reflected in the format of the work: ten main, sequentially numbered chapters are interrupted by three post-scripta, interjected after chapters 3, 5, and 9 and dealing with reactions by critics including Derrida and erstwhile teacher Gérard Granel. The fact that these post-scripta do not feature in their natural position at the end of the work might support that argument that, even in its first mainstream edition, it is presented as a thing of the past, and thus makes reference to the joint closure of the philosophical and the political of which it speaks (see below). Another effect of the positioning of the post-scripta is to accentuate the movement between chapters: when chapter 3, named '1933', closes, we might assume that discussion of Heidegger's relationship with Nazism during that year's rectorship of Freiburg University is over. And yet when chapter 4 resumes, after 'Post-scriptum 1', it is to continue to hammering away at this issue: its title is 'Faute' (translated in the English version as 'Doing Wrong'). This notion is carefully distinguished from that of error, for to speak of Heidegger's error in adhering to Nazism would be to see it as an errancy or aberration (the latter understood literally), i.e. a deviation from the core of his thinking. For Lacoue-Labarthe, however, this was no deviation, but instead something revealing the core of that thinking. In truth, this distinction between fault and error relies on the broader distinction in Lacoue-Labarthe's mind between everyday politics (*la politique*) and a broader mode of thought and engagement sharing its totalizing tendencies with metaphysical philosophy (*le politique*). These are the terms that enable us to continue to look at the condemnation of Heidegger in question.

La politique, le politique

Lacoue-Labarthe understands *le politique* or 'the political' in a particular way, i.e. as reproducing the totalizing mechanisms of metaphysical philosophy. This understanding is what led he and Nancy to write of 'la co-appartenance essentielle (et non accidentelle ou simplement historique) du philosophique et du politique' ['the essential (and not accidental or simply historical) co-belonging of the philosophical and the political'].[12] In order to further understand this certainly unusual sense of 'the political', it is useful to note that as well as being closely tied to metaphysical philosophy, it is also contradistinguished from *la politique*, the standard French term for politics. We can understand the latter term with relative ease as referring to the empirical field of established politics or political discourse. In this vein, in his discussion of Nancy Ian James frames this distinction in a useful way: '*La politique* is the empirical field of politics, the politics "of the Chinese Emperors, the Benin Kings, of Louis XIV, or of German social democracy". *Le politique* is a "specific dimension of alterity", prior to politics per se but fundamental to its possible modes of articulation or becoming.'[13] Other critics have read the distinction between the two positions as an unsatisfying one, ultimately leading Lacoue-Labarthe and Nancy to a privileging of the general, philosophical implications of *le politique* over the more pressing demands of *la politique*. Both Nancy Fraser and — although with greater sensitivity — Critchley adopt this position, which however leads them back to simply arguing for *la politique*, namely for what Fraser calls a 'good, old-fashioned, political fight'.[14] Even setting aside the question of whether the 'old-fashioned', traditional way of doing politics is 'good' — May '68 certainly thought otherwise —, this argument is surely misdirected. For it is not the case that being directed away from *la politique* as a concern with contemporary or timely demands necessarily entails a move towards the more general category of *le politique* and the untimely demands of what is to come. Whilst Lacoue-Labarthe and Nancy do indeed propose a move beyond *la politique*, this does not mean that *le politique* need be championed or adopted. The move between the two is a methodological one which must be carried out in order for them to be in a position to undertake a reading of *le politique* and its association with philosophy. This is to say that we cannot assume any prior decision or even inclination on the two thinkers' part in adopting *le politique*, at the expense of *la politique*, as a framework governing thought and action.

The distinction between these two approaches to political discourse is thus important for Lacoue-Labarthe throughout the 1980s, and especially so in relation to Heidegger. In terms of the latter's record, there is ample material demonstrating his adherence to Nazism in an everyday way (i.e. that of *la politique*), and on the basis of which in 1945 he was found guilty of political crimes and banned from university activities for five years. For instance, as Hitler was consolidating his grasp on power in 1933, the rector of Freiburg university was dismissed for declining to display 'the Jewish proclamation', and Heidegger took on the role in his place, eventually agreeing to display the proclamation. He went on to give numerous pro-Hitler speeches (which were published in Germany in 1960 and in France the following year).[15] He acted prejudiciously against Jewish students, and would later remove the dedication to his Jewish *Meister* Edmund Husserl from the 1941 edition of *Being and Time*. On resigning the rectorship after 10 months (following the 'night of the long knives' in summer 1934), he retained his Nazi party card until 1945. Beyond these elements, there is a reference in the 'Introduction to Metaphysics' (a 1935 lecture published in 1953) to Nazism and the 'the inner truth and greatness of this movement';[16] and no indication of remorse or apology was ever issued in relation to the concentration camps (the single reference uses them as an example of the technological nature of modern societies).[17] These elements are fully discussed in Lacoue-Labarthe's work. But whilst he condemns this vein of involvement with the Nazis, his thorough approach causes him to take into consideration the entirety of Heidegger's production following his resignation of the rectorship. Now, the mid-1930s would be significant in the thinker's work even if we knew nothing about his life: his first lectures on Hölderlin date from 1934–35 (renewed in 1941–42), and other key works are also begun at this time ('The Origin of the Work of Art', 1935–37; 'Overcoming Metaphysics', 1936–46, the lectures on Nietzsche 1936–41). Lacoue-Labarthe's interpretive strategy is to take all of these types of documentation into consideration. In doing so, he arrives at the view that whilst Heidegger's thought undergoes a renewal in the mid-1930s, it is not in any radically anti-Nazi way; and the argument (made by Heidegger in his famous 1966 interview with *Der Spiegel*) that this was due to the prevailing censorship is invalidated by his continued attitude post-1945. Rather, this renewal — I discuss below the theory of the *Kehre* or turn towards language — is seen by the French thinker as an increased engagement with the essence of Nazism, despite or due to the reduction in everyday participation in the movement.

In short, for *La Fiction du politique* and its treatment of Heidegger, the German thinker's relationship with the Nazi movement goes much deeper than the institutional and biographical facts with which it is sometimes confused. To this extent, Lacoue-Labarthe's study is therefore more weighty than Farias's *Heidegger et le nazisme* and other journalistic reactions in the late 1980s; indeed, Janicaud wrote of it that '[u]n livre se détache du lot et ouvre même un nouvel horizon philosophique, une phase plus intéressante du débat autour de "l'affaire" [...] *La Fiction du politique* [...] est le premier [essai] à proposer une lecture philosophique permettant de comprendre la "politique" de Heidegger' ['[o]ne book rises above the others and even opens a new philosophical horizon, a more interesting phase of the "affair" [...] *The Fiction of the Political* [...] is the first [work] to propose a philosophical reading that allows us to understand Heidegger's "politics"'].[18] Whilst condemning outright Heidegger's unambiguously Nazi actions and statements — particularly the post-war attitude, which he describes as 'scandaleusement insuffisan[t]' (FP 58; ['scandalously inadequate', HAP 34]) —, Lacoue-Labarthe also seeks to take the accusation further. This is to say that rather than addressing simply *la politique*, i.e. distinct political actions, he seeks to base his accusations in the wider realm of *le politique*, i.e. that which mirrors the totalizing Western notion of philosophy. In his mind, whilst Heidegger's politics are reprehensible and should be condemned without hesitation, it is *le politique de Heidegger* that presents the truly lasting difficulty, precisely to the extent that it involves his wider thinking, above and beyond biographical or institutional actions. Whilst Heidegger did have some prominence as rector at Freiburg, his reputation and influence as a thinker is greater by many scales of magnitude. It is thus on this second terrain that the discussions must take place.

The Philosophico-Political

Throughout Lacoue-Labarthe's thinking, 'philosophy' is endowed with a very specific set of connotations, making it clear that it is not the genre or discipline to which his investigations belong in any straightforward way. Nowhere is this more the case than in his reflections on the political, both preceding *La Fiction du politique* and in that work. In truth, the philosophical and 'the political' are approached in strikingly similar terms; we are told that the political needs to be given the full attention of deconstructive thought, and a 'déconstruction du politique' (FH 495; ['deconstruction of the political']) is proposed. In practice, this means that the same language that deconstruction adopts regarding philosophical tradition will appear in discussions of the political. Just as deconstruction designates the closure of philosophy understood as a metaphysical system, so do Lacoue-Labarthe and Nancy demand 'que soit reconnu un certain accomplissement du politique ou, pour user d'un autre lexique, qu'on prenne acte (mais ni par résignation ni par dépit) de la *clôture du politique*' ['that one recognizes a certain completion of the political, or, to use another vocabulary, that one takes note (but neither in resignation nor through vexation) of the *closure of the political*'].[19] This is a notable usage of the term *clôture*, meaning a closure or in literal terms an enclosure or fence. In short, philosophy and the political are addressed on the same model, namely that of a dominant, totalizing system which prevents us from thinking our shared existence in a radical or open way. In order to grasp how such statements on *le politique* or 'the political' are possible, it will be necessary to look in greater detail at Lacoue-Labarthe's understanding of that term (as distinct from *la politique*). For now, however, let us limit ourselves to noting that the same model is seen at work in philosophy and in the political.

Of course, this was not at all the first time that analogies between the two domains had been drawn. Since Plato there has been a tradition of seeking to shape the political order according to conclusions arrived at in philosophy, or at least to think it philosophically. Lacoue-Labarthe and Nancy attempt to avoid entering into a reiteration of this tradition by stating that 'nous n'avons aucune prétention à la *théorie politique*, c'est-à-dire à tout ce qui pourrait se réclamer d'une "science politique" ou d'une "politologie"' ['we have no pretension to *political theory*, and that is to say, to anything that could evoke a "political science" or a "politology"'].[20] What they instead propose to do is to underline the analogy between philosophical and political discourses. Rather than simply analysing political life in philosophical terms — as '"politology"' might do —, their approach is to argue that a specific understanding of 'philosophy' also subtends political discourse. This philosophy represents a metaphysical system intent on comprehending the variety and difference of existing beings — whether inanimate objects or living creatures — within a single horizon of sameness, namely a horizon formed by what they share precisely insofar as they *are* (or insofar as they are 'beings', *Seienden* or *étants*). Now, Lacoue-Labarthe and Nancy largely take this understanding of philosophy from Heidegger. Although his work engages in a version of this approach, underlining how this irreducible, common Being is radically other to and interruptive of our rational horizons, Heidegger also condemns the dominant models of it. Arguing for the need to overcome metaphysics, he sets out how this totalizing system has come to dominate all aspects of modern life, via ideologies (whether capitalist or Marxist) presenting themselves as inheritors of the tradition of Western reason. Whilst this might seem difficult to digest, we must remind ourselves of the dominance today — not only in the West but globally —, of market capitalism, one of the logics Heidegger railed against. This thinking is not alien to Nancy's later work in *La Création du monde*;[21] and indeed he and Lacoue-Labarthe ventriloquize Heidegger's thinking of philosophy or 'le philosophique' as follows:

> [*l*]e philosophique désigne une structure historico-systématique générale — ce que, jusqu'à ces derniers temps, on pouvait appeler l'Occident — dont la philosophie est chaque fois la thématisation, la préfiguration ou l'anticipation, la réflexion (critique ou non), la contestation, etc., mais qui déborde largement le champ d'exercice au fond très restreint du philosopher proprement dit.

> [[*t*]*he* philosophical designates a general historico-systematic structure — which, up until recently, one could have called the West — of which philosophy is each time the thematization, the prefiguration or the anticipation, the reflection (critical or not), the contestation, etc., but which far overspills the basically restricted field of operations of actual philosophizing].[22]

On this view, philosophy goes beyond 'actual philosophizing', meaning that whenever we come across discussions drawing on this Heideggerian thought, it cannot be understood neutrally or innocently. The 'general historico-systematic structure' described in this way, rather than any more localized philosophical investigation, provides the model on which the political will be understood. In short, on this reading of Heidegger, one cannot speak of the political without the philosophical, because political discourse (e.g. that of representation and democratic elections) is profoundly inflected by ideologies (e.g. market capitalism) ultimately leading back to Western reason understood as a rationalization or a calculation.

Lacoue-Labarthe and Nancy follow Heidegger in his diagnosis of the unavoidable association of philosophy and the political, even stating that 'c'est *la* figure philosophico-politique comme telle, ou la figure *du* philosophico-politique que nous entendons soumettre à notre interrogation' ['it is *the* philosophico-political figure as such, or the figure of *the* philosophico-political that we are intending to question'].[23] However, they update this diagnosis by drawing on a contemporary example: they criticize the slogan 'tout est politique' ['everything is political'] which was associated with May '68 revolts, doing so despite their involvement at university level. Indeed, they refer to this slogan as '[le] "tout est politique" par quoi l'on peut qualifier notre enfermement dans la clôture du politique' ['the "everything is political" which can be used to characterize our enclosure in the closure of the political'].[24] Here the significant term *clôture* is again used as part of the deconstruction of the argument that all aspects of existence should be approached in terms of a single measure, namely the measure of the political. They see this measure or model as representing the totalizing or dominant force of 'the political', arguing that the latter 'domine à peu près universellement aujourd'hui' ['which near enough universally dominates today'].[25] Their reflection on this notion and its underlying complicity with philosophy, which as deconstructive thinkers they seek to destabilize, therefore creates in their minds a responsibility: that of seeking out out non-totalizing modes of thinking, and indeed in their words to 'affronter le Politique' ['confront the Political'].[26] What is at stake here is a sense of responsibility — the word is not too strong, given their statement that 'il s'agit pour nous [...] de ce qu'il n'y a pas si longtemps on aurait appelé un "engagement"' ['[f]or us [...] it is a matter of what not so long ago would have been called a "commitment"'].[27] What's more, this sense of a responsibility to adopt a contestatory, polemical approach produces a resistance not only to totalizing models of the political, but also to 'philosophy', understood as totalization and systematization.

Against 'Philosophy'

We have begun to see that Lacoue-Labarthe's (and Nancy's) early-1980s elaboration of the notion of *le politique* drew heavily on Heidegger and his account of meta-physical philosophy as a totalizing system, before being turned against the thinker by Lacoue-Labarthe in *La Fiction du politique*. A sense of the wrench that it represents for him to criticize Heidegger's thinking (or *le politique*) — rather than simply the actions of the man (or *la politique*) — is found in the statement that: 'je ne suis "entré en philosophie", si j'y suis entré, que pour avoir subi le coup ou le choc [...] de la pensée de Heidegger' (FP 11; ['I only "entered philosophy" — if indeed I did

enter it — after experiencing the impact or shock [...] of Heidegger's thinking',
HAP ix, trans. mod.]). There is thus no other philosophical figure, not even
Nietzsche or Derrida, to whom Lacoue-Labarthe ascribes so much importance in
his own development (Hölderlin lies in a different category, although even then
the readings of him act as a counterweight to Heidegger's readings of the poet
in the *Elucidations*).[28] What's more, Heidegger not only determines the existence
of Lacoue-Labarthe's interest in philosophy, but its direction, which is to say its
contestatory outlook regarding Western metaphysics. This sense of contestation
explains why in the statement above he provides the instant qualification of 'if
indeed I did enter it'; he remains on the threshold or margins of this discourse.

In this vein, Lacoue-Labarthe's early readings of Heidegger set the latter up
as a crucial influence, insofar as he established the possibility for a 'thought' or
'deconstruction' overspilling the confines of philosophy. In this vein, *La Fiction du
politique* thus describes Heidegger as '[le] plus grand penseur, sans conteste, de ce
temps' (FP 14; ['without doubt the greatest thinker of the age', HAP 2, trans. mod.]).
Beyond its clarity, this statement is valuable insofar as we see Lacoue-Labarthe
describing Heidegger as a thinker rather than as a philosopher. And this distinction
draws on a reading of Heidegger's notion of *Dasein*: an approach to human
existence (literally *Da-sein*, there-being or being-there) which concentrates on its
minimal, irreducible status rather than on the identities which can subsequently be
constructed. In any case, Heidegger's self-distancing from philosophy is presented
as one of the reasons for the French thinker's long-standing admiration for him:
'M'impressionnaient la puissance de sa pensée et ce qu'à l'époque je devais appeler
sa "radicalité critique", l'âpreté du combat qu'il menait contre la philosophie' ['I was
impressed by the force of his thought and by what at that time I must have called his
"critical radicality", the bitterness of the combat he waged against philosophy'].[29]
Indeed, the work opens with a chapter named 'Philosophie' (the English version
proposes a different title, 'The Age's Modesty') in which the issue is taken beyond
the simple exegesis of Heidegger and established as a principle affecting the entirety
of the contemporary scene. The chapter opens as follows:

> Ces pages, en toute rigueur, ne prétendent pas à la philosophie.
> Il y va tout d'abord de la plus élémentaire modestie: à quel titre, de quel droit
> pourrais-je bien me revendiquer comme 'philosophe'?
> Ecartons toutefois ce qui relève du cas singulier. Ou de l'anecdote.
> La modestie dont je parle devrait être celle de l'époque, qui en manque
> décidément plus que toute autre: devant ce qui s'est instauré et déployé sous le
> nom de philosophie, devant ce qu'a représenté, dans un tel déploiement, l'app-
> arition de ce qui fut reconnu par la tradition comme des philosophes, devant ce
> qu'a signifié et impliqué, chaque fois, l'acte de philosopher, comment ne serait-
> il pas dérisoire, aujourd'hui, de se réclamer encore de la philosophie ou — pire
> — de se proclamer philosophe ? (FP 13)

> [Ultimately, these pages do not claim to be philosophy.
> This is due, in the first instance, to the most elementary modesty: what
> entitles me or gives me the right to claim to be a 'philosopher'?
> Yet let us leave aside what concerns individual cases. Or the merely
> anecdotal.

The modesty I am speaking of ought to be that of the age, which decidedly lacks it more than any other: faced with what has been established and deployed under the name of philosophy, faced with what, in that deployment, were traditionally taken to be philosophers, and what their appearance represented, faced with what each act of philosophizing signified and implied, how would it not be derisory today to still lay a claim to philosophy or — worse — to declare oneself a philosopher? (HAP 1, trans. mod.)].

Although he does not directly name 'what has been established and deployed as philosophy', it is important that the phenomenon alluded to by these words — i.e. totalizing or metaphysical knowledge — is described precisely as establishing itself (*instaurer*) and deploying itself (*déployer*). This is the language of military dominance and occupation, chosen by Lacoue-Labarthe to refer to what he sees as the totalizing violence of metaphysics. For this reason, it is not enough to simply become aware of or to describe this situation in order to alter it. Adopting a territorial metaphor, he continues:

> Nous habitons encore en terre philosophique et nous ne pouvons pas, tout simplement, habiter ailleurs. Cela ne veut pas dire qu'il n'y a pas, en droit, un au-delà de la limite mais que, envisagé d'ici, soit de la philosophie même, cet au-delà, toujours soupçonné, est strictement indécelable. (FP 16)

> [We are still living in philosophical country and we cannot just move to live somewhere else. This does not mean that there is no *de jure* place beyond the limit, but that, envisaged from here, i.e. from philosophy itself, this place beyond, although always half-glimpsed, is strictly undiscoverable. (HAP 3, trans. mod.])

Thus the situation not only of Heidegger, not only of the contemporary scene in general, but specifically of the discourse within which Lacoue-Labarthe situates himself — the 'here' to which he refers — is a complex one. This discourse is at once, as it were, trapped within philosophical territory, and able to glimpse — 'soupçonn[er]' — something beyond it.

La Fiction du politique contributes to this debate on the limitations and the closure of philosophy less by suggesting a positive way of stepping beyond it, than by condemning Heidegger for not having done so. This is to say that the work is set up as a criticism or reading, rather than the basis of a foundational, original thinking (if the latter is indeed possible, and it is an axiom of deconstruction that it is not). These are the stakes of the following passage, which is useful regarding the surprising and very specific sense in which Lacoue-Labarthe comes to understand 'philosophy':

> à deux reprises au moins Heidegger, de lui-même, s'est prêté à la philo-sophie.
>   Une première fois, massivement, et de manière, tout bien considéré, absurde [...] dans la circonstance précise de l'engagement politique de 1933–1934.
>   Une seconde fois, mais ce n'est probablement que le revers de cet avers, en s'autorisant de Hölderlin et, dans une mesure moindre, de Trakl pour franchir le pas au-delà du strict questionner ou de la simple annonce d'une 'autre pensée' et produire, de cette 'autre pensée', les premiers linéaments (FP 26–27).

> [on two occasions at least, Heidegger, by his own choice, gave himself over to philosophy.

A first time, massively, and in a way that was, all in all, absurd [...] on the precise occasion of his political commitment of 1933–34.

A second time, but this is probably merely the other side of the same coin, when he used the writings of Hölderlin and, to a lesser extent, Trakl to take a step beyond strict questioning or the simple heralding of 'another kind of thought', and produce the first outlines of that 'other kind of thought' (HAP 12, trans. mod.)].

The reason that this passage is so surprising is surely that it uses the language of political condemnation — 'on two occasions [...], Heidegger gave himself over' — to describe, in addition to his actions as rector of Freiburg University in 1933–34, the German professor's relationship to philosophy. This rejoins Lacoue-Labarthe's strategy of criticizing Heidegger for his work (namely, his philosophy and its inevitable association with *le politique*) rather than simply on the basis of his actions (namely *la politique*). In other words, his argument is that the radical nature of the thinking in question and the positive reception it had duly gained — not least in moments of his own thought — means that discussions about Heidegger and the political needed to take place on the basis of that thinking, if the issue was to be debated in a proper way, and if the conclusions arrived at were to be durable. This means that we must remain vigilant even with regard to Heidegger's later work, i.e. that written after the rectorship of 1933–34, after the supposed turn to language and poetry of the mid-1930s, and after the Second World War.[30]

We have thus seen how *La Fiction du politique* treats Heidegger's position in relation to radical, deconstructive thought on the one hand, and 'philosophy' on the other, as more than an initial determination of the terrain on which the main discussion is subsequently to take place: rather, the location of this terrain forms a large part of this main discussion. This being said, locating this terrain would not represent the whole picture; doing so would not fully address how Lacoue-Labarthe characterizes Heidegger's work as 'philosophical'. A lead is provided by the passage quoted above and its identification of this philosophy as that which 'used the writings of Hölderlin [...] to [...] produce the first outlines of that "other kind of thought"', i.e. that which instrumentalizes poetry to philosophical ends. This lead suggests that when we move from the general discourse Heidegger is painted as employing to the specific usage he makes of it, we come across the importance of art or poetry (*Dichtung* for Heidegger), which Lacoue-Labarthe addresses via the notion of *la fiction du politique*.

The Fiction of the Political

At first sight, the Heidegger of *Dichtung* or poetry is where Lacoue-Labarthe's interest in the thinker seems to lie; we can recall Nancy's statement that when role-playing with his regular co-author, he would adopt the persona of the early, ontological Heidegger whilst Lacoue-Labarthe would adopt that of the later, poetry-influenced period. The same line is taken by the latter thinker in an interview when he states that '[c]'était moins les thèmes existentiaux que le deuxième Heidegger, la pensée de l'histoire de l'être, qui m'intéressait en profondeur' ['it was less the existential themes than the second Heidegger, the thought of the history of being, that deeply interested me'].[31] This division of roles relies on a certain reading of the thinker's work, where for the earlier Heidegger metaphysical philosophy was assigned the role of thinking this radically other Being, whilst at a later stage this process took places through and as art, with the work of art crucial to the process of *aletheia* or the literal un-forgetting of Being.

However, whilst these comments by both Lacoue-Labarthe and Nancy reiterate the division of Heidegger's career into distinct phases, Lacoue-Labarthe's written work avoids doing so. In addressing the feasibility of a phase-based reading — in which the passage between phases would be provided by the period of the mid-1930s — he recalls that Heidegger resigned the rectorship of Freiburg after only ten months, and thereafter began to write on art and poetry. Nonetheless, Lacoue-Labarthe does not adopt the hypothesis that these years represent a *Kehre*, or turning towards language and poetry (specifically that of Hölderlin).[32] Although he sees a shift in the mid-1930s from an emphasis on philosophy to one on poetry, he argues that the political horizons of Heidegger's thinking remain the same. On this view, despite the seeming move or turn away from philosophy, in truth a philosophical core remains; Lacoue-Labarthe's attentiveness to poetry leads him to eschew the *Kehre* hypothesis regarding Heidegger. Although Heidegger does certainly begin discussing poetry much more after his abandonment of *la politique*, the argument is that the broader philosophical underpinnings — and the sense of *le politique* they entail — remain.

For Lacoue-Labarthe to say this is to argue that the horizons of Heidegger's work are essentially unaffected by his withdrawal from the limelight of public life as a Nazi intellectual and university rector. Indeed, although it was not understood as doing so by those in the party, the argument is that his work went on to explore what it named 'the inner truth and greatness of the movement', in effect being truer to the *essence* of Nazism than were its official representatives. Despite — or more probably owing to — Lacoue-Labarthe's own interest in poetry and literature, he finds significant differences between Heidegger's approach and his own. In his view of the former, the emphasis is on creation and production, and this is where the 'fiction' in the expression *la fiction du politique* comes into play. But in fact, the artwork which Lacoue-Labarthe is discussing here is highly metaphorical: we are not dealing with real works of art, but rather with the way they can provide a metaphor for a political order. In truth, this gesture is already present in Heidegger, whose *Origin of the Work of Art* states that '[o]ne essential way in which truth establishes itself in the beings it has opened up is truth setting itself into work. Another way in which truth occurs is the act that founds a political state'.[33] Thus art, by providing the site for truth to be founded or created (Heidegger insists that this truth does not pre-exist the artwork, in the traditional sense of content pre-existing form), provides a model that can also apply in the case of a political state or order. Lacoue-Labarthe's term for this model or metaphor is *la fiction du politique*, the political order (not just political events or *la politique*) being seen as fiction. This term does not refer to the characteristic of being true or false, but instead underlines the process of creation or construction. In his words, '[l]e politique (la Cité) relève d'une *plastique*, formation et information, *fiction* au sens strict' (FP 102, emphases original; ['the political (the City) belongs to a form of *plastic art*, formation and information, *fiction* in the strict sense' (HAP 66)]. What is conveyed by this choice of the artwork or fiction as a metaphor is that this vision of the political order sees it as something totalized, able to be fully present in one place and one moment, without any remainder.

A second point regarding art, and on which Lacoue-Labarthe seeks to differentiate himself from Heidegger, concerns who or what is represented in the metaphorical 'art' being used as a way of discussing *le politique* or the political order. According to the theory of *la fiction du politique*, the artwork in question does not represent a topic chosen at random, but in fact ultimately represents the political community itself. Lacoue-Labarthe writes that:

> C'est la communauté elle-même [...] le peuple ou la nation, qui est œuvre, selon l'assomption romantique de l'œuvre comme sujet et du sujet comme œuvre [...]. L'infinitisation ou l'absolutisation du sujet qui est au principe de la métaphysique des Modernes trouve là son issue proprement opératoire: la communauté à l'œuvre et au travail [...] s'œuvre, si l'on peut dire, et se travaille elle-même, accomplissant de la sorte le procès subjectif par excellence, c'est-à-dire le procès de l'auto-formation et de l'auto-production (FP 111–12).

> [It is the community itself, the people or nation, that is the work according to the Romantics' adoption of the idea of the work as subject and the subject as work [...]. The infinitization or absolutization of the subject, which is at the heart of the metaphysics of the Moderns, here finds its strictly operational outcome: the community at its task [*à l'œuvre*] and at work [...] works on itself and works itself [*s'œuvre*], if you will, thus fulfilling the subjective process *par excellence*, the process of self-formation and self-production (HAP 70, trans. mod.)].

It is significant that the chapter from which this is taken draws on Hans-Jürgen Syberberg's *Our Hitler: a Film from Germany* (1977), doing so in order to discuss the mass marches and spectacles created under Nazism.[34] Both in these events and in the film, as well as in Heidegger's thinking, Lacoue-Labarthe sees the creation of an artwork as a necessary step in the process in which German society was engaged in the Nazi project. In this case, art serves not to question identity nor even to shore it up, but actually to create it in the first place; in Lacoue-Labarthe's words, this means that 'l'œuvre d'art [...] offre la vérité de la *polis* ou de l'Etat, mais [...] le politique lui-même s'institue et se constitue (et se re-fonde régulièrement) dans et comme l'œuvre d'art' (FP 98; ['the work of art [...] offers the truth of the *polis* or the State, but [...] the political itself is instituted and constituted (and regularly re-grounds itself) in and as the work of art' (HAP 64, trans. mod.)]. Using art as a metaphor or a model here makes it possible for an emphasis to be placed on the constructing or founding of the political order being discussed. And the term most often used to stand for these processes is that of 'fiction', understood in the etymological sense, namely as a creating or fashioning. Indeed, it is revealing that Lacoue-Labarthe will write not just of fiction but of a '*fictionnement* des êtres et des communautés' (FP 125, emphasis original; ['the *fictioning* of beings and communities'; HAP 82, emphasis original]); this is an active fiction*ing*, an ongoing process with the real — and dangerous — power to create. What is crucial here is that this aspect of

Heidegger's view of art is presented as being ultimately concerned with the fiction or fiction*ing* of identity — whether that of a community, a people, or a country.[35]

This analysis of art, or more precisely of the way art is utilized as a metaphor for political discourse, is aligned with Lacoue-Labarthe's desire to undertake a thoroughgoing critique of Heidegger — by which we should understand one not based simply on *la politique*, but also including the wider notion of *le politique*. The latter is seen as being intimately connected with Heidegger's understanding of Nazism, which Lacoue-Labarthe describes as follows: 'Le national-socialisme ne s'est à aucun moment présenté comme une politique déterminée [...], mais comme la *vérité* du politique' (FP 114, emphasis original; ['National Socialism at no point presented itself as a determinate politics [...], but rather as the *truth* of the political'; HAP 77, emphasis original]). In other words, because it was an extreme, totalizing project not working within any former political model but instead seeking to found a wholly new discourse — for instance dissolving all other parties, and well as the notions of Right and Left —, Nazism tells us 'the *truth*' about all such totalizing projects. For Lacoue-Labarthe to speak of truth here does not of course entail any approval on his part: he is simply suggesting that democratic societies do not create, forge, or present totalized figures of themselves in the same way as Nazism does. They do not have its metaphysical urge. In this way he takes up the breadth and tragically misplaced ambition of Heidegger's view of Nazism — let us recall the statement on the 'inner truth and greatness of that movement' —, with hugely different intentions, namely to deconstruct this broader process of *la fiction du politique*.

This shift of focus from the empirical to the essential aspects of Nazism, correlate with the shift from *la politique* to *le politique*, has been criticized in some quarters. Luc Ferry and Alain Renault, for instance — who participated at *Les Fins de l'homme* before their marked differences from Lacoue-Labarthe, Nancy, Derrida et al. caused them to leave the conference early — make these criticisms in *Heidegger et les modernes*. Rather than seeing Heidegger's essentialized or spiritualized version of Nazism as associated with modern metaphysics, Ferry and Renault paint it as a reaction against the modern (they underline his hostility to both capitalism and communism). Their argument concentrates its attacks on Lacoue-Labarthe's notion that Heidegger's Nazism is the expression of a modern metaphysics of the subject — and therefore of the figure of 'mankind'. They state that

> si comme l'affirme posément un élève de Derrida [Lacoue-Labarthe], 'le nazisme est un humanisme' (*sic*), il faut considérer que c'est sous l'emprise d'une tradition humaniste et spiritualiste alors encore insuffisamment déconstruite que le Heidegger de 1933 a été conduit, *naturellement*, au nazisme [...].
>
> L'énoncé de cette thèse est quelque peu ridicule, trop dépendant qu'il est d'une polémique contre notre propre livre [*La Pensée '68: essai sur l'antihumanisme contemporain*, 1985]. Pour nous, le temps des polémiques est passé: réprimant la tentation d'ironiser, il nous paraît plus utile d'indiquer, d'emblée, à la fois ce que cette thèse signifie dans son fond et pour quelles raisons elle exprime à sa manière non seulement une erreur philosophique, mais peut-être l'erreur par excellence de la scène philosophique française contemporaine.

[if, as one student of Derrida's [Lacoue-Labarthe] coolly asserts, 'Nazism is a humanism' (*sic*), we should conclude that the Heidegger of 1933 was naturally led to Nazism because he was still in the grip of a humanistic and spiritualistic tradition he had not yet adequately deconstructed [...].

The wording of this claim is somewhat ridiculous, for it stems from a polemic against our own book [*French Philosophy of the Sixties: an Essay on Antihumanism*, first published 1985]. For us, the time for polemics is past; resisting the temptation to deride, we think it more fruitful to indicate at the outset just what this claim basically means and how in its way it typifies not just a philosophical error but perhaps *the* error par excellence of contemporary French philosophy].[36]

Despite announcing that 'the time for polemics is past', Ferry and Renault's position is both sweeping and provocative in the oldest polemical tradition. Lacoue-Labarthe is not only denounced as being mistaken, but as revealing '*the* error par excellence of contemporary French philosophy'. Whilst Lacoue-Labarthe's reading of Heidegger was certainly addressed by Derrida, Lyotard, and other major figures, it is surely an exaggeration to place him as such a central influence on contemporary thought. Perhaps Ferry and Renault's reaction is the inevitable counterpart of the aphoristic, provocative nature of statements such as 'Nazism is a humanism'. If so, it is disappointing that Lacoue-Labarthe's efforts to look at Heidegger's work in addition to his biography, i.e. at *le politique* as well as *la politique*, on this occasion produce a heated reaction which refuses to consider whether the notion of *la fiction du politique* might have any relevance beyond making accusations in cases, such as Heidegger's, where history has already — rightly — made its condemnation.

The theory criticized by Ferry and Renault is consistent with a previous piece of work by Lacoue-Labarthe, a short text written together with Nancy and for a wider public, *Le Mythe nazi* (1980). The work sets itself the task of looking more widely than at one specific period in history — and it seems true that it is more challenging to criticize the present than it is the past. In this vein, the work tells us that:

> Il ne s'agit pas d'opposer — comme on l'a sans doute trop fait, sous l'impulsion, en elle-même irréprochable, de l'anti-totalitarisme, un certain style de pensée démocratique — la figuration propre aux régimes fascistes d'une part, et de l'autre l'imprésentabilité en tant que trait d'essence de la démocratie.[37]

> [It is not a question — as it has been probably too often, as a reaction, beyond reproach on its own terms, against totalitarianism and in favour of democratic thought — of placing in opposition the figuring proper to fascist regimes on the one hand, and on the other unpresentability as an essential characteristic of democracy.]

In other words, no criticism should be made from a position of *a priori* impunity, even — and especially — when the object of one's attention is, like Nazism, of such a horrifying nature. This causes Lacoue-Labarthe and Nancy to adopt a sceptical position regarding approaches that serve to paint Nazism in such a way that it is distanced from our current moment. They write of:

> notre méfiance et notre scepticisme, s'agissant du nazisme, à l'égard de l'accusation hâtive, brutale et la plupart du temps aveugle, d'*irrationalisme*. Il y a au contraire une *logique du fascisme*. Ce qui veut dire aussi qu'*une certaine*

logique est fasciste, et que cette logique n'est pas simplement étrangère à la logique générale de la rationalité dans la métaphysique du Sujet.

[our suspicion and scepticism, when Nazism is at issue, regarding the hasty, crude, and usually blind accusation of *irrationality*. There is, on the contrary, a *logic of fascism*. This also means that *a certain logic is fascist*, and that this logic is not wholly foreign to the general logic of rationality inherent in the metaphysics of the Subject].[38]

This is to say that those writing on Nazism should be wary of making accusations of irrationalism, because such accusations always rely upon an affirmation of one's rationality and the justness of one's own position. This is a notable point because it confirms that *Le Mythe nazi* is not a historical study: instead, it constitutes a philosophical reflection on the viability and the justifiability of the historian's standpoint. Indeed, to undertake specific historical investigations would be to miss the wider point that Lacoue-Labarthe and Nancy believe needs making, which can be seen in the care they take not to discuss the utilization of particular myths within Nazi discourse — for instance, Norse mythology or Indo-European linguistic or ethnographical theories about Aryans. In this light, we can read that '[l]'identification doit donc passer par la construction d'un mythe, et non par un simple retour à des mythes anciens' ['[i]dentification must therefore take place through the construction of a myth, not by a simple return to ancient myths'].[39] This is to say that empirical content of a myth is less important than the performative process of its construction, which allows — or forces — one to identify with it. The aim of *Le Mythe nazi* is therefore neither to outline the particular myths utilized by Nazism (i.e. Nazi myths), nor to argue that 'Nazism was a myth', i.e. that its ideological groundings were false (and that, implicitly, that those alternative groundings relied upon to make such a statement are correct). Instead, the work takes as its object what can be expressed as 'the myth that was Nazi' or 'the myth that was at work in Nazism but that could also be at work elsewhere'.

Returning to *La Fiction du politique*, it is by widening the horizons of his investigation that Lacoue-Labarthe raises the possibility of a condemnation of Heidegger that would be more thoroughgoing, insofar as it touches on more than biography. Indeed, this wider condemnation is based on *le politique* and touches on what he names 'the general logic of rationality inherent in the metaphysics of the Subject'. This means that it takes on the status of a concept able to operate beyond the confines of Heidegger's thinking, for instance in Lacoue-Labarthe's more critical views of Jena Romanticism ('nous ne sommes pas sortis de l'époque du Sujet', AL 27; 'we have not left the era of the Subject'; LA 16), or even regarding his own political itinerary: in the film *The Ister*, he declares that 'je n'ai pas envie de l'accuser [Heidegger] stupidement d'avoir été nazi' ['I do not wish to stupidly accuse him [Heidegger] of having been a Nazi'], before proceeding to evoke his own, early Leninism, which he says is equally open to criticism.[40]

Two further examples can illustrate the importance for Lacoue-Labarthe's thinking of the concept of *la fiction du politique*, as elaborated in his work on Heidegger, for his thinking as a whole. The first draws on the violent or even iconoclastic tendency which he tends to exhibit when initially approaching a particular cultural form or discourse — as we shall see in terms of the status quo in poetry ('j'exècre ce qu'on range de manière emphatique sous le nom de "poésie"', PH 19; ['I loathe what is emphatically classed under the name of "poetry"']) or a similar status quo in theatre (which he dismisses as 'de la gesticulation verbale', AN 192; ['mere verbal gesticulation']). This tendency is explicitly related to his thinking of fiction or figure — let us recall that both stem from the Latin *fingere*, to fashion or form — when he states that: 'Je serais tenté de couper court et de dire: de même qu'il faut casser le spectacle, il faut casser — j'allais écrire: la figure (quel programme!). Disons donc plutôt: il faut tenter d'enrayer le processus fictionnel' ['I would be tempted to cut short and say: in the same way that one must smash spectacle, we must smash — I was going to say: figure [*la figure*] (what a proposal!). Let us therefore say instead: we must attempt to halt the fictional process'].[41] Although he self-ironizes here about the expression used, *casser la figure* meaning both to deconstruct the figure or figurality, and in everyday French 'to smash someone's face in', it remains the case that his thinking has led him to this point. He retreats only a short distance, stating that 'the fictional process', i.e. the process of the fiction or fiction*ing* of the political must be halted. The second example underscores this violence or iconoclasm which seems to be instinctive in Lacoue-Labarthe's approach, but is also raised to the status of a concept by his investigations. It is taken from an unpublished public debate featuring Lacoue-Labarthe and Nancy, in which the former made the straightforward but far-reaching assertion that 'la figure est toujours fasciste' ['figure is always fascist'].[42] Jean-Luc Nancy recalls that his hesitations, shared with those of Jean-Christophe Bailly, were not able to dissuade Lacoue-Labarthe from thinking in this direction.

In any case, it is clear that Lacoue-Labarthe's thinking of *la fiction du politique* passed beyond both Heidegger's biographical relationship with Nazism (i.e. in the domain of *la politique*), and — although it addressed this also — beyond what he saw as the metaphysical aspects of the thinker's approach to art as a metaphor for political narratives, fictions, or state-building. Above and beyond these areas of resonance, his thinking saw attendant dangers in past, present, and future invocations and instrumentalizations of art. This is the point Lacoue-Labarthe arrives at in *La Fiction du politique*, having drawn on his and Nancy's work on *le politique*, as well as on a deconstructive distancing from metaphysical 'philosophy', a distancing that we can say to be timely insofar as it presents its 'modesty' as one which 'devrait être celle de l'époque' (FP 13; ['ought to be that of the age'; HAP 1]).

Lacoue-Labarthe, then, responds to Heidegger's use of art or the artwork as metaphor for various orders of the political with an alternative strategy which involves establishing the aim of stepping beyond 'le fictionnement' ('fictioning') or 'la "politique-fiction"' (FP 125–26; ['"fiction-politics"'; HAP 82, trans. mod.]). This alternative strategy can be found in his particular understanding of the notion of 'mimesis', which emerged from 1975's collective volume *Mimesis: des articulations* whose contributors included Nancy, Lacoue-Labarthe, Derrida. To be mimetic is to be forced to speak indirectly, through imitation and dissemblance, rather than as a controlling or calculating subject. In this vein, Derrida would later write a text for Lacoue-Labarthe named 'Désistance': by coining this term, Derrida envisages an existence which would consist entirely in a withdrawal from the processes of 'fiction' whereby a subject can fix its essence by identifying with a larger construction. In this way he takes up and develops *La Fiction du politique*, in which Lacoue-Labarthe identifies the eponymous notion as a major ground on which Heidegger should be criticized. We therefore see that the work finds a resonance in Derrida's mind — but this is far from being his only interaction with Lacoue-Labarthe. Let us now turn to explore the others.

Notes to Chapter 2

1. In *Rejouer le politique*, p. 20; *Retreating the Political*, p. 114.
2. '[C]onseilliste' refers to a belief in small-scale workers' councils. The divergences between the pair are mentioned here: 'l'un (J.-L. N.) est passé par *Esprit* et la CFDT, l'autre (Ph. L.-L.) s'est longtemps retrouvé sur les positions de *Socialisme ou Barbarie* et, pour une part, de *l'Internationale situationniste*', in *Rejouer le politique*, p. 16n ['the itinerary of one of us (J.-L. N.) runs through *Esprit* and the CFDT [the French Democratic Confederation of Labour], whilst the other (Ph. L.-L.) for a long time found himself in accord with the positions of *Socialisme ou Barbarie* and, for a long while, of *The Situationist International*'; *Retreating the Political*, p. 179n].
3. *Le Mythe Nazi* (1980; La Tour d'Aigues, 2005). An associated project was for a *Cahier de l'Herne* around the question of Blanchot and politics. Lacoue-Labarthe and Nancy sought collaborators for this in 1984–85, but did not find the right number of quality contributions. Nancy gives his account of this abortive project, as well as presenting a long letter from Blanchot, in *Maurice Blanchot: Passion politique* [*Maurice Blanchot: Political Passion*; Paris: Galilée, 2011].
4. Lacoue-Labarthe and Nancy's writings from the two volumes are translated in *Retreating the Political*. For its part, *Les Fins de l'homme* had featured figures from Ferry and Alain Renault (whose anti-Derridean stance saw them leave the conference early) to Lyotard, passing through Werner Hamacher, Luce Irigaray, Gayatri Spivak, Barbara Johnson, Denis Hollier, and numerous others.
5. The work has been described by Richard Wolin as 'brazenly tendentious' and 'extremely weak from a philosophical standpoint', in *The Heidegger Controversy: a Critical Reader*, ed. by Wolin (1991; London: MIT Press, 1993), pp. 276, 279; and in terms of its 'irritante platitude' ['irritating platitudes'] by Ferry and Renault, in *Heidegger et les modernes* ([*Heidegger and Modernity*]; Paris: Grasset, 1988), p. 39. For an overview of the 'affair', see Janicaud, *Heidegger en France*, vol. I: *Récit* ([*Heidegger in France*, vol. I: *Narrative*]; Paris: Albin Michel, 2001), pp. 347–90; Heidegger's pro-Nazi texts including the Rectorat speech are included in *The Heidegger Controversy*. Ferry and Renault give an overview of discussion of Heidegger's politics prior to Farias, by Sartre and orthodox Heideggerians; see *Heidegger et les modernes*, pp. 19–27.
6. Victor Farias, *Heidegger et le nazisme* (Lagrasse: Verdier, 1987); Derrida, *De l'Esprit: Heidegger et la question* ([*Of Spirit: Heidegger and the Question*]; Paris: Galilée, 1987); Hugo Ott, *Martin Heidegger: a Political Life*, trans. by Allan Blunden (London: HarperCollins, 1993).
7. A debate held in February 1988 featuring Derrida, Lacoue-Labarthe, and Hans-Georg Gadamer has recently been published as *La Conférence de Heidelberg (1988): Heidegger, portée philosophique et politique de sa pensée*, ed. by Mireille Calle-Gruber (Paris: Lignes/IMEC, 2014). Individually, Lacoue-Labarthe published 'L'Ampleur du désastre' ['The Extent of the Disaster'], in *Libération* (12 March 1987), 31; and Derrida 'Heidegger, l'enfer des philosophes' ['Heidegger, the Philosophers' Hell'], in *Le Nouvel observateur* (6–12 November 1987) as well as a text in *Le Monde* (9 February 1988).
8. See 'Ponctuations: le temps d'une thèse' (1980; ['Punctuations: the Time of a Thesis']), in *Du Droit à la philosophie* ([*Who's Afraid of Philosophy? Right to Philosophy*]; Paris: Galilée, 1990), pp. 439–60. Interestingly, the surviving examiner's reports are divided on the issue of whether *La Fiction du politique* represents a Thesis in the strict sense: Lucien Braun argues that it does, whilst Lyotard argues that it is radical because it avoids adopting such a position.
9. In 'La Fiction du biographique', p. 203.

10. Critchley, in 'Re-tracing the Political: Politics and Community in the Work of Philippe Lacoue-Labarthe and Jean-Luc Nancy', in *The Political Subject of Violence*, ed. by David Campbell and Michael Dillon (Manchester: Manchester U. P., 1993), pp. 73–93 (p. 83).

11. This hardened position towards Heidegger led to the 1988 play *Sit Venia Verbo* (Paris: Bourgois, 1988) which Lacoue-Labarthe worked on together with Michel Deutsch. The play is set in 1945–46 and features a disgraced German philosopher modelled unambiguously on Heidegger. Its title means 'pardon the expression', and seems to refer to a 1947 Éric Weil article which refers to 'le langage nazi, la morale nazie, la pensée (*sit venia verbo*) nazie, le sentiment nazi' ['Nazi language, Nazi morals, Nazi thought (*sit venia verbo*), Nazi sentiment']; see Janicaud, *Heidegger en France*, vol. I: *Récit*, p. 373.

12. In *Rejouer le politique*, p. 14; *Retreating the Political*, p. 109.

13. In *The Fragmentary Demand*, p. 165. He is quoting from *Le Retrait du politique*, pp. 186, 193.

14. In 'The French Derrideans: Politicizing Deconstruction or Deconstructing the Political?', in *New German Critique*, 33 (Autumn 1984), 127–54 (p. 142).

15. Heidegger, 'Discours et proclamations', trans. by Jean-Pierre Faye, in *Médiations: Revue des expressions contemporaines*, 3 (Autumn 1961), pp. 139–50.

16. In *An Introduction to Metaphysics*, trans. by Ralph Manheim (Garden City: Doubleday, 1961), p. 166.

17. In Heidegger, 'Insight into that which is', cited in Wolfgang Schirmacher, *Technik und Gelassenheit* (Freiburg and Munich: Albers, 1983), p. 25. See *La Fiction du politique*, p. 58. Derrida spoke on the issue of Heidegger's failure to express remorse following the war in the 1988 Heidelberg conference — the exploratory nature of his remarks perhaps explaining the 25-year hiatus before the text was recently published. His statement is as follows: 'Je crois que, peut-être, Heidegger s'est dit: je ne pourrai prononcer de condamnation contre le nazisme que si je peux la prononcer dans un langage non seulement qui soit à la mesure de ce que j'ai déjà dit, mais aussi à la mesure de ce qui s'est passé là. Et cela, il n'en a pas été capable. Et ce silence est peut-être une manière honnête de reconnaître qu'il n'en était pas capable. C'est une hypothèse très risquée: j'ai dit que je l'improviserais ce soir' ['I think that Heidegger perhaps said to himself: I will only be able to condemn Nazism in a language able to measure up to what I have said in the past, but also able to measure up to what happened. And he was not capable of doing that. This silence is perhaps an honest way of recognizing that he was not capable of doing that. This is a very risky hypothesis: I said that I would be improvising this evening'], in *La Conférence de Heidelberg*, p. 82.

18. In *Heidegger en France*, vol. I: *Récit*, p. 370.

19. In *Rejouer le politique*, p. 15 (emphasis original); *Retreating the Political*, p. 110 (emphasis original).

20. In *Rejouer le politique*, p. 13 (emphasis original); *Retreating the Political*, p. 108 (emphasis original).

21. See Nancy, *La Création du monde ou la mondialisation* ([*The Creation of the World or Globalisation*]; Paris: Galilée, 2002).

22. In *Le Retrait du politique*, p. 186 (emphasis original); *Retreating the Political*, p. 124 (emphasis original).

23. In *Rejouer le politique*, p. 28 (emphases original); *Retreating the Political*, p. 120 (emphases original), trans. mod.

24. In *Rejouer le politique*, p. 18; *Retreating the Political*, p. 112, trans. mod.

25. In *Le Retrait du politique*, p. 188; *Retreating the Political*, p. 126.

26. In *La Panique politique*, p. 60.

27. In *Rejouer le politique*, p. 19; *Retreating the Political*, p. 113 (trans. mod.).

28. Heidegger, *Elucidations of Hölderlin's Poetry*, trans. by Keith Hoeller (Amherst: Humanity, 2000).

29. In 'La Fiction du biographique', p. 200 (emphasis original)

30. Wolin's reading of the approach by Lacoue-Labarthe and Derrida differs from mine on this point; he states that the two thinkers 'intentionally seek (unlike the blatant apologists) to link up the philosophy of the early Heidegger with his pro-Nazi phase in order the better to save him: the early Heidegger, whose thought is in any case overly saturated with superfluous metaphysico-humanist residues, can be safely jettisoned in order that the post-humanist

Heidegger — the Heidegger of the Nietzsche lectures and the "Letter on Humanism" — can be redeemed unscathed', in *The Heidegger Controversy*, p. 285. Wolin's position does not take into account Lacoue-Labarthe's criticism of Heidegger's metaphysical attitude in his readings of Hölderlin, nor the sense of *le politique* with its applicability to diverse moments of Heidegger's — and our own — thinking.

31. In Janicaud, *Heidegger en France*, vol. II: *Entretiens*, p. 199.

32. For the *Kehre* hypothesis, see William Richardson, *Heidegger: Through Phenomenology to Thought* (The Hague: Martinus Nijhoff, 1963).

33. In 'The Origin of the Work of Art' in *Martin Heidegger: Basic Writings*, rev. ed. (London: Routledge, 1993), pp. 139–212 (p. 186).

34. *Our Hitler: a Film from Germany* (1977; Berlin: Film Galerie 451, 2004).

35. Lacoue-Labarthe also uses the term 'le national-esthétisme' ('national-æstheticism') to describe this process; chapter 7 of *La Fiction du politique* uses it as its title.

36. In *Heidegger et les modernes*, pp. 11–12 (emphasis original); in *Heidegger and Modernity*, trans. by Franklin Philip (London: University of Chicago Press), p. 2 (emphasis original), trans. mod.

37. In *Le Mythe nazi*, pp. 11–12.

38. In *Le Mythe nazi*, p. 25 (emphases original); in 'The Nazi Myth', trans. by Brian Holmes, in *Critical Inquiry*, 16:2 (Winter 1990), 291–312 (p. 294, emphasis original).

39. In *Le Mythe nazi*, p. 45; 'The Nazi Myth', pp. 301–02.

40. Barison, David and Ross, Daniel, *The Ister*, featuring Lacoue-Labarthe, Jean-Luc Nancy, Bernard Stiegler and Hans-Jürgen Syberberg (Australia, 2004).

41. In *Scène* suivi de *Dialogue sur le dialogue*, p. 24.

42. In correspondence with the author of 12 April 2014, Nancy confirmed that the debate took place in January 1997 at the Odéon in Paris.

CHAPTER 3

L'Écriture

The collaborations between Lacoue-Labarthe and Nancy were both oriented towards timely developments in contemporary thought and configured around the untimely (Jena Romanticism, Nietzsche, Heidegger, and others). But whilst on many levels theirs is a community of two, there are numerous other contemporary figures and groups who inform their community from a slight remove. Jacques Derrida is the foremost of these. His interaction with Lacoue-Labarthe is not simply an instance of one-way traffic between a *maître* and a junior partner: key moments in his own work are inflected by the thinking being done in Strasbourg. This two-way or reversible model of influence suggests that this is a relationship grounded in exchange rather than hierarchy, and as such one that shares common features with the notion of *l'écriture*, the major nexus through which the two thinkers interact.

It seems worthwhile establishing some biographical reference-points for this interaction. Born in 1930, Derrida was ten years Lacoue-Labarthe's senior. He never taught him, although came close to doing so when posted to teach at the *lycée Montesquieu* in Le Mans the year after Lacoue-Labarthe left the town to pursue his studies in Bordeaux (the energies the latter devoted to exploring Hölderlin's stay in that town could therefore have been employed as one of Derrida's first students). Lacoue-Labarthe read Derrida's first articles as they appeared in the early- and mid-1960s, and his early encounters with Nancy were marked by Derrida's texts (mainly *De la Grammatologie* [*Of Grammatology*] for Lacoue-Labarthe, mainly *La Voix et le phénomène* [*Voice and Phenomenon*] for Nancy). In 1970–71 the pair invited Derrida to speak at a conference in Strasbourg and he presented 'La Mythologie blanche' ['White Mythology'], a text which in Lacoue-Labarthe's words 'me laissa abasourdi, terrassé, bégayant, honteux, lorsqu'il me fallut prendre la parole' ['left me dumbfounded, floored, tongue-tied, ashamed, when I was asked to speak'].[1] From this point, a large number of projects linked Derrida to Lacoue-Labarthe (often together with Nancy, up to the mid-1980s at least). Some interpretations have it that the Strasbourg thinkers were simple acolytes of Derrida — for instance critics such as Nancy Fraser, Luc Ferry and Alain Renault, or Jacques Lacan who reacting to their book on his work (*Le Titre de la lettre*, 1973) dismissed them as deconstructive 'sous-fifres' ('second fiddles').[2]

The majority of the evidence, however, points to a more collaborative view, with the community of Lacoue-Labarthe and Nancy forming as it were the central group, in which Derrida and/or Sarah Kofman, or these two plus others still, took part according to the situation. For instance, the book collection 'La Philosophie en effet' ['Philosophy Indeed'] was founded by Lacoue-Labarthe, Nancy, Kofman, and Derrida, forming in the latter's words 'un TGV philosophique entre Paris et Strasbourg' ['a philosophical TGV between Paris and Strasbourg'].[3] One of the first works to appear under this imprint was a collective volume featuring all four editors named *Mimesis: des articulations*.[4] The title's partitive article 'des' connotes plurality, but still leaves open the possibility of other approaches than those included in the volume, in a way that the alternative title *Mimesis: les articulations* would not have done. In other words, these are *some* articulations of mimesis, but not an exhaustive or total account of all those possible. What's more, this 'des', thanks to the liaison meaning that the 's' must be pronounced as a /z/, can lead to the title being heard homophonically as *Mimesis: désarticulations*. This phonetic transformation of 'des' to 'dés-' serves to suggest that it is by participating in a plural and open group of thinkers that philosophical discourse can be disarticulated, dislocated or put out of joint.[5]

Such group projects continued to multiply in following years: from the Cerisy conference organized by Lacoue-Labarthe and Nancy, *Les Fins de l'homme: à partir du travail de Jacques Derrida* (1980) to the founding of the *Collège international de philosophie* (1983-), and from Derrida examining the *doctorat d'état* theses of both Lacoue-Labarthe (*La Fiction du politique*, 1987) and Nancy (1988), to his long text on Lacoue-Labarthe, 'Désistance' (1987; ['Desistance']).[6] It is possible to follow individual threads showing how Derrida's work is influenced by these opportunities for collaboration — for instance in a text on Blanchot named 'La Loi du genre', first given at a 1979 Strasbourg conference on genre, or with *Spectres de Marx* (1993), a work that returns to Lacoue-Labarthe's challenge to engage with the work and reception of Marx: 'Je ne suis pas persuadé qu'on rende le meilleur service à la décon-struction [...] en tenant le marxisme à l'abri de la déconstruction' (FH 496; ['I am not convinced that deconstruction is best served [...] by keeping Marxism sheltered from deconstruction']). What's more, it seems that for Derrida, Lacoue-Labarthe and Nancy represented both an alternative group and way of thinking to *Tel Quel*, from whom he split in the early 1970s. He writes of this period as follows:

> c'étaient déjà les prémisses de ma rupture irréversible avec le mouvement *Tel Quel* — non pas avec la revue à laquelle je n'ai jamais appartenu, mais avec un groupe qui supportait de plus en plus mal mon indépendance politique, aussi bien quant à leurs positions pro-PCF, et pro-soviétiques en 1968 au moment de l'invasion de Prague, et, un peu plus tard, quant à leur conversion tout aussi dogmatique à un maoïsme caricatural, aveugle, accompagné d'un terrorisme intellectuel un peu puéril. Ces moments de solitude furent difficiles pour moi. Dès lors, la complicité affectueuse et hospitalière de Philippe et de Jean-Luc commença en effet à faire de Strasbourg, pour moi, le symbole d'une ville-refuge.[7]

> [these were already the grounds for my irreversible rupture with *Tel Quel* — not with the journal, to which I never belonged, but with a group which found my political independence more and more unbearable, both in terms of their pro-French Communist Party and pro-Soviet positions in 1968 at the time of the invasion of Prague, and later, in terms of their conversion, which was just

as dogmatic, to a caricatural and blind Maoism which was accompanied but a somewhat puerile intellectual terrorism. These moments of solitude were difficult for me. From that time on, the affectionate and hospitable complicity of Philippe and Jean-Luc indeed began to make Strasbourg, for me, into the symbol of a city of refuge.]

Such a move away from *Tel Quel* therefore moves him towards Lacoue-Labarthe and Nancy, who, as we have seen, themselves had doubts regarding Sollers's group — these doubts forming one motivation for their work on Jena Romanticism as an avant-garde group interested in *la théorie de la littérature* (the subtitle of *L'Absolu littéraire*, 1978) and the self-reflexivity of modern writing. On a historicized account of Derrida's thinking there is therefore a turn towards Lacoue-Labarthe and Nancy, informing his texts from the mid-1970s onwards.

Beyond this, it is notable that in the text from which this passage is taken, Derrida attempts to move beyond the anecdotal — not abandoning the autobiographical mode of writing as he does so, but bringing it into dialogue with philosophical and political thinking. These are the implications of his interactions with the two Strasbourg thinkers, forming what Derrida names 'notre trio' ['our trio'].[8] The text in question is drawn from a volume arising from Derrida's final visit to the town, and named *Penser à Strasbourg* (translatable, of course, both as *Thinking in Strasbourg* and as *Thinking about Strasbourg*).[9] The title of his intervention is also polysemic: 'Le Lieu dit: Strasbourg' both playing on the French idiom of the 'lieu dit', a fixed expression introducing a particular place, and suggesting that is place — or *le lieu*, the wider category of 'place' itself — speaks or is speaking. In other words, this second reading of the title 'Le Lieu dit: Strasbourg' presents Strasbourg as a name being enunciated by the place (or by place in general: *le lieu*): i.e. it becomes something beyond just another city, instead having some sort of wider importance.[10] This importance is to be found, for Derrida, in the political domain: he states that '[c]e que Strasbourg, la ville et mes amis, mes premiers hôtes [...] m'ont donné la chance de partager avec eux, comme je ne l'ai jamais fait avec d'autres, c'est aussi [...] une expérience politique' ['[w]hat Strasbourg, the city and my friends, my first hosts [...] allowed me to happily share with them, as I have never done with others, is also [...] a political experience'].[11] This statement can be read in two ways: first, as an allusion to Derrida's shared sympathies with the Strasbourg thinkers on the wider scene, from a broad (though indirect) sympathy with May '68 to a reading of the more radical elements of Heidegger (Lacoue-Labarthe stated that '[q]uand j'ai découvert Derrida, je me suis dit que c'était enfin la première lecture "de gauche" de Heidegger'; ['When I discovered Derrida, I said to myself that here finally was the first "left-wing" reading of Heidegger']).[12] The second reading of the statement takes the reference to 'a political experience' not as referring to the wider political scene, but instead to the community or *polis* represented by the numerous seminars and conferences in Strasbourg and elsewhere. Derrida gives the cue for this reading, although tellingly he does not use the Greek model of the *polis* to conceive of the community in question, but instead that of a synagogue. He writes that '[un] souci [...] nous appelait ensemble, à vivre et à venir ensemble, à *convenir* dans quelque chose comme une synagogue. Vous le savez, c'est le premier sens du mot: une synagogue, c'est le rassemblement, le lieu dit qui dit ou dicte de se rendre ensemble' ['[a] concern [...] called us together, to live and to come together, to *convene* in something like a synagogue. As you know, this is the first meaning of the word: a synagogue is a gathering, the place [*lieu dit*] which speaks [*dit*] or dictates a coming together'].[13] Such a convening or coming-together in the community of Lacoue-Labarthe and Nancy therefore represented for Derrida a way of responding to the demands of (the) place — to what 'le lieu dit' —, and this quotation of Creon's words in Antigone establishes (with some irony) these demands as those for a just and peaceable way of living together. Derrida is thus invoking both Jewish and Greek traditions of thought; interestingly, it is the former that is picked up by the analogy used by George Steiner to describe the relations of Derrida, Nancy, and Lacoue-Labarthe — but with disparaging intent. He writes of 'l'aura, pour moi toujours suspecte, du cénacle local, de l'encensement mutuel' ['the aura, which for me is always suspect, of the local cenacle, of mutual anointment'].[14]

As a whole, Derrida's 2004 paper raises various problems. The first is simply that of historical accuracy: the emotional setting of the paper, in what would clearly be his final visit to Strasbourg given his failing health (he died the following year), means that many statements are incompatible with the historical record. For instance, '[s]ans cette amitié [entre Lacoue-Labarthe, Nancy, et moi-même], je sais, moi, que je n'aurais jamais osé m'avancer dans ce que j'appelle encore, pour faire vite, la pensée et l'écriture' ['[w]ithout this friendship [between Lacoue-Labarthe, Nancy, and myself], I personally know that I would never have dared to strike out into what I still call, to keep things short, thought and writing'].[15] In reality, however, Derrida famously published three works in 1967 — *De la Grammatologie, L'Écriture et la différence,* [*Writing and Difference*] and *La Voix et le phénomène* — before having met the two younger thinkers, who had yet to publish a single article. The second problem is that the relationship between the 'trio' of Derrida — Nancy — Lacoue-Labarthe, presented as a political one and as a 'synagogue', risks becoming a community rooted in what Steiner named 'mutual anointment' (and an all-male one at that, the occasional presence of Sarah Kofman notwithstanding). And thirdly, the question arises of what lasting importance such interactions might have for those who were not present; to what degree can they be relevant to those who seek to follow Derrida's thinking of *l'écriture*, one understanding of which is as a distancing from speech, from charismatic, lived presence? Ultimately, can the texts produced in and around the interaction between Lacoue-Labarthe, Nancy, and Derrida, be read in and of themselves, in the as it were impersonal, post-hoc time of reading, fragmented as it is across different contexts and different times? If we are to ask these questions — which we must —, we realize that alongside a discourse that does veer dangerously close to a communitarian self-reinforcement, there is a more durable strand in the interaction between these figures. Derrida gives voice to it as follows:

> Ce que je partage avec Lacoue-Labarthe, nous le partageons aussi tous deux, quoique différemment, avec Jean-Luc Nancy. Mais je m'empresse aussitôt de le rappeler, malgré tant de trajets et de travaux communs entre eux deux et entre nous trois, l'expérience de chacun reste, dans sa singulière proximité,

absolument différente, et c'est malgré sa fatale impureté, le secret de l'idiome. Le secret, c'est-à-dire en premier lieu la séparation, le sans-rapport, l'interruption. Le plus urgent, j'essaierai de m'y employer, ce serait de rompre ici avec les airs de famille, d'éviter les tentations généalogiques, les projections, assimilations ou identifications. [...] L'assimilation ou la projection spéculaire, voilà ce contre quoi Lacoue-Labarthe nous met sans cesse en garde.[16]

[What I share with Lacoue-Labarthe, we also both share, though differently, with Jean-Luc Nancy. But I hasten immediately to reiterate that despite so many common paths and so much work done in common, between the two of them and between the three of us, the work of each remains, however singularly close to the others it might appear, absolutely different; and this, despite its fatal impurity, is the secret of the idiom. The secret: that is to say, first of all, the separation, the non-relation, the interruption. The most urgent thing — I'll try to work on this — would be to break with the family atmosphere, to avoid genealogical temptations, assimilations, or identifications. [...] Assimilation or identificatory projection: these are what Lacoue-Labarthe constantly puts us on guard against. (TYP 6–7, trans. mod.)]

In other words, behind or to one side of a discourse that on a sceptical reading can appear to be that of a community based around presence, the interaction between Lacoue-Labarthe and Derrida directs us towards a thinking of language — 'the idiom' — and 'the separation, the non-relation, the interruption' that are associated with it. In what follows I hope to set out precisely this mode of thinking, which most often in Lacoue-Labarthe's written interactions with Derrida goes by the name of *l'écriture* (a term which I most often retain in the French). In doing this, we shall see that neither Lacoue-Labarthe nor Derrida can be definitively associated with either pole of the dualism of philosophy and literature — *l'écriture* standing precisely for what questions such binaries, instead remaining in movement or *différance* and thereby providing an important iteration of deconstruction as slippage between discourses.

The first section of what follows will set out how *l'écriture* is oriented in relation to these debates on the interactions between discourses. We shall then move to look at some of Lacoue-Labarthe's earliest articles, in which the influence of Derrida is marked. In these texts Nietzsche acts as an untimely *tiers* allowing us to triangulate between Lacoue-Labarthe and Derrida, with his work providing a model for the delays and deferrals of *l'écriture* whereby the metaphysics of presence could be set aside. The chapter's second section then looks at the interactions between Lacoue-Labarthe and Derrida at *Les Fins de l'homme* in 1980. Although still performing detailed readings of the older thinker, Lacoue-Labarthe now felt able to challenge him, using the issue of style and clarity to do so. Here, it is Heidegger who acts as the untimely *tiers* allowing us to triangulate between the two; partly through a reading of the German thinker, Lacoue-Labarthe asks whether *l'écriture*, with its emptying-out or exhaustion of the process of naming, is a suitable tool in the struggle to set aside the imposition of philosophy as a mode of discourse and of *l'homme* as the ultimate horizon of the so-called *sciences humaines*.[17]

Orientations of *L'Écriture*

Why this term rather than another? Many have emphasized that the challenge presented by Derrida's thinking lies in its mobility: his insistence on deferrals, slippages, and uncertainties mean that attempts to locate a centre or essence to his thinking are bound to fail. And the same can be said of attempts to define a single, central term that might provide a solid starting-point or ground from which his œuvre can be read. As Lacoue-Labarthe and Nancy state in the invitation to *Les Fins de l'homme*, the conference loosely organized around Derrida's work and taking its title from it, '[l]e problème [du colloque] aurait [...] cette forme: que font "les fins de l'homme" dans l'ensemble constitué par "le texte", "la trace", "le gramme", "la différance", "la dissémination", "l'hymen" [...]? Que font-elles dans cet ensemble et à cet ensemble? Et réciproquement?' (FH 20; ['The problem [of the conference] would have the following form: what do "the ends of man" do in the ensemble made up of "text", "trace", "gramma", "differance", "dissemination", "hymen" [...]? What do they do within this ensemble, and to it? And reciprocally?']). There is therefore only limited use in setting out, as it were, on a mushroom hunt for terms such as *différance, trace, écriture*, and so on, in Derrida's work: the latter instead rewards sensitivity to the particular configuration, at a particular moment, of a given conceptual framework. Bearing in mind the inadequacy of any single term, we can nonetheless note that in Lacoue-Labarthe's work, it is the Derridean notion, motif or principle of *l'écriture* that is most fully explored: again in the invitation to *Les Fins de l'homme*, we read that 'c'est au motif de "l'écriture" qu'on rattache avant tout le nom de Derrida' (FH 20; ['Derrida's name is associated above all with the motif of "writing"']). I therefore concentrate my attention on *l'écriture* — by which is understood not literature in any received sense, but instead something like a heterogeneous ensemble of meaning within which function multiple patterns of delay and deferral.

As we shall see, Lacoue-Labarthe's reading of *l'écriture* is a major vector both in his relation to the timely or contemporary scene, and in his readings of Nietzsche and Heidegger, both thinkers of the interaction between the timely and the untimely (not least in the former's *Untimely Meditations*). The question of where to situate *l'écriture* shows that Derrida and Lacoue-Labarthe share common ground. Each has reservations about being qualified as a philosopher in the Western tradition, if by that term is understood a metaphysician (interested in essences rising above historical contingency), or a dialectician (oriented towards binding difference into a final resolution). Nonetheless, each engages extensively with the corpus of philosophy, often doing so in the name of 'thought' or 'deconstruction'. This can be seen particularly regarding *l'écriture*, given that two of the term's major orientations stem from readings of Plato.

The first orientation is the idea of *l'écriture* as a synonym for literature, i.e. a tradition or a discipline distinct from philosophy and standing in a relationship of symmetry or opposition to it. Famously, Plato's position in *The Republic* is that poets must be excluded from the city in order to assure its governability; as Lacoue-Labarthe ventriloquizes in his autobiographical text which — notably — opens with this rift between philosophy and poetry, 'les mythes et les faiseurs de mythes (les poètes) seront pratiquement tous condamnés. Et dans quelques pages encore, ce sera au tour de l'homme de théâtre, de l'acteur-auteur tragique, d'être rituellement expulsé' ['myths and myth-makers (poets) will practically all be condemned. And a few pages further on, it will be the turn of the theatre man, of the tragic actor-author, to be ritually expelled'].[18] However, the deconstructive way of reacting to this exclusion is not to simply champion poetry or literature against the claims of philosophy. To do so would be merely to invert the hierarchy that Plato establishes, therefore confirming it. For, the argument goes, this model of literature was only created in and by Plato's act of exclusion; to champion it is therefore to fall into a trap, to have always already accepted a straightjacket from which there is no subsequent escape. The better approach is to identify characteristics of l'écriture (such as heterogeneity, multiplicity, deferral), and then be attentive to their presence in a range of texts or moments of textuality, whether or not the latter are part of literary, philosophical, or other canons.

Plato's second contribution to our understanding of l'écriture concerns the status of writing as a new technology at the time, i.e. something providing a supplement to voice and memory. Again, the philosopher's gesture is one of exclusion: he rejects writing, worrying that reliance upon it will lead us to lose our capacity to remember. What is more, when a thought is written down, there is a danger that the reader will mis-interpret it, given the absence of the original author and his inability to explain the underlying intention. The ultimate model in this regard is Plato's maître Socrates, who simply taught, leaving Plato to write down the resulting dialogues (in doing so of course complicating his denunciation of writing; Derrida's Carte postale takes its cue from a postcard representing the two Greeks in which the roles have — perhaps accidentally — been reversed). In De la Grammatologie, especially, Derrida argues against this privilege given to the voice or 'phonocentrism'. He seizes on the danger or risk that Plato sees as inherent in writing, presenting this as the radical good fortune — or chance — that writing makes available. But again, the argument is not simply an empiricist one, suggesting for example that speech should be outlawed and all interactions conducted on the page. Instead, Derrida's approach suggests that l'écriture is a quality of all discourse, whether it happens to be empirically written or spoken: the quality whereby our language, by definition, escapes our intention and control and lies open to misinterpretation. In Geoffrey Bennington's words,

> 'écriture' implique répétition, absence, risque de perte, mort; mais aucune parole ne serait possible sans ces valeurs; d'ailleurs, si 'écriture' a toujours voulu dire signifiant qui renvoie à un autre signifiant, et si, nous l'avons vu, tout signifiant ne renvoie qu'à d'autres signifiants, alors 'écriture' nommera proprement le fonctionnement de la langue en général.

> ['writing' implies repetition, absence, risk of loss, death; but no speech would be possible without these values; moreover, if 'writing' has always meant a signifier referring to other signifiers, and if, as we have seen, every signifier refers only to other signifiers, then 'writing' will name properly the functioning of language in general].[19]

So, in order to explore the idea that language exceeds the control of any individual, the possibility of that individual's metaphorical 'death' is raised. *L'écriture*, in this light, is a principle of uncertainty inherent in language. Users of language understood as *l'écriture* can never be entirely sure of how, where, and by whom it will be heard; or in other words, they can never be entirely certain of where it will end up, of its destination. In other words, *l'écriture* is a more mobile notion than that of literature understood as given works issuing from and illustrating the thoughts of their authors. Instead, it reconfigures itself ceaselessly as it engages in something like an errancy, lacking destination, outside the security of authorial control.

After Nietzsche

Lacoue-Labarthe's thinking responds on a different level to this principle of errancy insofar as the influence of Derrida does not sit in its own, sealed compartment within it: instead, this strand in his work is in constant communication with others. One of these is the atmosphere which, following Situationism's prominence in Strasbourg and then May '68, contributes to his contestation of prevailing philosophies. Another strand is his work on Nietzsche, a thinker who in this period, in the French thinker's words, 'avait pratiquement envahi la totalité de la scène philosophique française' ['had invaded practically the entire French philosophical scene'].[20] The Nietzschean desire to both inhabit the corpus of philosophy and move beyond it, as well as the readings of writing and textuality that can emerge from his work, mean that he provided a key platform through which Lacoue-Labarthe's engagement with Derrida was played out in the early publications. These range from his first article on philosophy — 'La Fable (littérature et philosophie)' (1970; ['Fable (literature and philosophy)']) — to his participation in the 1972 Cerisy conference *Nietzsche, aujourd'hui* (Derrida and Nancy were amongst the other participants). Beyond this, he and Nancy published a small anthology of their translations of Nietzsche texts as *Rhétorique et langage* [*Rhetoric and Language*, 1975], and also gave numerous seminars on the thinker in this period. Lacoue-Labarthe for instance taught seminars on *The Birth of Tragedy*, and published a translation of the work in 1977.[21] In this section we shall encounter a sample of this work, namely two articles that are particularly illuminating regarding the notion of *l'écriture* and its broad reach within Lacoue-Labarthe's thinking.

'La Fable (littérature et philosophie)'

This text represents several firsts: it is at once Lacoue-Labarthe's first published article, it appears in the launch issue of the review *Poétique*, and it opens his first solo book on its collection in *Le Sujet de la philosophie* (1979).[22] But despite what these more or less contingent details might suggest, the article in fact challenges the notion of making a clean start, or founding a discourse from first principles. As we saw above with the example of Plato, the foundation of the Western philosophical tradition takes place in and through the exclusion of its other, which we can refer to simply as 'literature'. This amounts to saying that literature is a necessary condition for the birth of philosophy, precisely because such importance is placed on excluding the former from the City. What is more, we can ask whether such an exclusion can ever be definitively successful; and this is the scenario on which Lacoue-Labarthe's text opens. It reads:

> On voudrait ici poser à la philosophie la question de sa 'forme'; ou, plus exactement, jeter sur elle ce soupçon: et si, après tout, elle n'était que de la littérature? On sait en effet avec quelle insistance la philosophie, la métaphysique, s'est en général déterminée contre ce que nous appelons la littérature. On sait aussi à quel point, depuis Nietzsche surtout, le combat mené contre la métaphysique a pu s'accompagner d'un effort proprement littéraire ou même s'identifier avec lui. (SP 9)

> [We would like to enquire here into the 'form' of philosophy; or more precisely, to cast upon it this suspicion: what if, after all, philosophy were nothing but literature? We know how insistent philosophy — metaphysics — has generally been in defining itself against what we call literature. We also know to what extent, particularly since Nietzsche, the struggle against metaphysics has been coupled with, or has even identified itself with, a specifically literary effort. (SP2 1)]

Here we encounter the line of questioning, familiar to readers of Derrida, that calls into question philosophy's pretention that it thinks in entirely abstract or conceptual terms, i.e. that it is able simply to sideline the difficulties posed by language. In this light, the category of literature returns from the exile to which it had been banished, and provides a mode of analysis or reading more able to cope with the particular rhythms, idiosyncrasies and problems of translation that arise when we begin to look at the text of philosophy (which is to say, at philosophy as text). And indeed, the reference to Derrida is wholly explicit, coming no later than the article's second page: 'Dans la mesure en effet où le désir d'un dire pur est lié au refoulement de l'écriture [...], le soupçon porté ici sur la métaphysique est celui-là même que porte Derrida.' (SP 10; ['To the extent, indeed, that the desire for a pure saying is linked to the repression of writing [...], the suspicion we cast upon metaphysics is the very one cast upon it by Derrida;' SP2 1, trans. mod.])

But given that the article takes Nietzsche as its most explicit subject for discussion, we must remember that Lacoue-Labarthe's is a double gesture, writing as it were 'after' Derrida but on the subject of Nietzsche. If he is to avoid repeating the emphasis that metaphysics places on fixed essences, there must be an effort to proceed otherwise than by *applying* Derrida's thinking retrospectively to the German philosopher. Neither Derrida nor Lacoue-Labarthe can be described as addressing the untimely simply in terms of the timely (i.e. contemporary thought), in the way such an 'application' would suggest. In this light, the article in question discusses one of Nietzsche's aphoristic formulations, which Lacoue-Labarthe translates as follows: 'Parménide a dit: "on ne pense pas ce qui n'est pas"; nous sommes à l'autre extrême et nous disons: "ce qui peut être pensé doit certainement être une fiction"' (SP 12; ['Parmenides said, "one cannot think of what is not"; — we are at the other extreme, and say: "what can be thought of must certainly be a fiction"', SP2 3]). According to Nietzsche, the situation of contemporary philosophy — that pertaining to 'us' in this aphorism — is the mirror image of the one described by Parmenides. Between this pre-Socratic philosopher, standing at the outset of philosophy, and we who stand at its point of closure, a reversal has taken place. And this reversal concerns the confidence placed in thought: Parmenides's statement suggests that simply because we think something, it must be true — human reason has a privileged relation to truth, ultimately being immune from error. (This, at least is the view of Parmenides as translated and presented by Nietzsche and then Lacoue-Labarthe; the latter translates the original Greek rather differently, as 'c'est le même, en effet, penser et être', SP 12; ['thinking and being are, in effect, the same'; SP2 3]). For Nietzsche, on the other hand, it is simply because we think something that it can be designated as fiction, as that which is excluded from truth; this is an absolute lack of confidence in human reason's ability to access truth. This view therefore privileges fiction rather than truth as the mode of human knowledge: in short, an operation has taken place whereby one epistemological regime has replaced another, and in this fragment Nietzsche is equally sure of his negative assertion as Parmenides was of his positive one. We can therefore define this as a simple reversal of the hierarchy between truth and fiction. In Lacoue-Labarthe's words, '[l]e thème est connu: Nietzsche, c'est le renversement du platonisme, et donc encore du platonisme, — et finalement l'accomplissement de la métaphysique elle-même. Et il est vrai qu'un texte comme celui-ci [...] autorise une interprétation de ce genre' (SP 15; ['the theme is well known: Nietzsche is the reversal of Platonism and therefore still a Platonism, and ultimately the accomplishment of metaphysics itself. And it is true that a text such as this one [...] justifies an interpretation of this kind', SP2 5]). To argue that human thought is necessarily fiction rather than truth recalls the argument that all philosophy is always already literature; Plato's hierarchy between the two is neatly reversed, but not challenged in any more rigorous way. But this is not what the French thinker is searching for here; he soon moves on to present a more subtle and ultimately more valuable aspect of Nietzsche's thinking. This is to be found in the statement which when translated by Lacoue-Labarthe reads: 'Le "monde-vérité", nous l'avons aboli. Quel monde nous est resté? Le monde des apparences peut-être?... Mais non ! *Avec le monde-vérité nous avons aussi aboli le monde des apparences!*' (SP 16, emphasis original; ['The "truth-world" — we have abolished. What world has remained? The world of appearances, perhaps? But no! *With the truth-world we have also abolished the world of appearances*'; SP2 5, emphasis original, trans. mod.]). Here the initial stage of the abolition of what Nietzsche calls idiosyncratically the 'truth-world' — the true world or the world as truth —, takes place as it did previously. But what is different is that this world is not replaced by a view of fiction as the dominant epistemological regime; instead fiction has been abolished along with truth, doubtless because it is little more than an inversion or dialectical opposite of it.[23] (N.B. the sense of 'fiction' here is distinct from the fictioning or *fictionnement* he addresses in *La Fiction du politique*). Whilst one aspect of Nietzsche's thought reverses philosophical hierarchies, another seeks to get beyond even the oppositional or alternative thinking that is produced in this way — the hierarchy between truth and fiction is not just turned round once, as it were, but set in a continual spin or revolution.

For Lacoue-Labarthe, the interest of this second approach is considerable. The way he aligns his text with Derrida's thinking suggests that, as part of the enterprise of unsettling metaphysical philosophy, he might be wont to privilege literature as an alternative to it. However, as also for Derrida, we soon discover that literature is too readily seen as a creation of that same metaphysics, albeit a creation made in the act of exclusion from the City. This is the situation in which *l'écriture* becomes an attractive notion, insofar as it demands that we look beyond binaries or dualisms, even and especially those in which it might commonly be thought to be implicated: those of writing and speech, or literature and philosophy. In this light, we can read the passage where Lacoue-Labarthe brings Nietzsche's challenge to the dualism of truth/fiction to bear on his own thinking of *l'écriture*. We read:

> il y a peut-être un moyen d'arracher la littérature à la domination de la métaphysique et de briser le cercle dans lequel on était au départ. Mais il ne s'agit plus évidemment de la 'littérature'. Fiction, mythe, fable, sont des mots provisoires. Mieux vaudrait sans doute parler d'*écriture*. Mais on n'en est pas encore là. Ou plutôt, on voit bien que si l'on veut suivre cette voie, il ne faut pas brûler les étapes. On devrait en effet distinguer entre deux tâches:
>
> (1). Retourner contre la métaphysique (dans la métaphysique), sous le nom de littérature, ce contre quoi elle-même s'est retournée, ce à partir de quoi elle a voulu se constituer. C'est de bonne guerre.
>
> (2). Entreprendre de forcer ses limites, c'est-à-dire, si l'on veut déplacer la barre qui sépare symboliquement littérature et philosophie (littérature/philosophie) de telle sorte que de part et d'autre littérature et philosophie soient toutes deux barrées et s'annulent en communiquant: littérature philosophie (SP 22).

> [there may be a way of wresting literature from the domination of metaphysics and of breaking the circle in which we found ourselves at the outset. But it is obviously no longer a question of 'literature'. Fiction, myth, and fable are provisional words. It would doubtless be better to speak of *writing*. But we are not there yet. Or rather, it is clear that if we want to follow this path, we must not take shortcuts. We should in fact distinguish between two tasks:
>
> (1). Turning against metaphysics (within metaphysics), under the name of literature, that against which metaphysics itself has turned, that from which it has striven to constitute itself. Fair enough.
>
> (2). Undertaking to force open the limits of metaphysics, that is, displacing the bar that symbolically separates literature and philosophy (literature/philosophy) in such a way that on each side literature and philosophy are both crossed out and cancel each other in communicating. Hence we would have: literature philosophy; SP2 9, trans. mod.].

In other words, *l'écriture* can only be arrived at by an essentially dual mode of thinking. On the one hand, this involves inverting hierarchies: not to do so would be to risk remaining stuck within the traditional perspectives of metaphysics, and there is therefore some value in a combative, oppositional stance. On the other hand, we must not be content once the hierarchy has been reversed. This second aspect of the approach suggested by Lacoue-Labarthe is a continuation of the process of reversal: one must reverse the new hierarchy one has established, then the one arising from this second reversal, and so on. In this case, this leads not to replacing philosophy with literature, but first writing and then effacing both terms by striking them through, i.e. placing them *sous rature* or under erasure. In general terms, then, two approaches must be combined if we are to arrive at *l'écriture* — and the shifts and recalibrations between these approaches will be an important part of Lacoue-Labarthe's understanding of *l'écriture* in relation to Derrida and Heidegger. The distinction we can draw between literature and *l'écriture* is therefore that the former is a positive entity, defined by a set of characteristics setting it apart from philosophy; whereas the latter instead exists as and through an iteration of characteristics belonging to both literature and philosophy. There is no defining feature by which we could grasp it (or by which, having grasped it once, we could do so a second time). On this point, Lacoue-Labarthe writes that 'on ne peut pas "en venir" au texte: car le texte est précisément sans rivage' (SP 27; ['one cannot "come to" the text, for the text is precisely without a shore', SP2 12]). Textuality or *l'écriture* — the two are synonymous here — is not some positively available, alien continent to be conquered. And in a similar vein, at the end of the article it is not Derrida's name that is invoked, but that of Blanchot:

> peut-être s'agit-il seulement de faire l'aveu de l'*impossible*, qui n'est ni la parole ni le silence, ni le savoir ni l'ignorance, ni la force ni l'impuissance, dont on ne peut rien dire sinon qu'il nous livre à ce murmure infini, infiniment disjoint mais infiniment recommencé, à ce que Blanchot nommait d'un mot qui désignait bien pour nous ce qu'est devenue, ce qu'a toujours été l'injustifiable et nécessaire entreprise de l'écriture: le *ressassement éternel* (SP 27–28, emphases original).

> [perhaps it is simply a question of admitting the impossible, which is neither speech nor silence, neither knowledge nor ignorance, neither strength nor impotence, something of which one can say nothing except that it gives us over to an infinite murmur, infinitely disjointed but infinitely renewed, to what Blanchot calls by a name that designates for us what the unjustifiable and necessary enterprise of writing has become, what it has always been: *ressassement éternel* [eternal rumination]; SP2 13].

Here we see a series of dualisms being posited and then stepped beyond, with the effect of underlining that the thought emerging from Lacoue-Labarthe's reading of Nietzsche here is one reaching beyond any single dualism, for instance philosophy and literature. This process is named a *ressassement éternel*, drawing on Blanchot's work of the same title (itself a re-presentation of two previously-published *récits*, i.e. already a minimal, emptied-out act of writing). And given this note of *ressassement* on which the article ends, it comes as little surprise to find Lacoue-Labarthe soon returning to the question of Nietzsche and *l'écriture*.

'La Dissimulation' a.k.a. 'Nietzsche apocryphe'

As we have begun to see, one of the main ways into Derrida's thinking of *l'écriture* is via the interface of writing and speech, following the phonocentrism — or privileging of speech — demonstrated by a range of philosophers from Rousseau to Husserl. However, Derrida does not simply invert these thinkers' hierarchy between writing and speech; counter-intuitively but importantly, *l'écriture* should not be taken as synonymous with writing when the latter is understood as one pole in a dualism with speech. Instead, *l'écriture* is what defies definition in such dualistic terms, always already being at play even in its supposed opposite. In putting forward this thinking, Derrida is reading the canonical texts of early Greek philosophy in a particular way. For whilst Plato approaches the interface of writing/speech in a thematic way (expressing reservations over writing as a new technology that would not aid memory but in fact replace it), he also does so in the very gesture of writing his dialogues. For the latter feature the figure of Socrates, whose existence as a historical person distinct from Plato has long been a topic of discussion. Plato is therefore in danger of inconsistency: on the one hand arguing against writing, and on the other hand, writing Socrates's words down for posterity. And indeed, the durability of writing as a technology has meant that whilst we possess these written accounts, some thinkers have called into question the very historical existence of Socrates: might he be Plato's fictional creation, an idealized version of himself? In brief, the interface between Socrates/Plato — explored at length by Derrida in *La Carte postale* — is another way of approaching that between writing/speech, and indeed the *écriture* that exceeds and escapes this dualism.

We can now turn to 'La Dissimulation', a paper first given by Lacoue-Labarthe at the 1972 Cerisy conference *Nietzsche, aujourd'hui* and then collected in *Le Sujet de la philosophie* (1979) as 'Nietzsche apocryphe'.[24] Here he looks at the unstable status of the relationship between 1) Plato the philosopher and 2) Socrates the character in Plato's work, and uses it to cast light on the relationship between 1) Nietzsche the philosopher and 2) Zarathustra the character in Nietzsche's work. In this analogy, Socrates is to Plato as Zarathustra is to Nietzsche. In each case, the strategy of the philosopher (whether Plato or Nietzsche) is said to be the creation of a 'figure interposée' ('interposed figure'), of which examples are then given. This comparison between the two contexts is what allows Lacoue-Labarthe to write of: 'Socrate, Zarathustra, pour rester dans le même exemple' ['Socrates, Zarathustra, to remain with the same example'].[25] Such a figure, interposed or acting as a mask for the philosopher, would provide the 'dissimulation', the title under which the article in question first appeared. In other words, we are dealing with the dissimulation of Nietzsche by the figure of Zarathustra, or of Plato by the figure of Socrates. The question that arises is therefore: where exactly we are to draw the line between — for instance — Nietzsche and Zarathustra? And in presenting us with this uncertainty, how does Nietzsche's text, standing at the closure of Western metaphysics, reiterate the gesture made by Plato at its beginning? This leads on to a second question which is of direct interest to our current reading of Lacoue-Labarthe's response to the notion of *l'écriture*: whether Nietzsche's *Thus Spake Zarathustra* can be said to be a leading example of a work written according to the movement, the differences and deferrals, of *l'écriture*.

If it were such a work, this would be in part due to the dissimulation of its author Nietzsche by the figure of Zarathustra, blurring the boundaries between authorial presence ('speech') and fictional creation ('writing') in line with *l'écriture* as a non-dialectical principle — scrambling, as it were, binary or dualistic distinctions. Already Lacoue-Labarthe, writing together with Nancy, had presented Nietzsche's work in general as 'une pratique incessante de l'écriture' ['an incessant practice of *l'écriture*'].[26] And in terms of *Zarathustra* specifically, when Lacoue-Labarthe is thinking in shorthand form, the hypothesis that this thinker practises or represents *l'écriture* seems to be defended:

> Nietzsche était [...] celui qui, de tous les 'philosophes' (Kierkegaard compris), s'était le plus systématiquement distingué, malgré lui pour une part, mais avec la rage ostentatoire que l'on sait, par sa pratique contradictoire et multiple, énigmatique, et, disons bouleversante, de l'écriture. Au point que sans lui, la 'question' du texte n'aurait jamais sans doute fait irruption (SP 80).

> [Nietzsche, of all the 'philosophers' (Kierkegaard included), was the one who distinguished himself the most systematically (partly in spite of himself, but with his usual ostentatious rage) by his contradictory and multifarious, enigmatic and, let us say, disruptive practice of writing. Indeed, without him the 'question' of the text would doubtless never have emerged so forcefully; SP2 39].

On this evidence, the issue seems clear enough: Nietzsche blazes the trail for textuality and *l'écriture*. Yet things become more nuanced once we begin to look at the various facets of the argument made in the article. For instance, is it not ultimately contradictory to search for an exemplar of *l'écriture*, if the latter is truly to represent that which always lies elsewhere, escaping views of it as being located in one particular work rather than another? Instead of such a localizable nature, i.e. one capable of being posited or representing a *position*, this motif should always remain in movement. If *l'écriture* is to remain *l'écriture*, rather than simply writing (i.e. the opposite of speech) or literature (i.e. the opposite of philosophy), then surely it must be always mobile, moving past individual positions within systems of identification.

Once again, therefore, we should recall that the positive entity, canon, or discourse of literature cannot be taken to explain what Lacoue-Labarthe sees at work in *l'écriture*. However, in a marked difference to 'La Fable', Lacoue-Labarthe in 'La Dissimulation' sets up his investigation as explicitly distinct from Derrida's. Given the approach to the question of whether Nietzsche's *Zarathustra* can exemplify *l'écriture*, we might have taken the question of the thinker's style, and any different style it makes necessary for anyone writing in response to that work, to be important. But this is not the case. In the debate following his paper, Lacoue-Labarthe makes it clear that:

> Cette question du style, je n'ai pas voulu l'aborder autrement que de manière théorique, ou discursive. [...] [C]ette question [...] appartient encore à l'esthétique, c'est-à-dire à la philosophie. [...] Il aurait fallu, d'entrée de jeu, attaquer d'une tout autre manière, tourner ou forcer la clôture esthétique (philosophique, métaphysique) de la question du style en posant le style comme l'a fait Derrida au début de son texte. Je ne suis pas Derrida, et c'est évidemment ce que je n'ai pas fait.[27]

> [I have not attempted to address this question of style otherwise than in a theoretical or discursive way [...] [T]his question [...] still belongs to aesthetics, which is to say to philosophy. [...] From the word go, one would have had to attack things from a completely different angle, turning or forcing open the closure [*clôture*] of aesthetics (of philosophy, metaphysics) represented by the

question of style by positing style as Derrida did at the beginning of his text. I am not Derrida, and that is what I obviously did not do.]

This is notable: Lacoue-Labarthe here accepts the language, the advantages but also the constraints, of aesthetic philosophy or a discursive approach. In fact, the emphasis lies on the constraints, the 'clôture' — a term meaning both '(en)closure' and more literally 'fence' — of aesthetic philosophy; we sense that this attempt to distinguish himself from Derrida's approach has merely led him back within the philosophical language from which *l'écriture* escapes. He would soon move past even this uneasy truce with philosophy, however, and it would be the question of mimesis that would allow this to happen.

This much can be seen when we come to realize the significance of the reflection on the relationship between the philosopher — or the subject of philosophy, to reiterate the title of Lacoue-Labarthe's collection — and the work he/she produces. Now, we have seen Lacoue-Labarthe establish two avenues for exploring this: that of Nietzsche/Zarathustra, and that of Plato/Socrates (I will not address, although he does, the second-order question of Nietzsche's reading of Plato). Analogy is certainly present in the French thinker's mind: whereas Nietzsche is discussed for his 'incessant practice of *l'écriture*', Plato too is read otherwise than as the philosophical tyrant he sets out to be. We read that:

> le critère distinctif ou le trait pertinent du modèle platonicien [consistait], conformément à l'infidélité de Platon à sa propre doctrine, dans la *dissimulation* de l'auteur (du sujet de l'écriture) en personnage. Dans le dialogue platonicien, ce n'est pas Platon lui-même qui parle ou qui intervient en son nom propre (SP 105, emphasis original).

> [the distinctive criterion or relevant feature of the Platonic model [consisted], in accordance with Plato's unfaithfulness to his own doctrine, in the *dissimulation* of the author (of the subject of writing) as a character. In Platonic dialogue, Plato himself does not speak or intervene in his own name; SP2 54, emphasis original].

This statement confirms that the second, mimetic element in Plato's work is in conflict with 'his own doctrine', i.e. his exclusion from the City of representation or art (e.g. poetry and theatre). But it also proposes the more radical of two possible readings of this tendency in Plato's work — rejecting the hypothesis that such dissimulating figures, Socrates most of all, might ultimately act as mouthpieces for philosophers' arguments. Instead, Lacoue-Labarthe's reading is that the existence of these masks, these 'interposed figures', effects a crucial change in Plato's status in relation to the dialogues. On this view, the dissimulation that is at work would be not merely a process of (self-)disguise, but one of self-alteration. Or, as a section heading in his article puts it shortly afterwards, there is a short step between two concepts: 'La dissimulation — la dissimilation' ['[d]issimulation — dissimilation']. This is to say that the process of (dis-)simulation means that similarity is always being unworked or if you will dis-similated; there is no sameness or identity in this realm of difference.

Such is the reading of the Plato/Socrates relation that emerges from Lacoue-Labarthe's account; but we still need to address the question of Nietzsche/

Zarathustra, and its attendant implications for *l'écriture* (i.e. the model where neither pole of the dualism between two identities ultimately predominates). We have seen how Lacoue-Labarthe picks up on Nietzsche's view that Plato juxtaposes various genres; in this light it is notable that the French thinker mentions 'cette condamnation de l'auteur "apocryphe" dont parle Platon au livre III de la *République* (393 a-e) lorsqu'il s'agit de définir, entre le récit simple et l'imitation pure, entre le dithyrambe et la tragédie, le récit, mêlé d'imitation, de l'épopée' (SP 105; ['that condemnation of the "apocryphal" author Plato brings up in Book III of *The Republic* (393a-e), where it is a question of defining, between simple narrative and pure imitation, between dithyramb and tragedy, the epic as a narrative mixed with imitation', SP2 54]). In other words, Plato sees the author of the mixed genre of epic as essentially apocryphal (he would doubtless have rejected Nietzsche's view that he was precisely such an author of 'novel[s]' or mixed-genre writing). And this term gives us pause for thought — it stems from Greek *apokryphein* (to hide away), and developing from there into *apokryphos*, 'hidden, (hence) of unknown authorship, spurious' (*OED*). Plato's use of this term to designate the author of mixed-genre writing or epic doubtless referred to the indirect way in which such an author was represented in such works: not through direct speech or exposition (*diegesis*), but instead via the detour provided by the different genres and the various figures they contain (*mimesis*). This usage doubtless already contained the seed of denigration that the designation 'apocryphal' would later gain in Christian and especially Protestant discussions of various marginal biblical texts. In any case, we can note that when Lacoue-Labarthe's 1972 paper is collected in *Le Sujet de la philosophie*, it is renamed as 'Nietzsche apocryphe'. This act of renaming suggests that in setting up his own double in Zarathustra as the figure of the prophet-philosopher, Nietzsche rehabilitated the term 'apocryphal' which Plato had denigrated. Thus through a reading of Nietzsche as an 'apocryphal' writer, as 'Nietzsche apocryphe', Lacoue-Labarthe attempts to show that the act of creating a fictional philosopher is not simply a dissimulation of some underlying authorial essence, but rather a dissimilation, an admission that the real author is only ever absent or apocryphal.

Lacoue-Labarthe's reading of Nietzsche therefore explores the view of the thinker as a radical exemplar of *l'écriture*. It is worth noting that such thinking informs the way he presents his own position as an author in 'Typographie' ['Typography'], a related text published in 1975's *Mimesis: des articulations* (a collaboration with Nancy, Derrida, Sarah Kofman, Sylviane Agacinski, and Bernard Pautrat, all of whom had participated in *Nietzsche, aujourd'hui*). Whilst all six authors agreed to omit their names from the table of contents, and the texts were arranged in alphabetical order, Lacoue-Labarthe went further still, ensuring his text closed with a signature in inverted commas, '"Philippe Lacoue-Labarthe"'. In truth, this merely expresses a sense that this early period of his work can be read as proceeding from a desire to interrupt the identity of 'le sujet de la philosophie': we are left somewhere between the realms of autobiography and autothanatography. Derrida and Lacoue-Labarthe would continue to guide one another beyond Nietzsche, as they engaged around an untimely figure in the role of the third man.

After Heidegger

Les Fins de l'homme

The notion of *l'écriture*, as we have begun to see, introduces a delay or deferral between the subject of discourse and his or her ability to understand and be understood by others, even in the case of Socrates and his infamous personal charisma. This raises the question of the compatibility or otherwise of *l'écriture* with a community in which discourse would be addressed to one's fellow beings, and through them the more general entity of mankind. In other words, the issue is raised of mankind as the goal or destination of *l'écriture*, as the end towards which the latter is oriented — in French, *la fin de l'homme*. To broach this issue is to question the validity of mankind as such a destination: the idea that *l'écriture* might be at play underneath, or to one side of humanist discourse suggests that the latter has come to an end, meaning that one can speak of a different sense of *la fin de l'homme*. The play between these two meanings of *fin* or end was taken up by Derrida in his 1968 paper 'Les Fins de l'homme' ['The Ends of Man'], and then reiterated by Lacoue-Labarthe and Nancy in the 1980 conference they organized, naming it *Les Fins de l'homme: à partir du travail de Jacques Derrida*.[28] Their thinking prior to and at this conference enjoins Derrida both to maintain the subtlety of his approach to *l'écriture* and to make more explicit the political charge that he had himself announced in opening his 1968 paper with the words '[t]out colloque philosophique a nécessairement une signification politique' ('[e]very philosophical colloquium necessarily has a political significance').[29]

The notion of *la fin de l'homme*, in the sense of the ending or the closure of humanist discourse is strongly rooted in French thought of the period. Humanism was associated with the post-1945 dominance of Sartrean thought (resting for instance on Sartre's *L'Existentialisme est un humanisme*, 1945; [*Existentialism is a Humanism*]), and had already been displaced by numerous thinkers, not least Maurice Blanchot (*Le Dernier homme*, 1957; [*The Last Man*]) and Michel Foucault, who famously concluded *Les Mots et les choses* [*The Order of Things*] by writing that '[l]'homme est une invention dont l'archéologie de notre pensée montre aisément la date récente. Et peut-être la fin prochaine. [...] On peut bien parier que l'homme s'effacer[a], comme à la limite de la mer un visage de sable' ['[a]s the archeology of our thought easily shows, man is an invention of recent date. And one perhaps nearing its end. [...] One can certainly wager that man w[ill] be erased, like a face drawn in sand at the edge of the sea'].[30] In the broadest terms, Derrida can therefore be seen as part of a wider move towards a view of language as dehumanizing or alienating, once it is de-coupled from being simply the expression of human culture. In other words, language was beginning to be seen as more than a simple anthropological object. Indeed, the conference at which 'Les fins de l'homme' was given had as its subject 'philosophy and anthropology', two notions which, to put it bluntly, were at that time diverging from one another. This is to say that philosophical investigations — for instance those into language — could no longer be assumed to take place within an anthropological horizon; key structures such as the unconscious or power relations could be impersonal, inhuman, even dehumanizing. The bulk of Derrida's paper addresses Heidegger, exploring the thinker's rejection of Sartre's humanist reading of him (in the 'Letter on Humanism'). In this light, the radical nature of Heidegger's thinking is underlined: *Dasein* — the translation of which as *la réalité humaine*, adopted by Sartre, Derrida rejects — can be defined as that for which its Being is a question.[31] But what this Being is, or more precisely whether it can rigorously be said to *be* anything, is a complex affair. The challenge is presented by the idea that if this Being (*Sein*) is presented as one particular being (*Seiend*) rather than another, then it will have been misunderstood: Being is precisely that which is shared by all beings, without being reducible to the characteristics of any single one. Being can nonetheless be understood in a privileged way by *Dasein*, given that the latter is defined as that for which Being is a question. Such, therefore, is an initial reading of Heidegger in Derrida's article. But it is accompanied by a second reading, which suggests that the thinker's project of *Abbau* or *Destruktion* needs to be extended it if is to become a true deconstruction. This is to be found as Derrida questions the privileged role in relating to Being that Heidegger affords to *Dasein*. This privileged role is presented as that which is proper to mankind, i.e. that which it does not share with any other being (an animal, for instance, or a material object). Via this notion of properness, the opening that Heidegger makes possible towards a Being that is radically other, resistant to all circumscriptions and interpretations, is closed off once again. Being becomes appropriated as central to mankind's own (*propre*) identity rather than something destabilizing all identity. In other words, mankind's thinking of Being becomes a metaphysics. As for Heidegger, he argued that philosophy was mankind's major task because it enabled mankind to fulfil a role proper to it and therefore to elevate itself above the category of simple beings. In Derrida's eyes, this conception of philosophy — as opposed to thought or deconstruction — becomes part of the problem rather than the solution.

Now, it will be important to remember these models or categories: on the one hand an as it were horizontal plane of beings (*Seienden* or *étants*), and on the other a vertical transcendence of Being (*Sein* or *Être*), whether on the part of Being or of mankind in its philosophical understanding of that Being. For Lacoue-Labarthe, these two models, the horizontal and the vertical, will provide two possible readings of *écriture*, confirming that he approaches Derrida in the light of Heidegger (and vice-versa). Before we come to these readings, though, let us return to Lacoue-Labarthe and Nancy's presentation of the conference named after Derrida's paper 'Les Fins de l'homme'. In view of the latter's discussion of that which for Heidegger is *proper* to mankind, they state that their aim is to get away from this entire mode of thinking, and instead to move towards 'l'interrogation d'une non-essentialité ou d'une impropriété de l'homme' (FH 14; ['the interrogation of a non-essentiality or an impropriety of mankind']). Now, it seems that there is a major consequence of this move, concerning what Heidegger conceived as most proper to mankind in its interrogation of Being, namely philosophy. The latter would be the discourse of mankind's destiny as the being called upon to think Being, and as such would be a necessary step in a process of 'destination' (understood in the active sense of destin*ing*, a giving of destiny). Lacoue-Labarthe and Nancy are therefore seeking to move away from this model of the 'proper' and of destination, and a move away from philosophy is implied in their project. This is the light in which we should understand the importance of *l'écriture* in their thinking at *Les Fins de l'homme*. By this notion they do not mean literature as it is often understood, because this would be to fall back within the dualism Plato attempted to establish between philosophy and literature. Instead, *l'écriture* would be neither philosophy nor literature (the latter being simply the reverse-side of the former); as such it stands for a mode of thinking that is not subjugated in advance to a destination. Or at least, such is the hypothesis that they wish to test by holding the colloquium. In their words,

> Notre question est donc: de l'écriture — la destination.
> Autrement dit: comment des fins — les fins de l'homme — peuvent-elles être soumises à autre chose, qu'à une assignation, une position, une évaluation, une visée, une appropriation, etc? Comment *inscrire* les fins? (FH 14, emphasis original)

> [Our question therefore is: writing — and its destination.
> In other words: how can ends — the ends of man — be understood otherwise than via an assignation, a position, an evaluation, an aiming, an appropriation, etc? How can ends be *inscribed*? (emphasis original)]

Rather than thinking ends — in both senses of the term — via the various philosophical methods suggested (assignation, position, evaluation, and so on), the question is how to 'inscribe' or write them, i.e. how to see *l'écriture* as an alternative way of thinking. The contemporary situation which it seemed a pressing task to discuss in this way was twofold: first, the end or death of mankind given the post-humanist turn in French thought; and secondly mankind seen otherwise than in relation to its philosophical end or goal. With the premises for debate being set up in these terms by texts preceding and introducing the Cerisy conference, let us now see in more detail how the arguments themselves develop.

'Au nom de...'

Beyond the conference's various co-authored texts of invitation, introduction, and conclusion, Lacoue-Labarthe's intervention is a text named 'Au nom de...' ['In the name of...']; the subtitle '[à] Jacques Derrida' ['[t]o Jacques Derrida'] is added later, on its collection in *L'Imitation des modernes*. The paper begins with Lacoue-Labarthe stating that he wants to address a question to Derrida, and thus explicitly aligns itself with a thinking of destination. Indeed, there is a considerably theatrical element to this opening and how it sets up the relation between the two thinkers. Shortly after this opening, Lacoue-Labarthe states that: 'je crois obstinément, c'est-à-dire passionnément, à l'élucidation. Je ne me l'explique pas, mais je m'entends dire, constamment, il faut la clarté. Ce qui ne doit — ni ne peut — s'entendre simplement' (IM 230; ['I believe obstinately, which is to say passionately, in elucidation. I cannot explain it, but I constantly catch myself saying that there must be clarity. This must not — and can not — be taken simplistically']). Now, this is a concern often raised by readers of Derrida: that his performative, circumlocutionary style gets in the way of clear exposition. Most rejections of his work by Anglo-Saxon philosophy draw on such a position for their justification: it is therefore surprising to find these words in a text by Lacoue-Labarthe, a thinker notionally close to Derrida. But this is no accidental lapsus, for a few lines above, the same text reads as follows:

> ce à quoi [la question de la destination] touche [...] peut-être est-ce à la part idiosyncratique ou idiomatique de ce que tu écris, à un certain climat, à une aura étrange, à un style ou à un *ton*; peut-être aussi [...] est-ce à des sortes de choix, profonds, sourds, à des goûts, un habitus ou un éthos qui te sont, mettons, 'propres', mais dont on perçoit que tu ne les maîtrises ni ne les calcules vraiment, qu'ils s'entraînent d'eux-mêmes en t'entraînant (IM 229–30, emphasis original).

> [what [the question of destination] touches on [...] is perhaps the idiosyncratic or idiomatic element in what you write, a certain atmosphere, a strange aura, a style or a *tone*; it is perhaps also [...] certain kinds of deep, vague choices, tastes, a habitus or an ethos which are — let us say — 'proper' to you, but which perceptibly you cannot control or really calculate, and which are carried off by their own logic and carry you off with them (emphasis original)].

This is no small accusation: that Derrida is not fully in charge of his own writing. And what is more, the terms 'idiosyncratic' and 'idiomatic' are carefully chosen owing to their joint root of Greek *idios* (private, own, peculiar). Whilst Lacoue-Labarthe does not extend his range of words from this root — i.e. by calling Derrida's writing 'idiotic' —, doubtless to avoid a full-scale rupture, he is moving in that direction, the allegation being that the writing style in question is impenetrable to anyone except its author and deficient in its employment of philosophical generalities. In his response during the debates following Lacoue-Labarthe's paper (which are reproduced in the volume of conference proceedings), Derrida picks up the *idios* root and states 'je n'ai rien à dire sur ce que tu as appelé mon idiome' (FH 441; ['I have nothing to say about what you called my idiom']). This response can be read as non-committal, but it is perhaps better to see it as a playful, ironic — even sarcastic? — way of playing along with the suggestion that he had placed himself outside the general language of debate.

As already seen, Lacoue-Labarthe's text centres itself on issues of destination: 'la *destination* sera ma question' (IM 230, emphasis original; ['*destination* will be my question', emphasis original]). In doing so, it establishes its reading of Derrida in Heideggerian terms, but also in those of the latter's thinking of *l'écriture* — this emerges particularly in Lacoue-Labarthe's responses to questions posed in the discussion following the paper. For instance, when answering on the dynamics of the ontological difference between beings and Being and how that difference relates to *Dasein*, he states the following: 'Toute la difficulté tient à ceci qu'il faut un *Da* au *Sein*. C'est donc la question du privilège accordé, pour la thèse de l'être, à tel ou tel étant. Avec le danger toujours possible d'un arrêt, ou d'une fixation sur un étant déterminé' (FH 439; ['The difficulty stems entirely from the fact that a *Da* is required by *Sein*. This is therefore the question of the privilege given, by the thesis of Being [*l'être*], to such and such a being [*étant*]. With the ever-present danger of a stop, a fixation on a determinate being [*étant*]']). Here the situation described is one where the thought of Being as radically withdrawn from the (horizontal) field or plane of beings is not maintained, and instead a privilege is accorded to a particular being (namely Dasein or mankind). This giving of privilege is presented as a 'stop' or a 'fixation': by extension, the model of movement, fluidity, and deferral that emerges is a workable definition of *l'écriture*. Similarly, Lacoue-Labarthe's response to the question of whether he sees the word 'mankind' as having any positive referent is the following (the transcription of the debate is in the third person):

> Il ne s'approprie pas vraiment ce terme mais il l'utilise de manière à le faire communiquer avec tout ce qui ressortit au motif de la thèse, de la position, de l'installation — *Setzung, Stellung, Gestell*, etc. —, c'est-à-dire avec ce qui attire nécessairement l'être dans l'étant. Le danger, comme il l'a déjà souligné, est celui d'un possible arrêt sur tel ou tel privilège ontique (FH 440).

> [He does not really make the term his own, but in using it brings it into relation with everything which refers back to the motif of theses, positions, and installations — *Setzung, Stellung, Gestell*, etc. —, which is to say with what necessarily draws Being [*l'être*] into being [*l'étant*]. The danger, as he has already underlined, is that of potentially stopping at a particular, given ontic privilege].

Here again we are confronted with the privileging of a being (*Seiend* or *étant*) over Being (*Sein* or *Être*); this is the movement whereby Being is drawn in or attracted into the horizontal plane, i.e. that of being(s). Such a gesture of privileging is discussed in terms of 'mankind' being set up or installed as a figure, or alternatively we could say set down, posed or posited ('theses, positions, and installations'). And once again, a working definition of *l'écriture* emerges by extension from such terms: that which remains in movement, not set down, not a 'thesis' but an ongoing reflection. On this view, *l'écriture* is incompatible with the privileging of mankind, or to couch the same process in different terms, with a process of fiction or fictioning where one notion is, as it were, erected into a privileged position.

But this is not to say that Lacoue-Labarthe is setting up a simple opposition where Derridean *écriture* can be championed at the expense of Heidegger's thinking, from which it would be entirely separate. For his text, with its *tutoiement* of Derrida, suggests that: 'on pourrait tresser entre "Heidegger" et "toi" (entre les deux textes, et malgré les deux langues, au moins, et les deux styles) les liens les plus serrés,' (IM 252; ['the closest links could be drawn between "Heidegger" and "you" (between the two texts, and despite the two — at least — languages, and the two styles']) and then that 'Je le dis — je m'adresse à toi — parce que je ne vois pas ce que la pensée de l'écriture pense d'autre que l'être' (IM 253; ['I say this — I address you — because I do not see what the thought of *l'écriture* thinks other than Being']). This is a strong and counter-intuitive statement; in order to make sense of it, let us recall some characteristics of *l'écriture*: first, it cannot be limited to the canon of 'literature', as the latter is simply the reverse side of philosophy. Second, it cannot be neatly contrasted with speech, as it is always already at work in all manifestations of language. In other words *l'écriture*, rather than being any particular, identifiable discourse, would be that which escapes definition in dualistic terms. Here we are faced with a principle of movement or *différance*, that which is always moving elsewhere, bearing the trace of the past but remaining open to that which is to come, to 'ce qui arrive' ['what is happening or arriving'], to cite one of Derrida's definitions of deconstruction.[32] In this sense, it performs a similar role to Being when Heidegger thinks it in his more radical moments: that which can never be identified with any given being, on pain of altering fundamentally. Being, like *l'écriture*, is always moving elsewhere, and whilst it might be present in any given place or moment, it is always already elsewhere too.

The culmination of Lacoue-Labarthe's article relies on precisely this parallel between Being and *l'écriture*. He seeks to make sense of Derrida's attempts to move beyond humanism and the privileging of mankind as that being who has privileged access to Being thanks to its philosophy. We can there read: 'À la fin des "Fins de l'homme" [...] tu en appelais [...] à un "oubli actif" de l'être. [...] Mais d'où, aussi bien, est-il possible de dé-limiter l'humanisme, au-delà des délimitations hégéliennes et husserliennes, si ce n'est de la question de l'être?' (IM 253; ['At the end of the "Ends of Man" [...] you called [...] for an "active forgetting" of Being. [...] But at the same time, from where is it possible to de-limit humanism, beyond the Hegelian and Husserlian delimitations, if not from the vantage-point of the question of Being?']). This is to say that Lacoue-Labarthe cautions against setting aside altogether Heidegger's notion of Being, because its characteristics of radical otherness may be useful in resisting the privileged fictions created around mankind and philosophy. It is in this light that the article finishes with a question foreshadowing *La Fiction du politique* (where, as we have seen, Lacoue-Labarthe criticizes Heidegger's submission to 'philosophy'). Discussing Heidegger's 'fault', therefore, the article reads as follows:

> Mais peut-on échapper à une telle faute? Tout au moins à la forme générale d'une telle faute? Suffit-il — comme nous essayons tous, plus ou moins lucidement, de le faire — de changer perpétuellement de terrain? Suffit-il d'une sorte d'installation erratique dans l'étant? Suffit-il, dans nos discours, de substituer à l'infini les privilèges ontiques, d'affoler toute assignation et toute destination? Et si oui — et cela s'appelle 'écrire' —, *au nom de quoi?* Au nom de quoi le *faut-il*, si ce n'est quand même, ainsi que Heidegger l'aura presque toujours soutenu, en obéissant à cet appel sans appel, à cette injonction sans voix à la démesure de laquelle nulle réponse n'est en mesure de correspondre, mais à laquelle pourtant *il faut bien* mesurer notre impossible 'responsabilité' ? (IM 254–55, emphases original)

> [Can one avoid such a fault? Can one avoid at the very least the general form of such a fault? Is it enough — as we all, more or less lucidly, attempt to do — perpetually to change terrain? Is a sort of erratic installation in being [*l'étant*] enough? Is it enough, in our discourses, to infinitely find substitutes for ontic privileges, to throw into panic all assignations and all destinations? And if yes — and that is called 'writing' —, *in the name of what?* In the name of what is this *necessary*, if not — despite everything — as Heidegger almost always maintained, by obeying this call without call, this injunction without voice whose measurelessness is beyond any answer's ability to correspond, but against which it is nonetheless *necessary* to measure our impossible 'responsibility'?]

Once more, we have a definition of *l'écriture*, of that which 'is called "writing"', and it is the following: 'to perpetually change terrain [...] a sort of erratic installation in being [*l'étant*] [...] to infinitely find substitutes for ontic privileges, to throw into panic all assignations and all destinations'. Interestingly, there is a degree of scepticism expressed here, rejoining Lacoue-Labarthe's opening barbs to Derrida regarding his writing style ('there must be clarity'), but now placing the full weight of his argument behind them. It is suggested that even the errant heterogeneity famously explored by the digressions and circumlocutions of Derrida's text can be traced back to an underlying idea or motif, that of *l'écriture*. In other words, Lacoue-Labarthe questions the ability of even such a radical notion as *l'écriture* to break down the notion of 'destination'. It simply destines us to a different mode of writing. In this sense, even in setting himself at a distance from Derrida, Lacoue-Labarthe can be said to be thoroughly deconstructive: *even* the new mode of thinking is viewed with a rigorous scepticism, in the light of the practices of destination which it might continue or extend. This much is seen when Lacoue-Labarthe continues the passage quoted above: 'D'où pourrait-on refuser — dire non à la question: *au nom de...*? D'où pourrait-on — d'où pourrions-*nous* éviter de dire: *au nom de...*? Obstinément. En latin: *destinate*' (IM 255, emphases original; ['From where could one refuse — say no to the question: *in the name of...*? From where could one — from where could *we* avoid saying: *in the name of...*? Obstinately. In Latin: *destinate*', emphases original]). No straightforward answer is forthcoming to the questions asked in this passage, as the text ends with these words. However, they are revealing for several reasons: first, the presence of 'obstinately' recalls the challenge to Derrida with which the paper opened: 'je crois obstinément [...] à l'élucidation' (IM 230; ['I believe obstinately [...] in elucidation']). This is to say that he feels a responsibility not simply to accept at face value the non-referentiality of *l'écriture*: might it not bear metaphysical traits, beneath the surface? Second, the Latin plural past participle '*destinate*' can be translated as determined, destined, even destinated. The suggestion is that this is what we are, i.e. that our identity is given from an external source. Lacoue-Labarthe's recurrent thought of mimesis is surely resurfacing here: to think or to write is not to begin with a blank page, but to struggle with (and against) previous models and influences.

The attractiveness of *l'écriture* stems from its promise to free us of this mode of destination. And it is this issue that Lacoue-Labarthe addresses in proximity to Derrida via the text 'Au nom de...', having already, as we have seen, explored the notions of figures or models via the examples of Plato/Socrates and Nietzsche/Zarathustra. Nonetheless, at this stage in his thinking Lacoue-Labarthe demonstrates resistance to the notion of errancy that *l'écriture* represents, precisely insofar as the latter can take the form of a concept (albeit a radical one involving non-hierarchical horizontality). This resistance is what motivates his opposition to Derrida on the topic of clarity — although the latter should not be taken as straightforwardly philosophical: chapter 2 has already shown the distance Lacoue-Labarthe takes in the 1980s from that discourse. This was due in no small part to the investigations which had seen him take the spirit of *l'écriture* beyond the confines of what it was capable of as a concept. In other words, it was due to his investigations into untimely forms of writing in which mimesis could be given greater licence. We now turn to part II, in which these untimely meditations are explored, initially in the form of Lacoue-Labarthe's activities concerning the stage.

Notes to Chapter 3

1. In 'Hommage', p. 75. For an account of these early interactions as well as later ones, see Lacoue-Labarthe and Nancy, 'Derrida à Strasbourg' in *Penser à Strasbourg* ([*Thinking in/about Strasbourg*]; Paris/Strasbourg: Galilée/Ville de Strasbourg, 2004), pp. 11–20.
2. In Benoît Peeters, *Derrida* (Paris: Flammarion, 2010), p. 311. Their text was seen by the psychoanalytic figure as an exploratory mission, preceding Derrida's own text on Lacan (which was still conspicuous by its absence). 'Le Facteur de la vérité' ['The Deliverer of Truth/The Factor of Truth'] appeared two years later, in *Poétique*, 21, (1975), an issue co-edited by Lacoue-Labarthe and Nancy.
3. In 'Le Lieu dit: Strasbourg', in *Penser à Strasbourg*, pp. 31–59 (p. 47).
4. The authors discuss the text in a collective interview in *La Quinzaine littéraire*, 231 (15–30 April 1977), 19–22. Here (p. 21) Kofman declares that the project grew out of a reading of Derrida's text on Mallarmé's 'Mimique' ['Imitation'], in 'La Double séance' ['The Double Session'], which is collected in *La Dissémination* (*Dissemination*; Paris: Seuil, 1972), pp. 215–347.
5. Derrida would later return to the Hamletian notion of being 'out of joint'; see *Spectres de Marx: l'État de la dette, le travail du deuil et la nouvelle Internationale* ([*Spectres of Marx: the State of the Debt, the Work of Mourning, and the New International*]; Paris: Galilée, 1993), p. 19.
6. See also numerous other Cerisy conferences where the thinkers interacted, not least 'Nietzsche, aujourd'hui' (['Nietzsche, Today']; 1972) and 'Autour du travail de Jacques Derrida' ['Around the Work of Jacques Derrida'; 1997], which became *L'Animal autobiographique* ([*The Autobiographical Animal*]; Paris: Galilée, 1999). Derrida also relates *La Carte postale: de Socrate à Freud et au-delà* ([*The Post Card: from Socrates to Freud and Beyond*; Paris: Flammarion, 1980) to the Strasbourg thinkers, writing that it was as if 'les "Envois" de *La Carte postale* avaient toujours Strasbourg pour origine, destin ou destination', in 'Le Lieu dit: Strasbourg', pp. 52–53 ['[it was as if] the "Envois" [Sendings] in *The Post Card* always had Strasbourg as their origin, destiny or destination'].
7. In 'Le Lieu dit: Strasbourg', p. 45.
8. In 'Le Lieu dit: Strasbourg', p. 40. Nancy describes this trio as follows: 'il y a là quelque chose, une certaine typologie entre nous trois. Une typologie dans laquelle Philippe, tu serais du côté du *tragique*, Jacques de l'*indécidable*, et moi... je ne sais pas, peut-être du côté de l'*anastasis*', in Derrida, Lacoue-Labarthe, Nancy, 'Dialogue', in *Rue Descartes*, 52 (May 2006), 86–99 (p. 88, emphases original); 'I think there is something here, a certain typology, between the three of us. A typology in which you, Philippe, would be on the side of the *tragic*, Jacques on the side of the *undecidable*, and I... I don't know, maybe on the side of *anastasis*', in 'Discussion', trans. by Pascale-Anne Brault and Michael Naas in *For Strasbourg* (New York: Fordham University Press, 2014), pp. 17–30 (p. 19, emphases original).
9. See the recent publication *For Strasbourg*.
10. Derrida also tells us that 'le lieu dit' is an intentional misquotation of Creon in Lacoue-Labarthe's version of *Antigone*, who states that: 'C'est le lieu qui me dicte ce que je dois mettre en ordre' ['[i]t is this place that is dictating to me what I must set in order'], in 'Ex abrupto' in *Avant-guerre*, 2 (1st quarter 1981), 70. This statement refers to Creon's belief that in punishing Antigone he is acting in accordance with the spirit of the *polis*.
11. In 'Le Lieu dit: Strasbourg', p. 33.
12. In Janicaud, *Heidegger en France*, vol. II: *Entretiens*, p. 201.
13. In 'Le Lieu dit: Strasbourg', p. 34 (emphasis original).
14. In Lacoue-Labarthe and Steiner, 'Correspondance ouverte' ['Open Correspondence'], in *Journal de l'amicale de philosophie (Strasbourg)*, 3 (January 1989), 6–19 (pp. 6, 11). This analogy is rejected by Lacoue-Labarthe in the same correspondence with Steiner; we can thus imagine that he might have also had difficulties with Derrida's 'synagogue' comparison.
15. In 'Le Lieu dit: Strasbourg', p. 39.
16. In 'Désistance', pp. 602–03.
17. Blanchot provides a third point of triangulation between the two thinkers — see especially Lacoue-Labarthe's 'Fidélités' ['Fidelities'], in *Agonie terminée agonie interminable*, pp. 63–90,

written for the Cerisy conference 'Autour du travail de Jacques Derrida'. Derrida was close to Blanchot especially in the late 1960s, before going on to give numerous seminars on the writer in the 1970s. See *Parages* ([*Environs*]; 1986, 2003) and *Demeure* ([whose title is impossible to translate fully]; Paris: Galilée, 1998). I explore Lacoue-Labarthe's relation to Blanchot in chapter 5.

18. In 'La Fiction du biographique', p. 195. See the discussion of this exclusion in Matthew Potolsky, *Mimesis* (Abingdon: Routledge, 2006), pp. 15–31.

19. In *Derrida* (1991; Paris: Seuil, 2008), p. 51; in *Jacques Derrida*, trans. by Bennington (London: University of Chicago Press, 1993), pp. 49–50. This text plays with the relationship between *maître* and pupil, original thinker and scribe, as is described in the 'contract' between Bennington and Derrida with which it opens.

20. In the archive of Philippe Lacoue-Labarthe, IMEC, Abbaye d'Ardenne, Normandy. LAC 11.7 *Roman, opéra, Nietzsche* [*Novel, Opera, Nietzsche*]; 4. 'Nietzsche, histoire et mimesis' ['Nietzsche, History, and Mimesis'], p. 1.

21. 'La Fable' is collected in *Le Sujet de la philosophie*, pp. 7–30, as is 'La Dissimulation' from *Nietzsche, aujourd'hui*, although it is renamed as 'Nietzsche apocryphe' (['Apocryphal Nietzsche']; pp. 75–110), and various other articles on the philosopher. See also *Rhétorique et langage* (1975; Chatou: Transparence, 2008), and the translation of Nietzsche, *La Naissance de la tragédie* ([*Birth of Tragedy*]; 1977; Paris: Gallimard, folio/essais, 1992).

22. Ian James discusses this text in *The Fragmentary Demand*, pp. 20–26.

23. In 'Postface', a text written on his deathbed having already been pronounced medically dead, Lacoue-Labarthe returns to this issue. He discusses the poetic condition, stating that it 'n'est pas de traverser les apparences (il n'y a pas, précisément, d'apparences)' ['is not to go through appearances (precisely, there are no appearances)'], in *Préface à 'La Disparition'*, p. 46. In other words, there can be no appearances because there is no essential truth against which to define them; everything is at once *both* truth and appearance.

24. This change brings the article into closer proximity with Derrida's discussion of the crypt in 'Fors', his preface to Nicholas Abraham and Maria Torok, *Le Verbier de l'homme aux loups* ([*The Wolf Man's Magic Word: a Cryptonomy*]; Paris: Aubier-Flammarion, 1976), pp. 7–73, which had been published in the meantime.

25. In 'Précis', p. 148.

26. In 'Présentation', in *Poétique*, 5 (1971), 99–103 (p. 100).

27. In *Nietzsche, aujourd'hui*, vol. 2: *Passion* (Paris: U.G.E., 1973), pp. 9–36 (p. 45).

28. Derrida's paper is collected in *Marges de la philosophie* (Paris: Minuit, 1972), pp. 129–64.

29. In *Marges de la philosophie*, p. 131; *Margins of Philosophy*, trans. by Alan Bass (Brighton: Harvester, 1982), p. 111.

30. In *Les Mots et les choses: une Archéologie du savoir* (Paris: Gallimard, Tel, 1966), p. 398; *The Order of Things: an Archeology of the Human Sciences* (London: Routledge, 2002), p. 422. See Sartre, *L'Existentialisme est un humanisme* (Paris: Gallimard, 1945) and Blanchot, *Le Dernier homme* (Paris: Gallimard, 1957).

31. This translation was first proposed by Henri Corbin in 1938, before being adopted by Sartre in *L'Être et le néant: Essai d'ontologie phénoménologique* ([*Being and Nothingness: an Essay on Phenomenological Ontology*]; Paris: Gallimard, 1943).

32. In 'The Time is out of joint', in Anselm Haverkamp (ed.), *Deconstruction is/in America. A New Sense of the Political* (New York, New York U. P., 1995), p. 17, trans. mod.

PART II

Untimely Meditations

CHAPTER 4A

The Stage (Introduction)

Unlike in other major currents of modern French thought — from symbolism to absurdism — the theatre is often absent from narratives of deconstruction. Indeed, beyond Derrida's writing on Artaud in *L'Écriture et la différence*, few deconstructive reflections on the theatre come to mind: it therefore seems possible to present the period post-1960 as one in which theatre features as an untimely demand.[1] However, when it does feature, it punctuates, interrupts, or gives rhythm to the major timely or contemporary concerns of French thought post-1960; this is precisely what we find with the sustained attention paid to the theatre by Lacoue-Labarthe.

This was by no means an inevitable turn for his thinking to take, as is seen in a short autobiographical text, 'Bye bye farewell', which is striking in its depiction of his early dislike of the theatre. Its third-person narrative opens bluntly with '[i]l n'aimait pas le théâtre', (AN 191; ['He did not like theatre']) and proceeds to discuss productions of Racine which he found pompous in both gesture and diction. For him, these productions were grandiloquent and ridiculous, little more than 'de la gesticulation verbale — assez adéquate, du reste, à la gesticulation tout court qu'on pouvait voir sur le plateau' (AN 192; ['mere verbal gesticulation — which, what is more, matched the gesticulation pure and simple which could be seen on stage']). But whilst this is a clear rejection of traditional theatre practice, it does not automatically imply acceptance of alternatives to that tradition: in deconstructive terms, it is not enough to invert a hierarchy without also displacing it. This is shown by Lacoue-Labarthe's negative reaction — again recounted in the third person — to a production by experimental group The Living Theatre:

> (65? 66?): l'*Antigone* de Brecht par le Living: agitation incessante, vociférations, tout est hurlé — le comble du 'free', si l'on veut, au sens du free jazz. Et tout s'annule (vacarme au silence pareil). C'est de nouveau l'ennui, et une sourde colère. Il quitte la salle avant la fin — geste qu'il répétera désormais souvent (AN 194).

> [(65? 66?): Brecht's *Antigone* by the Living Theatre: endless agitation, clamourings, everything was shouted — the nadir of free style, if you will, in the sense of free jazz. And everything cancelled everything else out (a din equal to silence). Boredom once again, and a subdued anger. He left the auditorium before the end — a gesture that he would repeat often.]

In other words, it was not enough to replace the stiff formality of a traditional production of Racine with its opposite: one full of sound and fury, as it were, and signifying nothing. This is an important signal that Lacoue-Labarthe's approach to the stage — including his work on *Antigone*, productions of which by the Living Theatre (1960s) and by Brecht (1948) he held in widely differing esteem — will feel it necessary to detach itself from the new as well as from the old.[2]

As has often been observed regarding twentieth-century theatre, the possibilities for the stage were profoundly affected by the dominance of cinema. Lacoue-Labarthe's reaction to this was to accept that the former could not — and in fact did not need to — compete with cinema in terms of providing a spectacle. Indeed, setting aside 'le spectaculaire' represented an excellent opportunity:

> Le théâtre, contrairement à ce que dit le mot, ne lui [à Lacoue-Labarthe] paraissait pas essentiellement un art du voir (il partageait sur ce point la méfiance d'Aristote vis-à-vis de l'*opsis*) et il s'indignait de lire un peu partout confondus spectacle et représentation. Plus exactement: il soupçonnait, non sans obstination, que la représentation — la vérité de la présence — est très antérieure à l'installation d'un dispositif optique. La scène n'est pas forcément destinée à montrer. (AN 195)

> [Theatre, contrary to what the word tells us, did not seem to him [Lacoue-Labarthe] to be essentially an art of vision (on this point he shared Aristotle's distrust of *opsis*) and he objected to always finding spectacle and representation conflated. More precisely: he suspected, not without stubbornness, that representation — the truth of presence — by far precedes the installation of an optical framework. The stage does not necessarily have demonstration as its destiny.]

Here we see that Lacoue-Labarthe's initial aversion to certain types of theatre leads him to search for a form of expression not reliant on spectacle (*opsis* in Greek). It was clear in his mind that a different approach was required, whether we call this spectacular 'art of vision' *theatre* in the etymological sense relating to *theorein* (meaning to see or to behold), or a 'theoretical' theatre where clarity and oversight are thematized. Indeed, he explicitly distances himself from the mode of theatre that would be what he calls a 'mode *théorique* de la présentation' ['*theoretical* mode of presentation'].[3] Any such new approach needed to do more than simply provide an alternative theoretical or philosophical reading, for to do so would be merely to replace 'theatre' with 'theory' and thus to remain within the horizon of the gaze.

To say that Lacoue-Labarthe's investigations are principally concerned with 'theatre' is therefore to make assumptions that he strove to avoid. In this light, it is more fitting simply to present his interest and activities as concerning the 'stage'. The minimal quality of this description is better suited to his reflections on fundamental tensions between physical presence and speech; and indeed it features as the title of a text in which he discusses these questions with Nancy, named 'Scène: un échange de lettres'.[4] The respective personas emerging from this debate are that Nancy is more willing to identify himself as a philosopher, albeit one dedicated to thinking the relations of philosophical discourse to literature and the political, and of Lacoue-Labarthe as more hesitant and troubled, having abandoned his early dedication to literature and unable to define himself exclusively in terms of either literary, philosophical, or political thought. This division of labour would appear to be borne out in their approaches to the stage; Nancy is happier to accept that the *retrait* or withdrawing from myth, figuration, or fiction is at the same time a *re/trait* or re-drawing. As he writes to Lacoue-Labarthe in this public exchange,

> notre divergence sur l'*opsis* se rejoue ici: tu tends toujours, pour le dire très vite, vers un effacement de la 'figure' [...], tandis que je me sens toujours reconduit à l'exigence d'une certaine figuration, parce que l''interruption' du mythe m'a paru ne pas être une simple cessation, mais un mouvement de coupe qui, en coupant, trace un autre lieu d'énonciation.[5]

> [our divergence over *opsis* is back in play here: you always tend, to put it very simply, towards an effacement of 'figure' [...], whilst I always feel myself being drawn back towards the demand for some kind of figuration, because I have never seen the 'interruption' of myth as a simple ceasing, but as a cutting movement which, in cutting, traces out another site of enunciation.]

In other words, for Nancy there will always be some element of *opsis*, a spectacle that we see. If this is the case, then we would not expect Lacoue-Labarthe's aversion to spectacle and 'theatre' to manifest itself in an interest for the stage. However, this latter notion will provide a significant new iteration of the relationship between the two thinkers, and particularly of Lacoue-Labarthe's position or role. As Nancy states, 'le paradoxe veut que c'est toi qui as tenu à pratiquer de la "mise en scène", tandis que pour ma part je suis en général assez peu réceptif au spectacle du théâtre' ['paradox has it that you were the one who insisted on practising "*mise en scène*", whilst for my part I have generally little interest in theatrical shows'].[6] Lacoue-Labarthe's involvement in the theatre is therefore being presented by Nancy as paradoxical: it contradicts what the latter thought he had known about his writing partner, i.e. that he was opposed to representations, figures or fictions.[7] For Lacoue-Labarthe's part, our cue is to be found when later in the dialogue he states that 'je ne suis pas du tout persuadé que la scène produise inévitablement de la figure' ['I am not at all convinced that the stage inevitably produces figuration'].[8] This is to say that the stage need not enter into the category of figure or fiction, if we can learn to approach the stage as a space in which sheer appearance or emergence, as it were, can be explored; a minimal or irreducible human presence, the space or spacing in which we are exposed to one another, prior to constructed fictions of identity.

Lacoue-Labarthe's work in this area, then, moves away from the sight-based implications of 'theatre' and instead investigates the minimal, irreducible tensions suggested by the alternative term of stage or *scène*.[9] The work in question is wide-ranging and multifarious, consisting both in critical thought and in concrete stage productions, with each reflecting and refracting the other. These various elements are at play within each of the various strands of his interest in the stage — from various short, fragmentary scripts to his translation of and seminars on Nietzsche's *Birth of Tragedy*, or from his collaboration on the translation and staging of Euripides's *Phoenician Woman* (1982) to the scripting and staging of a play on Heidegger, *Sit Venia Verbo* (1988).[10] But there are above all two major ways in which his interest in theatre is pursued, which can be placed under the headings of tragedy (discussed in chapter 4b) and opera (see the companion chapter, 4c). The investigations into tragedy lead to critical discussion as well as to his French translations of Hölderlin's

German translations of Sophocles: *Antigone* and *Oedipus Rex*; Lacoue-Labarthe also collaborated on the *mise-en-scène* of each play.[11] It is notable that in the avant-propos to *L'Imitation des modernes*, Lacoue-Labarthe states that this experience of working on *Antigone* in the late 1970s caused his thinking as a whole to change direction fundamentally: 'mon travail s'est infléchi' (IM 9; ['my work shifted']). But this theory of a turning-point is called into question when we look at the second major area of his thinking of the stage, namely opera. For many of his earliest texts, from a decade or more before the proposed turning-point, address the operatic stage. And as I explore in chapter 4c, these investigations carry on in parallel to the work on tragedy, and culminate in the full-length work *Musica ficta (figures de Wagner)* (1991).

In historicizing terms, the two theses — that of a turning point, and the grad-ualist position — can be reconciled by stating that whilst the project on tragedy (Hölderlin/Sophocles) provided the best-known expression of Lacoue-Labarthe's thinking of the stage, the work on opera shows it did not do so in a void or starting from nothing. And in the area of Lacoue-Labarthe's contribution to thought, too, there is a common motif driving these two projects. For in each, as he moves from dominant narratives of the stage towards a more radical understanding of it, he seeks out alternative possibilities — or rather, sees the stage as functioning outside the totalizing domain of theatre and theory, of comprehension and possibility. Instead, with the stage we are plunged into mimesis: first because there is no direct speech (*diegesis*), only 'la dissimulation — la dissimilation' (SP 105) of characters and masks. But mimesis is also at issue in the sense of how, instead of constructing theories or fictions, we might attempt to relate or respond to what, or whatever, we are always already faced with.

Notes to Chapter 4a

1. Derrida, 'Le Théâtre de la cruauté et la clôture de la représentation' ['The Theatre of Cruelty and the Closure of Representation'], in *L'Écriture et la différence* (Paris: Seuil, 1967), pp. 341–68.
2. 'Bye bye farewell' details how his initial aversion to theatre was gradually softened by various productions: Japanese Nô theatre, Brecht's *Mother Courage* by the Berliner Ensemble, Giorgio Strehler's version of Goldoni's *Servant of two Masters*, Robert Wilson's *Einstein on the Beach*. Its title refers to the end of Jean-Pierre Vincent's tenure at the Théâtre National de Strasbourg. Lacoue-Labarthe had worked on *Antigone* at the theatre in 1978 (as we shall see), and wrote that 'la "vie" de Strasbourg c'était tout simplement le T.N.S.' (AN 124; ['the "life" of Strasbourg was quite simply the T.N.S.']). Cf. André Gunthert, *Le Voyage du T.N.S.: 1975–1983* (*The Voyage of the T.N.S.: 1975–1983*; Paris: Solin, 1983).
3. *Musica ficta*, p. 102 (emphasis original); *Musica Ficta*, p. 46 (emphasis original).
4. The text has recently been republished alongside the continuation of the exchange: see *Scène suivi de Dialogue sur le dialogue*. The second text reads Platonic dialogues as pieces of theatre by insisting on the presence of named interlocutors; the exchange refers back explicitly to Nancy's work on Plato's dialogues, *Le Partage des voix* (*The Sharing/Division of Voices*; Paris: Galilée, 1982). Since Lacoue-Labarthe's death Nancy has continued these reflections with 'Corps, théâtre', in *Passions du corps dans les dramaturgies contemporaines*, ed. by Alexandra Poulain [*Passions of the Body in Contemporary Dramaturgy*]; Paris: Septentrion, 2011).
5. In *Scène* suivi de *Dialogue sur le dialogue*, p. 13.
6. Ibid., p. 12.
7. On this aspect of Lacoue-Labarthe's thinking, Nancy wrote to me that: 'il y a là un léger

conflit ou bien une oscillation: d'une part, refus de la figure, d'autre part affirmation d'une représentation originaire. Le dépassement du conflit se trouve dans la pensée de l'apparition: d'une figure à l'état naissant, se figurant, non figurée... Cette apparition est l'"être" même ou bien le "théâtre originaire"' (correspondence of 27 November 2011; ['here there is a slight conflict or rather an oscillation: on one hand, the refusal of figure, on the other the affirmation of an originary representation. The conflict is overcome in the thought of appearing: of a nascent figure, figuring itself, rather than being figured... This appearing is "Being" itself or "originary theatre"'].

8. In *Scène* suivi de *Dialogue sur le dialogue*, p. 51.

9. Of course, *scène* can also be translated as 'scene', an episode within a narrative. As I explore in chapter 5, the psychoanalytic notion of *la scène primitive* has resonance for Lacoue-Labarthe — on one occasion, wordplay leads Nancy to describe the originary Greek theatre they are discussing as 'la scène primitive', i.e. the early stage; in *Scène* suivi de *Dialogue sur le dialogue*, p. 37.

10. Euripides, trans. by Lacoue-Labarthe and Claire Nancy, *Les Phéniciennes* ([*Phœnician Women*]; Paris: Belin, 2007); Lacoue-Labarthe and Michel Deutsch, *Sit venia verbo* (Paris: Bourgois, 1988).

11. *Antigone de Sophocle* (1978; Paris: Bourgois, 1998), henceforth abbreviated to AdS; *Œdipe le tyran de Sophocle* (Paris: Bourgois, 1998).

The Stage (Tragedy)

At first sight, one could be forgiven for seeing German poet and thinker Friedrich Hölderlin as marginal to French thought post-1960, especially if one had read the attack by Philippe Sollers of *Tel Quel* on a particular reading of Mao Tse-Tung's poems which, according to Sollers, imposed on the dictator's literary creations an 'écran bourgeois' ['bourgeois veneer'] by drawing on 'le Dit poétique hölderlinien' ['the Hölderlinian poetic Said'].[1] But if anything, Lacoue-Labarthe's decision to write on the poet risks being overdetermined — primarily by Heidegger's approach, which *La Fiction du politique* makes a point of criticizing as party to Heidegger's conception of the political, informing but also outlasting his biographical adherence to Nazism.[2] Indeed, this overdetermination of Hölderlin's work means that in his introduction to an edition of *Hymnes, élégies et poèmes* [*Hymns, Elegies, and Poems*], Lacoue-Labarthe is able barely to mention a single poem or line of poetry, instead devoting his discussion to philosophical readings of the poet.[3] But whether it is due to these overdetermining factors or in spite of them, Hölderlin occupies a special place in Lacoue-Labarthe's mind. More than Wagner and Heidegger, for whom his early admiration soured as his thinking progressed, and probably more than Nietzsche, this German poet and thinker is afforded a special status.

This is the case even to the point of Lacoue-Labarthe identifying with Hölderlin, and particularly with the so-called madness that dominated the final decades of the latter's life, which found an echo in Lacoue-Labarthe's alcoholism.[4] In this way, Lacoue-Labarthe can be said to mythologize Hölderlin. For instance, the cover blurb for his two French translations of the latter's German translations of Sophocles's *Antigone* and *Œdipus Rex* begins as follows: 'Ses traductions de Sophocle sont la dernière œuvre de Hölderlin. Lorsqu'il les fait paraître en 1804, assorties des "Remarques", Schelling, atterré, écrit à Hegel qu'elles "trahissent son délabrement mental"; et au comité de lecture du Théâtre de Weimar (Goethe, Schiller, Voss), on s'esclaffe' ['His translations of Sophocles were Hölderlin's final work. When he published them in 1804, accompanied by the "Remarks", Schelling, who was floored, wrote to Hegel that they "betrayed his mental degradation"; and in the reading committee of the Weimar Thatre (Goethe, Schiller, Voss), there were hoots of derision'].[5] It is noteworthy that Lacoue-Labarthe thus places in the most prominent position possible the myth of Hölderlin as a poet of madness or *poète maudit*, despite his perhaps more searching statement elsewhere that such an approach represents a myth and a 'malentendu' ['misunderstanding'].[6]

In terms of their relationship on the page, Lacoue-Labarthe takes as his main object an unusual area of Hölderlin's work, the translations of Sophocles, a subject (except the chorus on mankind from *Antigone*) given relatively little attention by Heidegger.[7] The two German translations were in turn translated into French by Lacoue-Labarthe (in 1977 and 1998); additionally, each was produced for the stage twice. *Antigone* was staged in different industrial ruins in Strasbourg in 1978 and 1979, and *Œdipus* first in the prestigious surroundings of the Avignon festival in 1998, then reprised in the same production in Sceaux in 1999 and in a different one in Évreux in 2005. We will look in turn at Lacoue-Labarthe's practice as a translator and as a dramaturg, before moving to his critical discussions of the two plays which he looks at in terms of their 'antagonisms'.

Translations

The interactions between ancient and modern, foreign and non-foreign must rely at some stage on translation. For Hölderlin dealing with Sophocles's Greek texts, this was more than a preliminary issue to be dealt with before moving on to the main discussion: translation was not merely a contingent practice, but something more conceptual. As such it is named by Lacoue-Labarthe 'métaphrasis', a Greek term originally meaning translation, but which also describes the actions of paraphrase, the actions of 'réfléchir ensuite, délibérer, examiner après mûre réflection' ['reflecting in due course, deliberating, examining after ripe reflection'].[8] In short, translation informs Hölderlin's account of the Greeks as having learnt sobriety as a response to their natural enthusiasm (and his complementary view of the moderns needing to do the opposite). This is to say that by translating from Greek Hölderlin was exploring the terms of these various antagonisms or non-resolvable dialectics between ancient and modern, enthusiasm and sobriety, absence (Dionysos) and presence or representation (Apollo). It is notable that he did so during or shortly following his stay in Bordeaux in 1802, when he wrote that 'the athleticism of people in the south, in the ruins of the ancient spirit, made me better acquainted with the true essence of the Greeks'.[9] It is perhaps not suprising that the radically non-standard, esoteric renderings of the Greek produced during this period prompted Schelling to express concern about Hölderlin's state of mind in a letter to Hegel, just as it prompted Goethe and Schiller's laughter; he was prounced clinically insane on his return to Germany.

On this topic, Lacoue-Labarthe writes that:

> Hölderlin, traduisant, ne visait pas à restituer l'explicite du texte (ce que dit le texte) mais son implicite, à savoir ce qui s'y était quand même dit mais sans que cela se fût jamais, mettons, proféré. D'où une grande violence vis-à-vis du texte, mais par laquelle surgit après-coup un sens originaire inouï (AN 157).

> [Hölderlin, translating, was not aiming to recreate what was explicit in the text (what the text said), but what was implicit in it, i.e. what it had said but without it ever being, shall we say, given voice. From here stems a great violence with regard to the text, but through which there appears, after the fact, an unheard-of originary meaning.]

This is to say that Hölderlin's translations of Sophocles are far from rigorous in any academic sense, instead demonstrating a freedom that comes from the collapse in his critical distance from the texts: he felt that his advanced understanding granted him licence. Numerous expositions of his choices and practice as a translator exist, and there is no need to redouble them here.[10] Suffice it to say that whilst the translations can be described as free, this quality is not accompanied by its usual correlate, namely naturalization, i.e. where the move away from the source text leads to more idiomatic phrasing in the target language. On the contrary, whilst Hölderlin's versions diverge from what we might expect of a translation, they do so in a different direction. This is to say that they are not faithful to either source or target language, but to the thinker's own conceptualizations of Greek tragedy. Lacoue-Labarthe flags up numerous examples of such divergences in Hölderlin's translations, of which we can mention just two: discussing the famous chorus in *Antigone* on mankind's ingenuity and ability to create and innovate, he writes that in the second of two translations that Hölderlin made of it, 'les écarts (nombreux) vont dans le sens d'une accentuation du "pessimisme" de ce chœur' (AdS 187; ['the (numerous) departures tend to accentuate the "pessimism" of this chorus']). Thus the chorus is altered from a celebration of mankind's technological ingenuity to a condemnation of it. And as for *Oedipus Rex*, Lacoue-Labarthe underlines that in the Greek text Tiresias tells Oedipus '*you* are the curse, the corruption of the land!', whereas in Hölderlin's version, he tells him that 'you speak with that tone which is a spot upon our land', thus suggesting that his despotism stems from a choice, a *tone* that is adopted, rather than being an unavoidable part of his personality or fate.[11] Oedipus's status as a modern, rational figure — explored further below — who is able to choose how he speaks rather than doing so instinctively or automatically is thus enhanced by Hölderlin's alteration of this point.

Translating in his turn the German versions of Sophocles into French, Lacoue-Labarthe invites us to ask whether translation requires foreignness to be naturalized, or alternatively represents an *épreuve de l'étranger* (to reiterate the title of Antoine Berman's study of translation).[12] These two alternatives can be understood further by looking at the comments and choices Lacoue-Labarthe makes as a translator of Hölderlin. For instance, he invites us to rule out the naturalizing approach, which would seek to appropriate the strangeness of the source text and render it culturally accessible by the use of idiomatic expressions, or by making the characters sound as if they were modern Frenchmen. For example, comparing his translation of Hölderlin's *Remarks* — the short, cryptic texts with which the poet accompanied each translation — to François Fédier's 1965 version, Lacoue-Labarthe states that he attempted to adopt 'un parti pris de plus stricte littéralité' (AdS 180; ['a policy of stricter literalness']).[13] This approach to translation represents a desire not to naturalize the source text, i.e. not to modernize or sanitize it: this is an implicit critique of speculative or dialectical philosophy with its appropriation of the other in terms of the same. Interestingly, however, Nancy has described the translations from German he and Lacoue-Labarthe carried out together in a way nuancing — even contradicting — the latter's avowed desire for literalness. Nancy has stated that he was the one who would unpack the more difficult German expressions, whereas

Lacoue-Labarthe 'faisait le saut dans la langue d'arrivée, trouvait une phrase à laquelle je n'aurais jamais pensé' ['would make the leap into the target language, came up with expressions I would never have thought of'].[14] This statement suggests that Lacoue-Labarthe's literalist approach should be seen as an *intention*, but not one always fulfilled in his *practice* as a translator (whether with Nancy, or separately). In order to explore further how — and whether — this desire on Lacoue-Labarthe's part is played out in practice, we must look at various moments of the main text of *Antigone de Sophocle* (which is more fruitful on this point than *Œdipe le tyran de Sophocle*).[15]

We can begin with line 21 which in Hölderlin's version reads '[w]as ist's, du scheinst ein rothes Wort zu färben?', and in Lacoue-Labarthe's, '[q]u'y a-t-il? Tu sembles broyer un pourpre destin' ['[w]hat is it? You seem to dye your words with red'].[16] This is an important element regarding the reception of Hölderlin's efforts, given that the German version reportedly made Schiller laugh out loud at its absurdity. Whether in spite of or due to this reception, Lacoue-Labarthe remains literal, pointing out in a note that he whilst wished to chime with the French idioms 'broyer du noir, un noir destin' he did not go so far as to include them in the text (AdS 183). Secondly, the famous opening word of Hölderlin's *Antigone* is provided by the neologism 'Gemeinsamschwesterliches!' which, in Steiner's words, 'constitutes a visual, auditive, semantic wielding of all the connotations of sorority, shared destiny, blood-relation, forced "oneness" which are set out serially and discretely in the Greek'.[17] Lacoue-Labarthe translates this term as '[s]œur de même souche' ('sister from the same root-stock'); in this case, he is being both less literal and less adventurous than Hölderlin. These qualities of his translation are confirmed by his note explaining that the German neologism is virtually untranslatable, and that a literal rendering of it would be: 'chose sororale commune' (AdS 183; ['communal sisterly thing']). This is an important admission: despite his hostility to naturalization and the privilege he therefore intends to give to literality, there is a line beyond which Lacoue-Labarthe as a translator is not prepared to go. Lastly, he makes several interesting choices chiming with the insistence in Hölderlin's translation on the notion of Creon's infidelity to justice (from Antigone's viewpoint at least). Now, this point demonstrates a salient point in Hölderlin's version — reproduced here, followed by Constantine's translation into English and Lacoue-Labarthe's into French:

> CREON: Wenn meinem Uranfang' ich treu beisehe, lüg' ich?
> HÆMON: Das bist du nicht, hälst du nicht heilig Gottes Nahmen. (AdS 90)

> CREON: If I stand by my first beginning am I lying ?
> HAEMON: You are not doing that not holding God's name holy.[18]

> CRÉON: A rester fidèle à mon origine, suis-je faux ?
> HÉMON: Fidèle, tu ne l'es pas. Tu ne tiens pas sacré le nom de Dieu. (AdS 91)

The French translation of *Antigone* here is significant because it diverges from the German, interpreting the situation in terms of fidelity or infidelity (Lacoue-Labarthe also adds a mention of infidelity in line 682). What is more, this divergence follows, as it were, the spirit of Hölderlin's own divergence from the Greek, when elsewhere he added a cognate of 'infidelity' — 'treulos' — to his translation of the Greek original (line 784).[19] This is to say that Lacoue-Labarthe is not only translating Hölderlin, but translating what he sees as the spirit of his text: this no longer entirely the literal translation we were promised. Instead, Lacoue-Labarthe is drawing on the concept of infidelity between gods and men as it is named by Hölderlin in the *Remarks* on *Oedipus* as an 'all-forgetting form of an infidelity'.[20] This non-literal act of translation is therefore not wholly misplaced given the many links that we have seen Hölderlin making between two of Sophocles's three Theban plays. But it nonetheless suggests that Lacoue-Labarthe's practice as a translator, although at times literal in the way he suggests, is at other times directly informed by his critical reading of Hölderlin. Translation, rather than being a simply contingent practice, is always already reflection, deliberation, or *métaphrasis*, the term used by Lacoue-Labarthe for the title of a text on the question of translating Hölderlin.

Dramaturgy

The tensions and negotiations between principle and practice in Lacoue-Labarthe's work can also be seen in his staging of the two plays emerging from his translations of Hölderlin's version of Sophocles. This activity gives rise to a number of articles — 'Traduction et histoire' (1999) follows the *Œdipus* production, as do 'Métaphrasis' and 'Le Théâtre de Hölderlin' — and indeed he writes that '[ils] sont en réalité distraits d'un travail "dramaturgique", au sens allemand du terme' ['in truth they are drawn from a single "dramaturgical" project, in the German sense of the term'].[21] Let us therefore look at this dramaturgical project, together with the suggestion that the split between practical and critical approaches is not contingent or due to some hesitation on Lacoue-Labarthe's part, but instead due to a thoroughgoing 'contradiction matricielle' (AdS 181; ['contradiction which serves as [a] matrix'] in his understanding of the stage. In positioning himself in relation to this, Lacoue-Labarthe attempts to maintain the state of contradiction or tension, unlike Hegel and Schelling (on the one hand) who resolved that tension, and like Hölderlin (on the other) who did not.

Antigone was twice staged by Lacoue-Labarthe and Michel Deutsch, first in 1978 and then also the following year, with the first production taking place in the abandoned Arsenal buildings in Strasbourg (which were demolished soon afterwards). A dossier on the two productions tells us that the space for the first was vertical, the actors speaking from several levels of the ruined warehouse. The 1979 production was based in a different abandoned building, the old forges of Strasbourg, and this time the space used was horizontal. This second 'stage' backed directly on to a canal, across which Tiresias's crucial entry onto the stage was made by boat. The productions present several further notable features: for instance, an actor played Hölderlin as a lost presence, wandering in the margins of the play's actions. Secondly, Nancy was one of the actors, playing one of the chorus of Theban elders (thus prefiguring the acting he has done more recently, for instance in the 2011 film *Les Chants de Mandrin*).[22] The dossier published on the productions contains Nancy's reflections, as well as those of spectators Roger Laporte and Derrida (who in doing so was returning to *Antigone*, having discussed the play in

Glas, 1974).[23] Interestingly given Lacoue-Labarthe's desire to move beyond the 'theoretical' spectacle and towards a minimal staging, Derrida states: 'Dire que je fus témoin [de la production] serait encore parler d'un spectacle or ce fut tout autre chose' ['To say I witnessed [the production] would still be to speak of a show [*spectacle*], whereas it was something entirely other'].[24] And this line of thinking is furthered by Derrida's comments on the relationship between the Arsenal buildings and the productions staged there: 'L'entrepôt parce qu'il était éventré ne gardait plus rien. Plus la moindre mise, ce n'était plus qu'une grande structure vide inapte à s'entremettre, entreposer ou imposer quoi que ce fût [...]. Dans cet état le mot lui-même vidé, comme l'entrepôt donnant lieu, me parut prédestiné à ce qui survint alors au défi de toute destination' ['The depot, because it had been gutted, no longer contained anything. Nothing was arranged in any way, it was no longer anything but a large empty structure unable to intervene, interpose, or impose itself in any way [...]. In this state were words themselves, also emptied, like the depot which was acting as a space; these words seemed to me to be predestined to what appears in such situations, above and beyond all destination'].[25] Derrida thus suggests that Lacoue-Labarthe was successful in his project of a stage-practice that would not allow the contradictions within it to rest within any ultimate resolution or fixed configuration. In other words, this would be a practice of movement, but one without ultimate goal or 'destination' (his latter use of this term of course recalls its prominence in 'Au nom de...', Lacoue-Labarthe's text addressing Derrida at *Les Fins de l'homme* in 1980, the year after Derrida had seen *Antigone* but the year before his text on it was published; see chapter 3).

There could hardly have been a greater difference in the setting for Lacoue-Labarthe's next production of his translation of a Hölderlin adaptation of Sophocles, the 1998 production of *Œdipe le tyran de Sophocle*, which opened the Avignon theatre festival in the *cour d'honneur* at the *Palais des papes*. (The production was reprised in Sceaux the following year, and Lacoue-Labarthe's translation was used for a different production in Évreux in 2005). Nonetheless, the production evinced similar minimalist qualities to those demonstrated by the two versions of *Antigone*; these similarities persist despite the apparent rupture between Lacoue-Labarthe and Jean-Louis Martinelli, the director (and then head of the Théâtre national de Strasbourg). This much can be seen thanks to Alain Dreyfus's review of the production for *Libération* which described the set as follows: '[u]ne voie étroite de béton gris traverse de part en part la démesure de la Cour d'honneur avec, en contrebas, la marge d'un terre-plein pour le choeur. Pas ou peu d'artifices: au fond, deux tours couleur de sang séché figurent le palais de Thèbes. Une rampe en diagonale pour les entrées et sorties' ['[a] narrow walkway of grey concrete crossed from one side to the other of the vastness of the *Cour d'honneur* with, as a base note, a margin of beaten earth for the chorus. There was nothing or little that was artificial: at the back, two towers the colour of dried blood represented the palace of Thebes. Also there was a diagonal ramp for entrances and exits'].[26] The journalist's position hardens as he closes the review, discussing the production in terms of 'ses options austères, voire rigides et figées, ou plus prosaïquement son manque d'imagination' ['its austere choices, which can even be called rigid and frozen, or more prosaically, its lack of imagination']. Such is the reaction produced by the desire, expressed repeatedly in Lacoue-Labarthe's thinking on the stage, to do away with the spectacle and return to a more essential appreciation of how text and stage interact; his aims were not seen to have transferred successfully to a concrete realization. We can also note that this production of a tragedy commented on its own status by featuring, in the reviewer's words, '[à] un bout de la scène, [...] la dépouille d'un bouc sacrifié. En vain. Les destins sont déjà noués' ['[at] one end of the stage [...] the carcass of a goat which had been sacrified. In vain. The fates had already been decided']. This element of meta-theatrical stage-setting is surely a reference to the theory that tragic theatre emerged out of ritual practices, and retains a trace of this emergence in its name (*tragos* being Greek for goat). Beyond these elements, Lacoue-Labarthe writes of the staging and his translation of Hölderlin as indissociable practices:

> L'*agôn* qui oppose Œdipe à Tirésias [...] n'est pas très long; ni, au fond, très complexe: Tirésias, malgré les soupçons et les insultes d'Œdipe, dit, sans le moindre détour ni la moindre formule 'énigmatique', *toute* la vérité (lorsqu'il quitte la scène, pour le spectateur du moins, il n'y a plus rien à apprendre). Œdipe, lui, refuse obstinément d'entendre. A mesure que l'*agôn* se déploie, le ton, comme il est de mise, ne cesse de monter. Elle-même, la traduction de Hölderlin, est abrupte, violente, comme écrite 'à l'arraché'. Le français n'est pas capable d'une telle brutalité, la mélodie racinienne l'emporte toujours. J'avais fait de mon mieux pour la casser.[27]

> [The *agôn* which sets Oedipus in opposition to Tiresias [...] does not last very long; neither, ultimately, is it very complex: Tiresias, despite Oedipus's suspicions and insults, says, without any indirectness or the slightest 'enigmatic' formulation, the *whole* truth (when he leaves the stage, for the spectator at least, there is nothing else to learn). As for Oedipus, he stubbornly refuses to hear. As is customary, as the *agôn* unfolds the tone continues to rise. Hölderlin's translation, for its part, is abrupt, violent, as if written 'against the odds'. French is not capable of such brutality, Racinian melodiousness always wins out. I did my best to smash it.]

Here as above we can see at work an aspiration to reproduce the abruptness of Hölderlin's German: a literal translation operating on the limits of the 'melodic' French language, would therefore be required. Beyond this, it is notable that Lacoue-Labarthe underlines the minimal qualities of the play: 'The *agôn* which sets Œdipus in opposition to Tiresias [...] does not last very long; neither, ultimately, is it very complex.' This reading serves to justify the minimalist characteristics of the play's staging which *Libération* would criticize. The idea of the stage being illustrated here is a stripped-down one, enabling attention to be concentrated on the underlying conflicts between physical presence and text, and perhaps even between the physical and the metaphysical.

In terms of what Lacoue-Labarthe's critical writing can tell us about his approach to dramaturgy, we can recall his dissatisfaction with the physical and verbal 'gesticulation' of traditional renderings of Racine, but also with the anarchic efforts of the Living Theatre. Beyond this, the following extract from an autobiographical text is revealing regarding Lacoue-Labarthe's relation to the stage; it begins by addressing his relationship with Michel Deutsch, director of the *Théâtre national de*

Strasbourg from 1975–83 and his collaborator on *Sit venia verbo* and *Les Phéniciennes*:

> Je pourrais dire qu'il m'a initié au théâtre. Ce n'est pas vrai: le théâtre est
> un art trop brutal, trop impitoyable. Il ne souffre aucune 'approche', il est
> immédiatement l'épreuve de la vérité, c'est-à-dire de la probité. [...] [T]raduire
> Hölderlin — et avec lui Sophocle —, le donner à prononcer, imaginer l'espace
> et les gestes, convoquer les objets, penser à ce qu'il faut donner à penser, ne pas
> céder à la beauté ni — surtout — à l'émotion, être juste, obligent à un courage
> dont même l'enseignement ne donne pas l'idée suffisante.[28]

> [I could say that he initiated me in the theatre. But it isn't true: theatre is
> too brutal, too pitiless an art. It allows of no 'approach', it is an immediate
> reckoning [*épreuve*] with truth, which is to say with probity. [...] [T]o translate
> Hölderlin — and Sophocles at the same time —, to offer him to enunciation,
> to imagine the space and the gestures, to provide the props, to think about
> what one must cause to be thought, not to give in to beauty nor — above all
> — to emotion, to be just, all of these require a courage about which not even
> teaching gives us an adequate idea.]

Despite the initial comment here that the theatre 'allows of no "approach"', we can
discern some characteristics of Lacoue-Labarthe's relation to it. For instance, on the
one hand the desire to resist aesthetic beauty reminds us that his interest lies not
solely in the empirical stage, but in how that stage can speak to us of a wider 'stage',
i.e. of exposition and appearance as categories through which we think. On the
other hand, the attempt to resist emotion or pathos seems to be directly taken from
Hölderlin's doctrine of sobriety, which is a recurrent motif in Lacoue-Labarthe's
work. Furthermore, this is not an aspect needing to be imposed on the German
translations from the outside, given that:

> La mise en scène d'*Antigone*, tout d'abord, l'épreuve du 'plateau' et de la
> diction du texte, le travail avec les comédiens, bref la sanction du jeu (elle est
> impitoyable), m'ont d'un coup révélé que Hölderlin savait ce qu'est le théâtre:
> sa 'traduction' n'est en rien un poème déclamatoire, ses *Remarques* sont d'une
> extrême précision dramaturgique.[29]

> [The *mise en scène* of Antigone, first of all, the experience of the 'boards' and of
> the text's diction, the work with the actors, in short what acting pitilessly makes
> necessary, suddenly revealed to me that Hölderlin knew what theatre was: his
> 'translation' is not at all a declamatory poem, his *Remarks* are extremely precise
> dramaturgically.]

This comment can serve as a signal that Lacoue-Labarthe's readings of Hölderlin's
Remarks could be informative as we reconstruct his dramaturgical practice. For
instance, given the emphasis Hölderlin places on the latter part of the play being
determined by the earlier part (*Antigone*), or vice-versa (*Oedipus Rex*), with Tiresias's
interventions providing the 'caesura' or hinge in each case, we can imagine how
the Tiresias scenes could be recreated with enhanced levels of lighting, acoustics,
or with other effects.

In Lacoue-Labarthe's mind, there is therefore a strong case that Hölderlin's texts
can and do work on the stage. But at the same time, he finds that they articulate
conceptual concerns in a way suggesting that the concrete, physical stage is not their
only horizon. An example of this second argument can be found when Lacoue-

Labarthe mentions how the German version of *Antigone* merges the Sophoclean roles of the guard, messenger, and servant into a single messenger. He writes:

> Le geste n'est pas de simple économie. Il en dit long tout d'abord sur la rigueur avec laquelle Hölderlin conçoit le partage, dans la tragédie, entre le dramatique proprement dit et le narratif (la scène et son 'dehors') [...]. Du moment où il confie à une voix unique la charge de rapporter ce qui ne peut être représenté, tout se passe en effet comme si Hölderlin voulait *aussi* contraindre la représentation à exhiber sa contradiction matricielle, c'est-à-dire ce qui explique que la ressource de la tragédie [...] ne soit rien d'autre que sa difficulté même (la tragédie ne s'affranchit jamais du récit et ne cesse de s'efforcer, douloureusement, vers une 'théâtralité' qu'elle ne peut accomplir). (AdS 181, emphasis original)

> [The gesture is not simply intended to save space. It says a lot about how rigorously Hölderlin conceives of the sharing or division [*partage*] within tragedy, between the dramatic in the proper sense and the narrative (the stage and its 'outside') [...]. Given that he confers upon a single voice the task of relating that which cannot be represented, it is as if Hölderlin also wanted to force representation to reveal the contradiction which serves as its matrix, a contradiction which explains why tragedy is resourceful [...], precisely because it is nothing other than its very difficulty (tragedy never liberates itself from narrative and constantly attempts to move, painfully, towards a 'theatricality' which it cannot complete.]

In other words, whilst tragedy might provide the platform for a reflection on the general category of *la scène*, constituting 'the dramatic in the proper sense', the fact that it must retain an element of 'narrative' proves to be a limiting factor. By unifying the three minor roles into a single character, Hölderlin pushes against this limit, seeking to avoid the physical comings-and-goings that might distract us from the 'contradiction which serves as [a] matrix' inherent in representation. In other words, the more minimalist a production is, the more we can appreciate its essence, the conflict between bare physicality and the metaphysical elements that inflect it. An unsympathetic reading of Lacoue-Labarthe's position here may see him as having a metaphysical or essentialist distaste for the concrete experience of the stage (this was the standpoint of Dreyfus on reviewing *Oedipus Rex* at Avignon). But in fact, for Lacoue-Labarthe there is no ultimate essence to the stage, only a 'contradiction which serves as its matrix': paradoxical though it may seem, it is in the nature of the stage to always be in contradiction with — or exposed to — what lies beyond the actors' physical presence.

Antagonisms

Lacoue-Labarthe's critical thinking of the stage in terms of an antagonism, i.e. a tension between divergent elements, sees it as a space 'où viennent "s'agonir" et "agoniser" des figures' ['where figures come to "agonate" each other and to "agonise"'], not least in his essay entitled 'L'Antagonisme' ['Antagonism'].[30] His thinking here is inscribed in relation to two main bodies of work: the first being speculative approaches to tragedy, which seek to resolve the tensions inherent in its divided format; the second is Hölderlin's thinking. Looking first at the speculative approach, its relevance begins to emerge in Lacoue-Labarthe's statement that 'la tragédie est le lieu où se révèle ce qui fait l'essence du savoir, et ce qui anime le désir du savoir: l'affrontement à la contradiction. En général' (IM 210; ['tragedy is the site where what makes the essence of knowledge is revealed, as well as what drives the desire for knowledge: confronting contradiction. In general terms']). The culmination of the tradition in which this takes place is seen in Hegel (writing on *Antigone*) and Schelling (writing on *Oedipus*).[31] This is the tradition that famously caused George Steiner to open his *Antigones* with the statement that '[b]etween c. 1790 and c. 1905' [at which point *Oedipus Rex* took precedence], it was widely held by European poets, philosophers, scholars that Sophocles's *Antigone* was not only the finest of Greek tragedies, but a work of art nearer to perfection than any other produced by the human spirit'.[32] To establish the existence of such a tradition is to argue that these thinkers' readings were not isolated, but instead represent the core of modern thinking when they use tragedy to privilege unity over fragmentation, and to convert negatives into positives.

For instance, Hegel's reading of *Antigone* is often taken to privilege Creon's claims for the rule of law over Antigone's special pleading (which would be to privilege the argument for leaving her brother Polyneices's body unburied as a warning to those who would defy the State, rather than the view that he should receive a humane burial whatever his actions in life had been). However, certain prominent critics have argued that this is too approximative a reading of Hegel, and does not do justice to the complexity of his dialectic. This second line of thinking led Steiner, for instance, to present the conflict between Antigone and Creon as a conflict between a divine law and a human law. And for his part Peter Szondi — whom Lacoue-Labarthe read on this topic — argues that '[i]n *Antigone*, Hegel sees the collision of these two manifestations of the ethical and, ultimately, the collision of the absolute spirit with itself in the process of returning to itself.'[33] This more nuanced reading advanced by Steiner and Szondi suggests that a dialectical reading of the interaction between Antigone and Creon must not peremptorily dismiss the claims of either. For his part (and again in a reading acknowledge by Lacoue-Labarthe), Schelling's reading of Oedipus advances an unexpected reading of the latter's fall and punishment:

> It has often been asked how Greek reason could bear the contradictions of Greek tragedy. [...] The fact that the criminal, who only succumbed to the superior power of fate, was *punished* all the same — this was the recognition of human freedom, an *honor* owed to freedom. [...] It was a *great* thought: to willingly endure punishment even for an *unavoidable* crime, so as to prove one's freedom precisely through the loss of this freedom and perish with a declaration of free will.[34]

Schelling's reading here re-locates its idea of 'Greek reason' in spite of prevailing contradictions, taking them to be merely apparent, a superficial distraction from the underlying positivity. In other words, Oedipus's suffering is not suffering pure and simple, but *tragic* suffering, unfairly imposed upon him by destiny. Although he gains no empirical freedom, his right to a *de jure* freedom is thereby established — it is almost as if the worse his punishment, the more just becomes his claim to deserve something better. Schelling's reading can thus be seen as a process of working one thing into the other, a conversion of positivity into negativity.[35]

The second body of work of interest to Lacoue-Labarthe in his reaction to modern approaches to the stage is that of Hölderlin. This thinker's work is of particular interest given his associated yet marginal relationship with the speculative thought just mentioned. For instance, in the introduction to Hölderlin's *Hymnes, élégies et autres poèmes*, Lacoue-Labarthe writes of the work in question as representing 'une pensée fulgurante, aussi forte que celle de Schelling ou de Hegel (auxquels il ouvre jusqu'à un certain point la voie), mais qui reste simplement ébauchée, lacunaire, qui ne se convertit pas en système ni même ne parvient à s'exposer' ['an overwhelming thought, as strong as that of Schelling or Hegel (towards whom he clears a path, up to a point), but which remains a simple sketch, incomplete, which is not converted into any system and does not even manage to demonstrate itself'].[36] And indeed, in looking at the work in question we can identify notable points of similarity with certain key characteristics of speculative or dialectical philosophy. For instance, in the 'Remarks on *Antigone*' Hölderlin says of poetry — by which he means both art in general, and tragedy in particular — that it 'treats the various faculties of a human being, so that the representation of these different faculties makes a whole, and the connection between the more independent parts of the different faculties can be called the rhythm, taken in a higher sense, or the calculable law'.[37] In this way Hölderlin sets up tragedy as an articulated or hybrid totality — and raises the possibility of there being two ways of placing the emphasis regarding tragedy. The first unifies the disparate elements that constitute it (thus aligning itself with speculative thought); the second underlines the hybrid, divided aspect (thus opening onto something more radical). In this light, Lacoue-Labarthe's questions concerning Hölderlin's pivotal position are the following: 'comment la démarque du spéculatif, dans Hölderlin, est-elle *aussi bien* sa marque (ou sa remarque)? Comment, autrement dit, le spéculatif se (dé)constitue-t-il — je veux dire, se défait et se déconstruit dans le mouvement même par lequel il s'édifie, s'installe et fait système?' (IM 43, emphasis original; ['how is it that the marking-down [*démarque*] of the speculative, is also its marking (or its remarking)? How is it, in other words, that the speculative (de)constitutes itself — I mean, dismantles itself, deconstructs itself in the same movement by which it erects itself, installs itself and constitutes a system?', TYP 212, trans. mod.]). In other words, Lacoue-Labarthe is asking whether Hölderlin can occupy a classically deconstructive position at the limit of a particular system, exploring that limit rather than simply passing to a new, alternative language. In order to explore this tracing or retracing of the limit — or its marking, remarking, or *démarque* (meaning marking-down, as in a retail sale) — let us look in more detail at this position at the limit of speculative thought, i.e. at the point where it opens beyond the enclosure represented by an ultimately self-same Subject. This can be done via two particular antagonisms that Lacoue-Labarthe sees as driving Hölderlin's thinking of the stage.

Antagonism 1: Two Greeces

The contradictions that speculative thought locates in Greek tragedy begin to form a pattern when they are aligned with Nietzsche's dualism of Apollo and Dionysos (even if the latter is a dualism where one of the two poles, Dionysos, is radically withdrawn, preventing any dialectical opposition being established).[38] And Lacoue-Labarthe also sees a similar pattern in Hölderlin's approach to the Greek stage. Indeed, this is an issue in which he had not only a critical and dramaturgical interest, but a biographical one. For Hölderlin's thinking of the Greeks as divided between two tendencies is informed by his voyage to Bordeaux: on return from his journey there in 1802, he felt he had seen 'the ruins of the ancient spirit'.[39] For his part, Lacoue-Labarthe — who was already reading Hölderlin — moved to Bordeaux in 1958, completing his *classe préparatoire* there. This coincidence led him to research Hölderlin's stay in the city and his translation from Greek of Sophocles and Pindar which the poet carried out during it.[40] This research grew into a film project entitled *Hölderlin à Bordeaux* — which although it did not appear as such, did feed into his translation of Hölderlin's 'Andenken' ['Remembrance'], a poem on the city which lends its name to a short 2002 film.[41]

In the thinking of the Greeks he carried out there, Hölderlin saw one pole of the contradiction that structured the Greek mind as the propensity for enthusiasm. He uses the term *Begeisterung*, which is translated literally by both 'enthusiasm' — from Greek *theos* — and 'inspiration' — from Latin *spiritus*. (It is notable in terms of his translating style that Lacoue-Labarthe rejects both of these wholly plausible options in preference of the even more literal 'possession par l'esprit'; AdS 169; ['possession by the spirit']). In any case, for Hölderlin this natural tendency of the Greeks causes them to act under the power of what Lacoue-Labarthe ventriloquizes as an 'élément oriental, "sauvage"' (AN 145; ['oriental, "wild" element']). The second pole consists in their propensity for art and representation. In Lacoue-Labarthe's words, this comes down to 'l'élément culturel ou artistique [...], ce que Hölderlin nomme la "sobriété" (tout le contraire, par conséquent, de l'ivresse dionysiaque)' (AN 146; ['the artistic or cultural element [...], what Hölderlin names "sobriety" (the exact opposite, therefore, of Dionysian drunkenness']).[42] An antagonistic relationship is therefore set up along these lines, and Hölderlin's argument is that it is because the enthusiastic element came naturally to the Greeks that they were forced to respond to it with its opposite, i.e. sobriety, clarity, and representation. For the moderns, things are the other way around: sobriety and careful exposition are what come naturally, meaning that they must learn what is foreign to them, namely enthusiasm.[43]

In parallel to this Hölderlinian approach, Lacoue-Labarthe also draws on a separate approach to this narrative of a modern tendency towards representation emerging out of an archaic, obscure enthusiasm. This other approach sees this as the issue of art's relationship to religion, according to the thesis that art emerged from the latter, in the process liberating itself from moral or theological purpose. Berthold Brecht is the thinker who makes this argument; he was a major influence on Michel Deutsch's group — including Lacoue-Labarthe — at the *Théâtre national de Strasbourg.* (This influence stems in part from his 1948 version of Hölderlin's *Antigone*; Lacoue-Labarthe also mentions Heiner Müller's 1969 staging of the poet's *Oedipus Rex* as a model). In any case, on various occasions the French thinker quotes Brecht on the relationship between art and religion, most extensively as follows:

> Brecht dit quelque chose du genre: quand on a dit que le théâtre est issu des cérémonies du culte, tout ce qu'on dit c'est qu'il en est sorti. [...] J'admire beaucoup Brecht, mais cette déclaration n'est rien de plus qu'une liquidation péremptoire de la question. Car le grand problème de l'art moderne, ce n'est pas qu'il se soit emancipé de la religion, ni même qu'il n'ait plus été à la hauteur de la religion. C'est conjointement que religion et art n'ont plus été à leur propre hauteur, et toute la grandeur de l'art moderne — toute sa fragilité aussi, ou son désarroi — est de tenter de répondre à cette situation sans aucun précédent, c'est-à-dire de répondre à ce que Hölderlin appelait la fuite ou le retrait des dieux, le 'défaut de Dieu' (AN 158).

> [Brecht says something like: when people say that theatre stems from cultic ceremonies, all they are saying is that it emerged from them. [...] I admire Brecht a lot, but this statement is nothing more than a peremptory liquidation of the question. For the great problem with modern art is not that it has gained emancipation from religion, but rather that it has not remained at the high level of religion. It is that, jointly, religion and art have both failed to live up to their own high level, and all the grandeur of modern art — all its fragility too, or its disarray — lies in attempting to respond to this completely unprecedented situation, which is to say to respond to what Hölderlin called the flight or the withdrawal of the gods, the 'lack of God'].

Brecht's assertion of course refers to the theory that Greek tragedy emerged out of cultic rituals — of which the dance and song of the chorus still give us some idea, not to mention other factors including the possible derivation of 'tragedy' from Greek *tragos*, meaning goat (the animal that was the object of ritual slaughter). In doing so, Brecht at once recognizes this theory and seeks to limit its importance: even if religion or ritual is the origin of tragedy, the argument is that precisely because it is its *origin* rather than the current form, tragedy as we know it cannot be reduced to these religious or ritual elements. Indeed, precisely because this is an exit from religion, it can even serve to underline or perform the modern stage's freedom from such a role in society. Now, Brecht's assertion performs a dialectical *Aufhebung*: the primitivist theory is taken up, but only in order to be rejected in the name of a subsequent stage of development. Whilst Greece provides the model for ancient or archaic religious sacrifice, it also overcomes that model with another one, representing philosophy, democracy, and modernity: the theory of the 'two Greeces' is not far beneath the surface here. Lacoue-Labarthe takes issue with what he thus sees as the dialectical nature of Brecht's assertion, expressing himself in strong terms: 'this statement is nothing more than a peremptory liquidation of the question'. For the French thinker, although Brecht's intention may be laudable insofar as it seeks to avoid the naïve return to the primitive or cultic origins of tragedy later seen in the Living Theatre's version of *Antigone*, the playwright is too complacent regarding the success that tragedy may — or may not — have had in leaving religion behind. Whilst Lacoue-Labarthe subscribes to Brecht's atheist aims, therefore, he does not agree with his analysis of modern art in general and of tragedy's role within it as successfully embodying this atheism. On this view, much thinking remains to be done before we arrive at the possibility of such an exit from religion, which is to say at an approach to the stage that lives up to Hölderlin's notion of the flight of the gods.

Antagonism 2: Ancient and Modern

The conflict forming the first antagonism we have explored, which can be expressed as that between enthusiasm and sobriety, or between religion and art, is also seen by Lacoue-Labarthe to exist between the ancient and the modern. Specifically, this second antagonism or conflict informs the differing roles that Hölderlin assigns to Sophocles's *Antigone* and *Oedipus Rex*. Although the Greek versions of these plays are of course historically contemporaneous — and Oedipus is the central character of the first two Theban plays (*Oedipus Rex* and *Oedipus at Colonus*) whilst Antigone, his daughter, features in the third —, in Hölderlin's account *Antigone* is presented as the more archaic play, and *Oedipus Rex* the more modern. Glossing this account, Lacoue-Labarthe writes of 'les deux tragédies de Sophocle que [Hölderlin] estimait idéalement représentatives de l'opposition — constitutive de l'histoire — entre l'ancien et le moderne (ou, dans son lexique, entre l'oriental et l'hespérique): *Antigone* et *Œdipe le tyran*' (AN 143; ['the two Sophocles tragedies that [Hölderlin] thought ideally representative of the opposition — which constitutes history itself — between the ancient and the modern (or, in his terms, between the oriental and the hesperian): *Antigone* and *Oedipus Rex*']). This is to say that *Antigone*, *pace* Simon Goldhill who has ascribed its popularity in the modern age to its lack of gods amongst the characters (which is unusual for a Greek tragedy), ultimately addresses the divine, whilst *Oedipus* reacts to their withdrawal or absence.[44] Lacoue-Labarthe writes that Oedipus's fate is not only that of Hölderlin in his madness, but is 'le "destin moderne"' ['"modern fate"'], which is to say 'le nôtre également, peut-être' ['ours too, perhaps']. He continues, making explicit what he understands this fate to be: 'Au comble de la fureur qui l'emporte, Œdipe ne fait l'expérience que d'une chose: le retrait du divin. Le dieu ne se manifeste plus qu'en cessant soudain de se manifester. Ce qui veut dire: en laissant l'homme à l'abandon' ['At the nadir of the fury that carries him away, Oedipus experiences only one thing: the withdrawal of the divine. The god now only manifested itself in suddenly ceasing to manifest itself. All of which means: by leaving mankind in abandonment'].[45] Accordingly, whilst the figure of Antigone is ultimately of limited interest to Lacoue-Labarthe, we are all Oedipus. This is not because, as Freud argued, we seek symbolically to murder our father and marry our mother; but because underlying this destiny lies a sense of being mistreated and abandoned by the gods.[46]

The original Hölderlinian reading underpinning this antagonism between ancient and modern draws on the view that the Greeks' nature could be located in a propensity for enthusiasm (possession by a god or spirit), and that this is demon-strated by Antigone. In the play, she comes into conflict with Creon over the issue of her brother's corpse; in arguing for his right to burial irrespective of his actions in life, she is arguing that certain humane values and familial bonds are irreducible. And in doing so, in Hölderlin's version of the play she invokes the divine: first when in a confrontation with Creon, she speaks of '*mon* Zeus' (AdS 57, emphasis original; ['*my* Zeus', emphasis original]), and secondly when in descending to the tomb in order to commit suicide, she compares herself to the mythological figure Niobe ('la Phrygienne, née | dans le sein de Tantale', AdS 101; ['the Phrygian, born in the bosom of Tantalus']).[47] Divine authority, i.e. an alternative and superior law, is therefore invoked in the struggle against State power as represented by Creon. To this extent, the play exemplifies in Lacoue-Labarthe's account of Hölderlin 'le traitement proprement grec du tragique' ['the properly Greek treatment of the tragic'].[48] This leads Hölderlin to identify Antigone and Creon respectively as *Nationelles* and *Antinationelles*, or as Lacoue-Labarthe translates, 'nationel' and 'antinationel' (AdS 169; ['nationel' and 'antinationel']). In doing so the poet avoids using the more common German *national* (meaning: pertaining to a nation), and this choice is glossed by Lacoue-Labarthe as follows: ' "Nationel": ce terme, démarqué du lexique révolutionnaire français, est d'un usage courant à l'époque. Le nationel est ici pensé au sens du naturel ou du natal (voire du "naïf", dans la terminologie de Schiller); l'antinationel désigne en conséquence [...] la culture (*Bildung*)' (AdS 207–08; [' "Nationel": this term, distinguished from the French revolutionary vocabulary, is in wide use in this period. The nationel is thought of here in the sense of the natural or the native (even of the "naïve", in Schiller's terminology); the antinationel therefore refers to [...] culture (*Bildung*)']). This is to say that *nationel* relates to being native, meaning in this case sharing a relation to birth (*natio* in Latin), which is particularly suitable for Antigone given her privileging of her familial duties to her dead brother. Creon, for his part, makes an argument based on the *anti-nationel*, given that he represents a model of society conceived otherwise than via blood and kinship. It seems clear that Antigone represents the relatively ancient or archaic element within this play, whilst Creon stands for the relatively modern, rationalized one. And whilst followers of Hegel (if not necessarily the philosopher himself, as we saw above) have argued that the latter as the ruler of Thebes represents a defensible, ethical principle, Hölderlin's reading — shared by many other readers — is that despite her downfall Antigone is the dominant figure in the play.

   Antigone, then, presents a dialectic of ancient and modern but Hölderlin (and Lacoue-Labarthe in his wake) emphasizes the ancient within that dialectic; *Oedipus Rex* shows us the same dialectic but with the emphasis placed the other way around, i.e. on the modern element. Indeed, the French thinker underlined what he sees to be the significance of these figures in the mind of the German thinker who spent time in Bordeaux and Paris and wrote on the contemporary events of the French Revolution. As we can read of Hölderlin's depiction of the ruler of Thebes,

> S'il a fait ce choix [d'*Antigone* et d'*Œdipe le tyran*], il me semble que c'est, pour l'essentiel, en raison de préoccupations politiques modernes. Œdipe, en particulier, était un personnage qui refaisait surface dans l'histoire, sous la forme du dictateur de la raison. C'était la Révolution française, Robespierre, Saint-Just, puis ensuite Bonaparte.[49]

[If he made this choice [of *Antigone* and *Oedipus Rex*], it seems to me to be essentially due to modern political concerns. Oedipus, particularly, was a character who was resurfacing in history, in the form of the dictator of reason. He was the French Revolution, Robespierre, Saint-Just, and then Bonaparte.]

Nothing could be more modern than Oedipus's role here: the invocation of figures from the French revolutionary period serves to underline the absolute value placed on Reason, as well as underlining that the absolute nature of this valuing is excessive and — paradoxically — unreasonable. This will form a key plank of Lacoue-Labarthe's reading of the play, which we can see as deconstructive in its attention for the edges and limitations of the discourse of reason. But whilst these are the stakes of the reading at hand, we have not yet established the basis on which Oedipus is presented as an essentially modern figure. Therefore let us hear the full argument concerning Oedipus and modernity, before we see how Lacoue-Labarthe, drawing on Hölderlin, attempts to glimpse something beyond it (just as he did regarding modernist avant-gardes from Jena Romanticism to *Tel Quel*).

To view Oedipus as a modern figure does not affect the fact that he is not free, his destiny being foretold by a prophecy, nor that this prophecy is then confirmed by his downfall. But this view does suggest a role for the protagonist going beyond that which we might expect of one who is passively punished or abandoned by the gods: for not only does Oedipus himself kill his father and marry his mother, meaning that he is the author of his crimes, but it is his own desire to identify his father's murderer that leads to them being revealed, provoking the *dénouement* of the drama. In Hölderlin's words on Oedipus's central dialogue with Tiresias, 'knowledge, when it has broken through its limits, as if intoxicated in its own magnificent and harmonious form [...] provokes itself to know more than it can bear or grasp.'[50] Therefore at some level it is this desire to know which is at fault (this reading does risk conflating the crimes themselves with the characters' knowledge of them; although this might confirm — after Foucault — that crime is an abstract, societal notion rather than an absolute). In other words, above and beyond parricide and incest, the desire to know is a crime; as Lacoue-Labarthe writes when giving an overview of speculative readings of the play,

> Œdipe fut d'abord, selon une interprétation possible de son nom (*oida*, j'ai vu, je sais), la figure du Savoir, au sens spéculatif du terme. C'est-à-dire le héros de la métaphysique, que celle-ci soit critiquée ou éprouvée dans sa possibilité, réinstaurée ou renversée, dépassée (surmontée) ou délimitée. C'est évident dans l'idéalisme spéculatif, pour lequel d'ailleurs la tragédie offre le premier modèle de l'ontologie dialectique: l'Œdipe de Schelling est l'affirmation de la liberté dans sa négation même; celui de Hegel est la relève, dans et comme la conscience-de-soi, de l'énigme orientale enfermée dans la pierre (le Sphynx).[51]

> [Oedipus was first of all, according to a possible interpretation of his name (*oida*, I have seen, I know), the figure of Knowledge, in the speculative sense of the term. This is to say that he was the hero of metaphysics, whether it is criticized or experienced as a possibility, restored or reversed, passed by (overcome) or delimited. This much is obvious within speculative idealism, for which, what is more, tragedy offers the premier model of dialectical ontology: Schelling's Oedipus is the affirmation of liberty in its very negation; that of Hegel is the

sublimation [*relève*], in and as consciousness-in-itself, of the oriental enigma contained within the rock (the Sphynx)].

This reading glosses an alternative reading of Oedipus's name (it is more commonly taken to refer to his feet being swollen following their binding when he was left on the mountain as a child). It also refers to the content of the myth from which Sophocles's play is drawn, i.e. Oedipus gaining the right to become King of Thebes and husband of Jocasta by solving the riddle of the Sphinx. In this view, this riddle-solving is a philosophical act, the self-affirmation of modern reason over 'the oriental engima' and an important one insofar as the answer was 'mankind': this is an episode of speculative self-recognition.[52] The key point is that Oedipus represents 'the figure of Knowledge, the hero of metaphysics', his desire to know making him a representative of philosophy itself. This desire enables both his rise to power and his subsequent fall. What is more, the philosophy with which he is associated is defined as essentially modern insofar as, even though his crimes are violent, archaic, and fulfill a prophecy, he establishes some degree of proto-freedom in at least becoming conscious of them, seeing them for what they are.[53]

Lacoue-Labarthe introduces Hölderlin's contribution to this debate by insisting on the aspect of vision, which is underlined by an alternative reading of Oedipus's name as having its roots in the Greek for 'I have seen', *oida*. He writes:

> Conformément à l'interprétation spéculative du nom d'Œdipe, celui qui sait — de *oida*, j'ai vu, je sais —, mais à une certaine distance de l'héroïsation philosophique que la pensée spéculative n'a cessé de faire d'Œdipe, Hölderlin insiste, à la grecque, sur la vue: c'est l'aveugle devin Tirésias qui vient dire à Œdipe l'aveuglante vérité: l'excès même de ton savoir, ton outrance dans la volonté de la vérité, est le signe de ta soillure et ta perte. C'est là, cette fois, tout le destin du savoir occidental qui est en jeu, et c'est bien ce que Hölderlin — la pensée de la césure — a opposé, sans op-position, obscurément si je puis dire, à Schelling et à Hegel.[54]

> [In accordance with the speculative interpretation of Oedipus's name, he who knows — from *oida*, I have seen, I know — but at a certain distance from the philosophical hero-making that speculative thought always undertook regarding Oedipus, Hölderlin insists, in the Greek manner, on sight: it is the blind seer Tiresias who comes to tell Oedipus the blinding truth: that the very excess of your knowledge, your immoderate pursuit of the will to truth, demonstrates your besmirching and your downfall. Nothing other than the entire destiny of Western knowledge is at stake here, and this is full well what Hölderlin — the thought of caesura — brings into opposition, without op-position, obscurely if you will, to Schelling and to Hegel.]

In other words, Hölderlin provides a way of resisting the speculative reading of the play because of the importance he places on Tiresias's intervention, which aims to discourage Oedipus from identifying his father's murderer. Of course, Sophocles's play already violently punishes the protagonist's desire to 'see', with the episode of his self-blinding. But beyond this, the readings of sight and vision provided by Hegel and Schelling on the one hand, and Hölderlin on the other, form the framework for the importance the latter places on the intervention of the blind sage Tiresias. In his *Remarks* accompanying the translations of the two plays, Hölderlin calls these moments, in both *Antigone* and *Oedipus Rex*, a 'caesura', a scission or interruption not only of the action of the play, but of the functioning or operation of speculative philosophy itself with its insistence on oversight and self-reflexion.

As a way of closing our account of the conceptual antagonisms at work in the reception of the two plays in question, it is worthwhile pausing to look at this concept of 'caesura' which for Lacoue-Labarthe is the most important one emerging from Hölderlin's work concerning the stage. The French thinker has written on the *Remarks* in various locations and attempting to provide an overview of them all would require considerable space, given the need to unpack Hölderlin's dense texts.[55] Nonetheless, we can look at one passage which begins with the motif of tragedy as an essentially divided form, thus raising the question of whether these parts will be articulated into a whole, i.e. via a dialectical resolution, or instead shown to be in irresolvable tension with one another. He states:

> c'est du point de vue de la structure, essentiellement, que la tragédie est fondée sur la règle de l'opposition (Nietzsche, évidemment, se souviendra de cette intuition): il y a deux espaces théâtraux (l'orchestre et la scène), deux langues ou deux traitements de la langue [...]; un système rigoureux d'échanges conflictuels entre les personnages ou plus exactement entre ce que représentent les personnages (c'est la structure agonale ou agonistique de la tragédie), que Hölderlin spécifie comme 'échange ou alternation (*Weschel*) des représentations'; la partition organique du poème tragique, assimilé à un vers ou à une phrase inégalement accentués et dont le rythme propre est assuré, comme en métrique, par une césure (qui correspond, dans chacune des deux tragédies, à l'intervention de Tirésias [...]) (AN 145).

> [essentially, it is thanks to its structure that tragedy is founded on the law of opposition (Nietzsche, of course, will remember this intuition): there are two theatrical spaces (the orchestra and the stage or *skene*), two languages or two ways of treating language [...]; a rigorous system of exchanges based on conflict between the characters or more precisely between what the characters represent (this is the agonal or antagonistic structure of tragedy), which Hölderlin specifies as an 'exchange or alternation (*Weschel*) of representations'; the organic partition of the tragic poem, which is compared to an unevenly accented verse or expression and whose own rhythm is based, as in metre, around a cæsura (corresponding, in each of the tragedies, to Tiresias's intervention [...]).]

What is being argued here is that Hölderlin brought to the fore the division or scission already present in Sophocles's tragedies and artificially reunified by speculative readings. It is significant that he should be doing so as a thinker associated with Hegel and Schelling (he had studied alongside them at Tübingen in the early 1790s), but whose thinking was ultimately more open than dialectics would allow. This allows him to refuse to extend the speculative reading of tragedy, i.e. to identify tragedy as 'theatre', if the latter is understood as a form self-reflexively seeing and grasping itself or producing the literal 'theory', i.e. the view or vision, of itself. Instead of any such resolution of parts into a total, unitary vision, the German poet describes a situation where, following an identification of the dualisms between the *orchestra* and the *skene* and between gods and men, '[e] verything is speech against speech, which mutually cancel each other out'.[56] And the final part of the passage quoted above refers to Hölderlin's 'assimilat[ion]' of the plays to a metrical verse. This refers to the opening parts of the *Remarks* on *Antigone*, which discuss the relative position in the two plays of what is named 'the counter-rythmical interruption' or the caesura, a commonly-used metrical term meaning cutting or scission (the term is also glossed in this way in the *Remarks* on *Oedipus*).[57] And in Hölderlin's words, 'in both plays, it is the speeches of Tiresias which constitute the caesura'; in *Antigone*, Tiresias the blind seer chastizes Creon for his actions, and in *Oedipus* warns the new King not to search for Laius's murderer.[58] This is to say that for the poet, this figure 'steps into the path of fate as the guardian of the natural power which tragically removes man from his orbit of life [...] to another world, and tears him off into the eccentric orbit of the dead'.[59] This identification of Tiresias as a figure who gives voice to the forces interrupting men's lives is important in understanding Hölderlin's work on the plays in its wider significance regarding speculative thought.

For Lacoue-Labarthe, it is not only the modern, rationalizing efforts of Creon and Oedipus respectively that are interrupted in this way, but also, by way of a meta-commentary, the readings of the plays provided by modern, speculative thought. This is not to say that any alternative thinking as such is being proposed — but rather that Hölderlin makes available a mode of thinking that might be other than a 'theory' (a seeing or vision). Accordingly, Lacoue-Labarthe's interest in his reiteration of Hölderlin is not so much in a tragic 'theatre' (place of vision) as in 'la scène', the space in which a tradition basing itself in clarity and insight can be exposed to its limits and limitations. In this sense, instead of projecting outwards or constructing a theory, Lacoue-Labarthe's interest in the tragic stage is a thinking that relates to that which precedes it and lies outside a control: a mimesis.

Notes to Chapter 4b

1. In 'De quelques contradictions' ['On Some Contradictions'], in *Tel quel*, 38 (Summer 1969), i–ix (p. vii). It is more common regarding Hölderlin to refer to 'le Dire poétique' or 'poetic Saying' — which precisely cannot be reduced to a 'Dit' or 'Said'.

2. See Heidegger, *Elucidations*. Following Heidegger, there had also been Blanchot's reading: see Leslie Hill, *Blanchot: Extreme Contemporary* (London: Routledge, 1997), pp. 77–91.

3. In Hölderlin, *Hymnes, élégies et autres poèmes*, trans. by Armel Guerne (Paris: Flammarion, 1983), pp. 7–20.

4. Nancy reports Lacoue-Labarthe as having stated to him: 'Je sais ce qu'il faut aujourd'hui pour être le Hölderlin de la fin du 20ᵉ siècle' ['I know what is necessary today to be the Hölderlin of the end of the 20th century']. To Nancy's reply, 'fais-le' ['do it'], Lacoue-Labarthe responded cryptically: 'mais tu te rends compte ? Horriblement difficile' ['do you have any idea ? Horribly difficult']. See film *Voyage à Tübingen: un Portrait de Philippe Lacoue-Labarthe*.

5. The 'Remarks' referred to are translated as 'Notes on the *Oedipus*' and 'Notes on the *Antigone*', in Hölderlin, *Essays and Letters*, trans. by Jeremy Adler and Charlie Louth (London: Penguin, 2009), pp. 317–32. I refer to them as the 'Remarks' in order to retain consistency with Lacoue-Labarthe's usage.

6. In 'Introduction', in Hölderlin, *Hymnes, élégies et autres poèmes*, p. 7. Derrida criticized Blanchot for assigning a similar role to Hölderlin's madness as the essence of poetry — see my 'Périmer d'avance: Blanchot, Derrida, and Influence', in *Questions of Influence in Modern French Literature*, ed. by Thomas Baldwin, James Fowler, and Ana de Medeiros (Basingstoke: Palgrave Macmillan, 2013), pp. 111–25.

7. See Heidegger, *An Introduction to Metaphysics*, trans. by Ralph Manheim (Garden City: Doubleday, 1961).

8. In *Métaphrasis suivi du Théâtre de Hölderlin* ([*Metaphrasis* followed by *The Theatre of Hölderlin*]; Paris: PUF, 1998), p. 8. Lacoue-Labarthe addresses translation in relation to Hölderlin in 'Traduction et histoire' (['Translation and History']; AN 141–50), and separately in 'De l'impossibilité de connaître Heidegger en français' ['On the Impossibility of Knowing Heidegger in French'], in *La Quinzaine littéraire*, 264 (1–15 October 1977), 18–20.

9. In *Essays and Letters*, p. 213.

10. For his part, Lacoue-Labarthe draws on the scholarly account Hölderlin's translation in the German version of the *Complete Works*, plus a stand-alone work by its editor, Friedrich Beissner, *Hölderlins Übersetzungen aus dem Griechischen* ([*Hölderlin's Translations from the Greeks*]; 1933; Stuttgart: Metzler, 1961). For a study of Hölderlin's translation in relation the other aspects of his work, see Charlie Louth, *Hölderlin and the Dynamics of Translation* (Oxford: Legenda, 1998).

11. Lacoue-Labarthe's observation is found in the original programme notes for his production; in Sophocles, *The Three Theban Plays*, trans. by Robert Fagles (Harmondsworth: Penguin, 1982), p. 179 (emphasis original); in *Hölderlin's 'Sophocles': Oedipus and Antigone*, trans. by David Constantine (High Green: Bloodaxe, 2001), p. 26.

12. Berman, *L'Épreuve de l'étranger: Culture et traduction dans l'Allemagne romantique, Herder, Goethe, Schlegel, Novalis, Humboldt, Schleiermacher, Hölderlin* ([*The Ordeal of the Foreign : Culture and Translation in Romantic Germany*]; Paris: Gallimard, 1984).

13. The text from which this passage is drawn is also used in the Notes for *Œdipe le tyran de Sophocle* (Paris: Bourgois, 1998), p. 228.

14. In an interview with the author, 27 July 2013.

15. The Oedipus volume also contains notes on Lacoue-Labarthe's translation, but there is less comment on the choices made during this exercise. Elsewhere, Lacoue-Labarthe's translation of Nietzsche's *Naissance de la tragédie* (1977) contains a glossary of key German terms (pp. 332–38), *L'Absolu littéraire* also contains a useful glossary (pp. 435–38), and the first section of *La Poésie comme expérience* discusses in detail the translation of two Paul Celan poems (see chapter 5). A Greek-French glossary is provided in 'Katharsis et Mathèsis' (2002) in *Europe*, 873 (May 2010), 72–94 (pp. 91–92).

16. The English is from *Hölderlin's 'Sophocles':Oedipus and Antigone*, p. 71.

17. In *Antigones: the Antigone Myth in Western Literature, Art, and Thought* (Oxford: Oxford U.P.), p. 85.

18. In *Hölderlin's 'Sophocles'*, p. 93.

19. Constantine's translation does not reproduce this term; in it, Haemon says to Creon: 'If you were someone else I'd say you'd strayed'; *Hölderlin's 'Sophocles'*, p. 94.

20. In *Hölderlin's 'Sophocles'*, p. 68. Cf. *Œdipe le tyran de Sophocle*, p. 225. Lacoue-Labarthe writes an article whose title is his translation of these words — 'La Forme toute oublieuse de l'infidélité' ['The Utterly Forgetful Form of Infidelity'], in *L'Animal*, 165–70.

21. In *Métaphrasis suivi du Théâtre de Hölderlin*, p. 1. The leaflet accompanying the production of *Œdipe le Tyran* (1998) credits Lacoue-Labarthe for translation and dramaturgy, and Jean-Louis Martinelli for *mise-en-scène*.

22. *Les Chants de Mandrin* [*Smugglers' Songs*], directed by Rabah Ameur-Zaïmeche (2011).

23. On Derrida's reading of Hegel in relation to *Antigone*, see Simon Critchley, 'A Commentary Upon Derrida's Reading of Hegel in *Glas*', in *Hegel After Derrida* (London: Routledge, 1998), pp. 197–226.

24. In 'Ex abrupto', p. 70.

25. Ibid., p. 70.

26. In *Libération* (13 July 1998). An interview with Charles Berling, the actor who played Oedipus, is available at: <http://www.youtube.com/watch?v=gFKccDNzR_A>. Lacoue-Labarthe wrote a homage to Philippe Clévénot, the actor who played Tiresias: '"Réfléchis!": un hommage' ['"Reflect!": an Homage'], in Jean-Christophe Bailly, *La Véridiction (sur Philippe Lacoue-Labarthe)* ([*Veridiction (on Philippe Lacoue-Labarthe)*]; Paris: Bourgois, 2011), pp. 81–90. Clévénot and Lacoue-Labarthe reportedly discussed a staging of Racine's *Bérénice*, but it never came about.

27. In '"Réfléchis!": un hommage', p. 86 (emphasis original).

28. In 'La Fiction du biographique', p. 203. For Deutsch's account of his work with Lacoue-Labarthe on *Antigone*, *Œdipe le tyran*, *Les Phéniciennes*, and *Sit Venia Verbo*, see 'Le Théâtre de Lacoue' ['Lacoue's Theatre'], in *L'Animal*, 199–202.

29. In *Métaphrasis suivi du Théâtre de Hölderlin*, p. 3.

30. In *Scène suivi de Dialogue sur le dialogue*, pp. 81–82. More widely, the conflict suggested by the Greek term *agôn* is present in texts from 'L'Agonie de la religion' ['The Agony of Religion'] to the volume in which it is collected, *Agonie terminée, agonie interminable*.

31. See the selection in Hegel, *Hegel on Tragedy*, ed. by Anne and Henry Paolucci (Westport: Greenwood, 1978); Schelling, letter ten of 'The Philosophical Letters on Dogmatism and Criticism', in *The Unconditional in Human Knowledge: Four Early Essays 1794–96*, trans. by Fritz Marti (Lewisburg: Bucknell U.P., 1980).

32. In *Antigones*, p. 1.

33. In *Essay on the Tragic*, trans. by Paul Fleming (1961; Stanford: Stanford U. P., 2002), p. 20.

34. In the last of Schelling's *Philosophical Letters on Dogmatism and Criticism*, quoted in Szondi, *Essay on the Tragic*, trans. by Paul Fleming (1961; Stanford: Stanford U. P., 2002), p. 7 (emphases original). Lacoue-Labarthe cites the same passage in *L'Imitation des modernes*, p. 48.

35. Cf. Sartre: 'La grande tragédie, celle d'Eschyle et de Sophocle, celle de Corneille, a pour ressort principal la liberté humaine. Œdipe est libre, libres Antigone et Prométhée. La fatalité que l'on croit constater dans les drames antiques n'est que l'envers de la liberté' (in *Un Théâtre de situations* (Paris: Gallimard, 1973), p. 19; ['Great tragedy, that of Æschylus or Sophocles, that of Corneille, has human freedom as its main wellspring. Oedipus is free, likewise Antigone and Prometheus. The fatality that is often noted in ancient drama is only the reverse side of freedom']. Nancy declares his bewilderment at the fact that Sartre wrote theatre despite wishing to subjugate literature to external forces; he refers to the possibility of he and Lacoue-Labarthe writing further on this (they did not); in *Scène* suivi de *Dialogue sur le dialogue*, p. 58.

36. In Hymnes, élégies et poèmes, p. 10.

37. In *Essays and Letters*, p. 325.

38. See Nietzsche, *The Birth of Tragedy out of the Spirit of Music* (1872), trans. by Shaun Whiteside (London: Penguin, 1993).

39. In *Essays and Letters*, p. 213.

40. Lacoue-Labarthe identifies the importance of Bordeaux's newly-erected (at the time) neo-classical architecture, as well as of the French Revolution. He argues that Hölderlin saw this as a model for Greece to throw off Turkish rule, and reads Hölderlin's novel in this light: '*Hyperion*, c'est ça' in the film *Voyage à Tübingen*.

41. Cf. *The Ister*, a longer film from 2004 featuring Lacoue-Labarthe, Nancy, Hans-Jürgen Syberberg, and Bernard Stiegler addressing Hölderlin's eponymous poem on the Danube. More recently, François Lagarde and Christine Baudrillon have directed *Altus*, featuring Lacoue-Labarthe's journeys to several *hauts-lieux* of philosophy. In an interview introducing the film, they state that together with Lacoue-Labarthe, 'Nous avions le projet de réaliser un film adapté de la nouvelle *Lenz* de Büchner dont nous avions écrit ensemble le scénario' ['[w]e had the project of shooting a film adapted from Büchner's novella *Lenz*, and whose script we had written together'], in 'Philippe Lacoue-Labarthe, *Altus*' (5 July 2013), <http://tinyurl.com/p3gxdrw> [accessed 27 July 2013].

42. Cf. the 'Remarques sur *Antigone*' (AdS 169–77), as well as Hölderlin's well-known letters to Böhlendorff before and after his stay in Bordeaux; *Essays and Letters*, pp. 207–09 and 213–15.

43. Cf. Heidegger, *Elucidations of Hölderlin's Poetry* and Avital Ronell, 'The Sacred Alien: Heidegger's Reading of Hölderlin's "Andenken"', in *The Überreader: Selected Works of Avital Ronell* (Champaign: University of Illinois Press, 2007), pp. 205–26.

44. In Goldhill, *How to Stage Greek Tragedy Today* (London: University of Chicago Press, 2007), p. 207.

45. In the leaflet accompanying the production of *Œdipe le tyran* (1998).

46. On the relationship of psychoanalysis to speculative or metaphysical thought and specifically on Lacan's reading of the play, see Lacoue-Labarthe's 'De l'Éthique: à propos d'*Antigone*' ['On Ethics: regarding *Antigone*'], in *Lacan avec les philosophes* ([*Lacan with the Philosophers*]; Paris: Albin Michel, 1991), pp. 20–36.

47. Steiner states that the translation '*my* Zeus' is 'certainly a grammatical error on Hölderlin's part', in *Antigones*, p. 82; Lacoue-Labarthe for his part states that the translation from Greek is unusual but 'autorisé, à la limite' (AdS 190; ['permissible, just about']).

48. In *Métaphrasis* suivi du *Théâtre de Hölderlin*, p. 18.

49. In 'De Hölderlin à Marx': Mythe, imitation, tragédie: Entretien réalisé par Bruno Duarte' ['From Hölderlin to Marx: Myth, Imitation, Tragedy: Interview with Bruno Duarte'], in *Labyrinthe*, 22 (2005), 121–33 (p. 125).

50. In *Essays and Letters*, p. 320.

51. In *Métaphrasis* suivi du *Théâtre de Hölderlin*, p. 11.

52. Cf. Giorgio Agamben, 'Oedipus and the Sphinx', in *Stanzas: Word and Phantasm in Western Culture*, trans. by Roland L. Martinez (London: University of Minnesota Press, 1993), pp. 135–40.

53. Freud's insistence on the inevitability of the underlying primal urges is therefore an opposing reading, arguing that Oedipus represents the ancient or the anti-modern, that which lies within us and does not allow us to be free.

54. In *La Réponse d'Ulysse*, p. 83.

55. See the second part of *Métaphrasis* suivi du *Théâtre de Hölderlin'* (pp. 35–73), and 'La Forme toute oublieuse de la fidélité' (AN 165–70).

56. In *Essays and Letters*, p. 323.

57. Ibid., pp. 325, 318.

58. Ibid., p. 318. Interestingly, Tiresias is excluded from Jean Anouilh's modernized 1943 version of *Antigone*, thus omitting what Hölderlin saw as its key element.

59. Ibid.

CHAPTER 4C

The Stage (Opera)

Lacoue-Labarthe's longstanding interest in opera nuances the narrative according to which his work on *Antigone* in the late 1970s acted as a moment of revelation regarding the stage; indeed it suggests that this was instead a moment when his previous thinking of it flooded into other areas of his work (for instance translation and the relation to philosophy). In any case, opera is treated in an uneven way throughout his career: much of his work on it remains unpublished, which rather than placing it as a secondary concern, suggests that it was a key issue on which he wished to publish only when ready. And in addition to the full-length work *Musica ficta (figures de Wagner)* (1991), opera is the horizon both of many of Lacoue-Labarthe's earliest texts (from the mid-1960s), and of the last published in his lifetime, *L'Allégorie'*. In short, although on an initial reading of his published output, opera might not seem greatly important, in truth it is something of a sleeping giant, one that develops the same distinction between 'theatre' and 'stage' that we have already seen operating in his approach to tragedy via Hölderlin and Sophocles.

In addition to textual traces, those who knew Lacoue-Labarthe speak of an early love of Wagner, and in 'Scène' he begins by recalling that his and Nancy's dialogues on the stage grew out of their interest in opera.[1] Nonetheless, despite his admiration of a range of canonical operas from *Don Giovanni* and *Così fan tutte* to *Tristan und Isolde*, his trips to the Bayreuth festival left him dissatisfied with contemporary practices of *mise en scène*. Indeed, he sometimes found greater inspiration in innovative practices at or beyond the traditional boundaries of opera: for instance *Einstein on the Beach* by Robert Wilson and Philip Glass (1976) or Syberberg's *Our Hitler: a Film from Germany* (1977).[2] Whilst Lacoue-Labarthe cites as influences these maximalist engagements with the stage or the spectacle, at other times he advocates minimalism stemming from his dissatisfaction with much contemporary opera, conceiving instead of a staging which he calls 'la "forme oratorio" ou "version de concert"' ['the "oratorio form" or "concert version"'].[3] This is noteworthy as it suggests that even before particular actions or gestures are performed, Lacoue-Labarthe's interest lies in the very relationship between disembodied or literally meta-physical music on the one hand, and on the other physical bodies on a physical stage.[4] As he states,

> Qu'un mot d'amour, le plus doux, obligeât à tant de contorsions du visage ou de la bouche, ou qu'en revanche une déclaration de haine — voix soudain blanche — pût s'accommoder, au comble de la brutalité, d'une face impassible, j'en

étais ému jusqu'aux larmes. Le reste — décors, costumes, même les éclairages, sans parler du 'jeu', souvent piteux ou grotesque, des acteurs-chanteurs — me paraissait *accessoire*.[5]

[That the gentlest word from one lover to another should make necessary so many contortions of the face or the mouth, or alternatively that a declaration of hatred — a voice suddenly livid with fury — could be combined, at the nadir of brutality, with an expression of impassibility, this shook me to the point of tears. The rest — the scenery, costumes, even the lighting, without mentioning the 'acting' of the actor-singers, which was often pitiful or grotesque — seemed to me to be *secondary*.]

In other words, his interest lies in a central tension within opera, in view of which many aspects of contemporary theatrical practice of the genre can be named as 'secondary'. Notably, this tension is not anything unitary or substantial in itself, but is rather a principle of conflict between two elements, which we might call the words sung ('[a] word from one lover to another', 'a declaration of hatred') and the body ('the face or the mouth'). In other words, what is paramount is precisely the sense that neither element can be privileged over the other: opera arises when the two come into tension. And the conflict is reiterated or redoubled when two or more characters interact on stage: 'toute l'intensité proprement dramatique se condensait dans l'*âgon* des voix' ['the intensity that was properly speaking dramatic was condensed in the *agôn* of the voices'].[6] In short, here we are presented with another version of the conflicts on the tragic stage that so held Lacoue-Labarthe's attention. And as with tragedy, with opera his interest will be in whether these conflicts are resolved into dialectical resolution, or whether they are instead allowed to clash antagonistically, outside any horizon of resolution.

The stakes raised by these two approaches to the conflicts arising from opera as an art form can be seen when Lacoue-Labarthe states that 'ce qui fait l'essence du savoir, et ce qui anime le désir du savoir [est] l'affrontement à la contradiction. En général' (IM 210; ['what makes the essence of knowledge [...], as well as what drives the desire for knowledge [is] the confronting of contradiction. In general terms']. In other words, the approach to contradiction is not simply a local issue concerning whether in a given operatic production the emphasis is placed on reconciliation or conflict between physical and metaphysical elements. Instead, it is an issue touching nothing less than 'the essence of knowledge' itself. But Lacoue-Labarthe does not merely *apply* this framework of what is essential to knowledge to opera as an art form; instead, his interest in the latter arises precisely because of its particular position on the boundary between the physical and the metaphysical (these are his terms, as we shall see). And the political implications or the political destination of this question are also important insofar as in *Musica ficta* with its approach to Wagner (whose totemic status for German nationalism barely needs to be recalled), he further explores his theses around 'fiction' and 'national-aestheticism' as developed in *La Fiction du politique*. Indeed, it is significant that he stated that 'mon "national-esthétisme" [...] est la figure que prend le destin allemand lorsqu'il cherche à se saisir et à se définir [...] dans son rapport au commencement grec' ['my "national-aestheticism" [...] is the figure taken by German destiny when it attempts to grasp and define itself [...] via its relation to the Greek beginning'].[7]

His work on the stage, specifically in the texts on Sophoclean tragedy and one named 'La Naissance (?) d'un opéra' ['The Birth (?) of an Opera'] in which dawn breaks over a Greek theatre, are thus attempts to relate to this 'Greek beginning' without establishing it as an origin, as part of a dialectic; instead he moves beyond such fiction or *fictionnement* to think the spacing and exposure of the stage without bending it into the logic of origins and beginnings.

This chapter is organized into four parts looking at distinct areas of Lacoue-Labarthe's writing in which these issues are addressed. First, we examine some unpublished texts from the 1960s which make clear the considerable level of his interest in opera, as well as demonstrating that this interest lies in the interface between the physical and the metaphysical. Second, we turn to *Musica ficta*, a work addressing four receptions of Wagner; specifically, we look at Baudelaire's reaction and how for Lacoue-Labarthe it shows Wagner to have been understood as a representative of the metaphysical or speculative theses associated with German Romanticism. Our third section then looks at another unpublished text, 'La Naissance (?) d'un opéra': part-way between a narrative and a critical reflection upon that narrative, this text makes clear how Lacoue-Labarthe associates opera with the conflicts in Greek theatre between 'ancient' and 'modern' which we saw in his writing on tragedy. The category of 'song' which emerges in this text provides the link to the final section, which looks at a text named 'L'"Allégorie"'. These narrative fragments feature an opera singer undergoing a medical emergency on stage; as such, they provide vivid and unexpected illustrations of this tension in opera between metaphysical song and physical body.

Opus metaphysicum

The collection of Lacoue-Labarthe's unpublished 1960s texts on opera, many of them fragmentary or in note-form, has disproportionate importance. This is largely due to the fact that it contains a series of sketches for a book or books on opera, which it is simplest to list by title as follows:

(1) *Opus metaphysicum* — with subtitle as either 'l'opération' ['operation'] or 'l'opéra, l'absence d'œuvre' ['opera, absence of work'].[8] This Latin phrase quotes Nietzsche's view that *Tristan and Isolda* is 'the real *opus metaphysicum* of all art'.[9]

(2) *Pourquoi pensons-nous à l'opéra?* [*Why do we Think of Opera?*], a title suggested shortly following a note asserting that '[c]e qu'il nous faut écrire aujourd'hui: un opéra' ['[w]hat it is necessary to write today: an opera'].

(3) *Théâtre* [*Theatre*] — with alternative titles given as follows: '(ou: *Opéra* — ou: *Le Simulacre* — ou: *Le Subterfuge*)' ['or: *Opera* — or: *Simulacrum* — or: *Subterfuge*]'. This third suggestion is developed into a plan for an opera, containing stage directions, references for texts on opera to be discussed (by Rousseau, Kierkegaard, Kafka), and elements from existing operas, e.g. Isolda's death from *Tristan and Isolda*.

(4) Between acts II and III of this third plan, we read the following: 'Ici viendrait se greffer *l'autre* livre (officieux), c'est-à-dire l'histoire de l'Écrivain et de la Cantatrice [...]: allégorie à rebours' (emphasis original; ['Here the *other* (unofficial) work would

be grafted on, i.e. the story of the Writer and of the Singer [...]: an allegory against the grain', emphasis original]). There is therefore a suggestion that this would be a multi-platform project, with one work resembling an opera — albeit a self-reflexive one containing numerous literary references — being intersected by another one that would be 'unofficial', containing some of the material that would eventually appear in *L'Allégorie*', which recounts the story of a *cantatrice* or singer.

Looking at these projects as a whole, it is striking that amongst the theoretical or philosophical accounts of opera we might expect, we find the project for an actual opera. This would surely have been written in collaboration with a composer, as there is no evidence that Lacoue-Labarthe had musical training. However, the involvement of a professor of philosophy had a certain pertinence, as opera as an art form recounts the struggle of music to transcend the stage, and as such mimics the transcendence of the world attempted by metaphysics. In such a light, the thinker would have had an important role, bringing out this metaphysical element — not necessarily privileging it, but instead using the stage in order to explore its conditions of possibility and its limitations.

As we saw, the first title listed above quotes Nietzsche's statement that '*Tristan and Isolda* is the real *opus metaphysicum* of all art'. In truth, the quotation occurs repeatedly throughout the archival material addressing opera, functioning as the insight driving Lacoue-Labarthe's interest. And this insight is that the music in Wagner's opera functions as a metaphysical force, transcending the local circumstances provided by the theatre building, the stage, the actors, and so on. One reading of this role being undertaken by music is that it confirmed Schopenhauer's doctrine that music represented the inner essence of the world. This therefore raises the question of how we are to read Lacoue-Labarthe's fascination with the 'opus metaphysicum' statement (evident in his frequent quotation of it): is he repeating the metaphysical gesture, seeking to write about opera — or indeed to write an opera — with transcendental aims, i.e. taking music to be some absolute, unchanging essence? Let us see how he addresses the issue:

> On pourrait faire l'hypothèse, concernant l'opéra, qu'il n'a jamais eu pour objet, pour sujet (dans ses plus hauts moments tout au moins) que la représentation, plus ou moins obscure et déchiffrable de sa propre essence, de ce qui le constitue comme 'l'art métaphysique par excellence': le combat de la musique contre le texte.

> [On the subject of opera we could hypothesize that it never had any object or subject (in its most lofty moments, at least) except the more or less obscure but nonetheless decodable representation of its own essence, of what constitutes it as 'the metaphysical art par excellence': the struggle of music against the text.]

This passage is important insofar as its use of the term 'struggle' causes us to nuance any view of Lacoue-Labarthe's argument as straightforwardly transcendentalist or metaphysical: the relationship between music and the text is not simply the prevailing of the former over the latter, but instead consists in tension and resistance. Nonetheless, there seems to remain a metaphysical tendency on Lacoue-Labarthe's part. For instance, we can also read that '[l]'horizon du texte, dans l'Époque de la métaphysique, c'est l'opéra, c'est-à-dire la disparition, l'effacement du texte dans le chant. | Disparition de la trace, de la marque, de l'inscription... dans la pure *Phonè*' ['The horizon of the text, in the Epoch of metaphysics, is opera, which is to say the disappearance, the effacement of the text in the singing. | The disappearance of traces, marks, inscriptions... into pure *Phonè*']. Here there is less an overcoming of metaphysics, to recycle Heidegger's phrase, than metaphysics overcoming the physical (whether the singer's body, or the text), and the situation is a generally applicable one: it is set up as nothing less than 'the horizon of the text, in the Epoch of metaphysics'. There are significant similarities here to Derrida's thinking of speech and writing, which of course denounced the belief placed in the voice as a guarantor of reliability as a phonocentric belief in presence, and a way of shutting down the transferability and iterability of a written text. But in Lacoue-Labarthe's interest in opera as a metaphysical art, the emphasis runs in the opposite direction to Derrida's contemporary publications; as someone still seeking to make his reputation, it is understandable why Lacoue-Labarthe in his mid-twenties might have seen these thoughts as too untimely for publication.

Another salient feature of Lacoue-Labarthe's unpublished material on opera concerns the notion of self-reflexivity. Writing about specific operas, he repeatedly arrives at formulations asserting that ultimately they do not address external subject matter, but rather their own processes, form, and genre. For instance, both *Tristan and Isolda* and *Così fan tutte* are referred to as 'l'opéra de l'opéra' ['the opera of opera']; *Don Giovanni* is said to be a '[c]omédie sur le comique, jeu du jeu, théâtre dans le théâtre' ['[c]omedy on the comic, play of play, theatre within theatre']: and remaining with this opera, we read (in note-form) of what is said to be the '[r]eprésentation de la représentation → apparence de l'apparence. | Le D[on] J[uan] est la représentation de l'art lui-même' ['Representation of representation → appearance of appearance. | D[on] J[uan] is the representation of art itself']. This self-reflexive structure of 'the X of X' signals that he sees opera as one development of the self-reflexivity that he and Nancy later located in Jena Romanticism. In other words, for the operas named above to represent themselves, and to comment on this representation, is for them to act simultaneously as object and subject. Effectively, they cast their gaze on themselves, creating a self-seeing, a 'theory' in the proper sense. In Lacoue-Labarthe's words, '[l]e sujet de l'opéra [est] la métaphore, l'allégorie de son essence. Autofiguration. Espace (figure) ajouté pour annuler le premier espace, la distance représentative, la séparation, la scission' ['The subject of opera [is] the metaphor, the allegory of its essence. A self-figuration. A space (or figure) added in order to cancel out the primordial space, the distance of representation, separation, scission']. This statement confirms that this self-reflexivity, self-theorizing, or 'autofiguration' comes into being as a reaction against the primordial separation or scission that is always already there. Lacoue-Labarthe identifies this as the 'sujet' *of* opera: i.e. this self-theorizing is the narrative recounted *by* opera, rather than opera itself. This is to say that the latter can also contain elements not reducible to that narrative, more redolent of the 'stage' than of 'theatre': for instance the mutual exposure to one another of the various voices, elements, or presences on the stage. *Musica ficta* will demonstrate this more fully.

Musica ficta (Figures de Wagner)

There are several ways in which this work occupies an important place in Lacoue-Labarthe's oeuvre. First, it is his most extensive work on the theatrical arts, both developing his longstanding interest in opera and forming a comparative viewpoint from which to see his work on Hölderlin and Sophocles. Second, it confirms that his field of interest is resolutely comparative, meaning here that opera is of interest primarily insofar as it mimics — and provides us with a way of reading — the transcendent movement inherent in metaphysical philosophy. Third, it develops this comparative approach by making wholly explicit the implications of the self-reflexive 'fiction' that opera as a metaphysical art carries out. This is to say that the same process of fiction or *fictionnement* is ultimately the object of both *Musica ficta* and *La Fiction du politique*.[10] And lastly, *Musica ficta* carries through Lacoue-Labarthe's interest in Jena Romanticism as the birthplace of a modern aesthetic ideology, of which an expression is found in the Wagnerian concept of the *Gesamtkunstwerk*.

The standpoint adopted by the work is not that of a monograph on Wagner, but rather as a collection of four essays detailing his reception by writers and thinkers. The two sections into which these essays fall are divided by nationality and by century, chapters one and two addressing Baudelaire and Mallarmé, and then three and four looking at Heidegger and Adorno.[11] The work's subtitle *Figures de Wagner* can thus be read as meaning 'figures *of* Wagner', but the alternative reading would be 'figures *from* Wagner', i.e. the type of figures or fictions that the composer contributed to modern aesthetic thought. Although this double genitive is surely intended to be polysemic, the latter interpretation is currently of most interest. For in Lacoue-Labarthe's mind the term 'figure' is associated with what he names the figuration or fiction of the political. And art's role in this process is far from incidental or neutral. As he writes, 'se jouent, ensemble, l'art et la politique, mais ni sous la forme d'une politique de l'art ni, encore moins, sous celle d'un art de la politique. Il s'agit, plus gravement, de l'esthétisation — de la *figuration* — du politique' ['art and politics are played together, but neither in the form of a politics of art nor, even less, in the form of an art of politics. It is a more serious matter, the matter of the aestheticization — the *figuration* — of the political'].[12] In other words, this aestheticization of the political — we recall the category of 'national aestheticism' — represents a process whereby the political order is thought of as a construction to be worked on, as one might work on an artwork. Raw materials are to be bent to its goals, cuts and excisions will be necessary, and most crucially, there is the assumption that this political order is to be built according to the thinking of presence which is in evidence less in art as an abstract category than in the art*work*. As Lacoue-Labarthe and Nancy write in *Le Mythe nazi*, a short work which addresses the process of the 'fiction' or the figuration of the political,

> Wagner, bien plus que Goethe, se pensera comme le Dante, le Shakespeare ou le Cervantès de l'Allemagne. [...] il visera délibérément, avec la fondation de Bayreuth, un but politique: celui de l'unification, par la célébration et par le cérémonial théâtral, du peuple allemand (unification comparable à celle de la cité dans le rituel tragique). Et c'est en ce sens fondamental qu'il faut comprendre

l'exigence d'une 'œuvre d'art totale'. La totalisation n'est pas seulement esthéti-que: elle fait signe en direction du politique.[13]

[Wagner, far more than Goethe, would think of himself as the Dante, Shake-speare or Cervantès of Germany. [...] With the foundation of Bayreuth, he would deliberately aim for a political goal: that of the unification, via celebration and theatrical ceremony, of the German people (a unification comparable to that of the City via tragic ritual). And the demand of a 'total work of art' must be understood in this fundamental sense. Totalization is not only aesthetic: it also gestures towards the political.]

Such are the dangers represented by an art form taking elements from different genres (music and theatre) and intervening in different domains (the artistic and the political). Rather than establishing a relationship of exposure whereby each element is inflected by the other and a play of *différance* is set in chain, a totalization or systematization occurs. The pluri-disciplinarity of such a Total Artwork only serves to reinforce its ability to serve politically as an exemplary myth of unification and homogenization.

Now, the two thinkers' analysis of Jena Romanticism saw it as privileging the artwork as part of the construction of a new mythology. This led the Romantic thinkers to insist on the effectivity of the artwork, the process whereby it becomes and is an artwork, which is named *l'opération littéraire* (in fact the original title for the work on Romanticism *L'Absolu littéraire*). As Lacoue-Labarthe's thought is developed in *Musica ficta*, he is able to return to his longstanding interest in opera. In other words, there is a level on which the Romantic *opération* and Wagnerian *opéra* produce the same effect. Lacoue-Labarthe gives a noteworthy account of the influence of this phenomenon on Baudelaire, as the latter reacts to this Romantic legacy. He writes that:

avec Wagner, de plein fouet, [Baudelaire] reçoit une *théorie*, au sens fort du terme [...] c'est de l'entrée de Wagner sur la scène française qu'il faut dater, en matière d'esthétique tout au moins, l'entrée en France de la métaphysique allemande et la divulgation des thèses fondamentales du romantisme spéculatif. Et c'est Baudelaire, le premier, qui en subit le *choc*.

Il faut ici parler de *choc*, une deuxième fois, parce que, sous-jacente à la révélation musicale, il y a cette autre révélation, difficilement acceptable, elle, et même scandaleuse: à savoir que si la musique atteint, chez Wagner, à une telle puissance, c'est dans l'exacte mesure où elle procède d'une volonté expresse et délibérée de supplanter, ou sinon d'accomplir, la poésie.

[with Wagner, [Baudelaire] is directly in the line of fire, hit by a *theory*, in the strongest sense of the term [...] it is from Wagner's arrival on the French stage that, at least in the matter of æsthetics, the arrival in France of German metaphysics and the divulgence of speculative romanticism's fundamental theses must be dated. And it is Baudelaire who first experiences its *shock*.

It is necessary to speak of *shock* a second time here, because underlying the musical revelation there is another revelation, difficult to accept and even scandalous, which is that if Wagner's music attains such power, it does so to the precise extent to which it proceeds with the express and deliberated will to supplant or otherwise to complete poetry].[14]

In other words, speculative Romanticism as reiterated in the work of Wagner presents a challenge to Baudelaire. It goes beyond any expectations he may have had of elements from the operatic genre usefully informing his work: the Romantic-Wagnerian project was not content with confining itself to a single art-form, but rather acted with the ambition of overhauling all art-forms, and creating a single, new mythology for the modern age. And this comes through clearly in Lacoue-Labarthe's description of how Wagner's programme repeats and reinforces the ambition of speculative thought:

> L'œuvre d'art, telle que la comprend et la propose Wagner, représente un [...] défi [...] à la poésie, en son sens restreint, qu'elle met en concurrence avec la musique, renversant [...] la hiérarchie métaphysique (logocentriste) des arts [...]. [C]e renversement n'est pas sans porter la marque, comme ce sera encore le cas dans *La Naissance de la tragédie*, de l'opérativité dialectique elle-même: ce qu'on commence déjà à traduire par l'"œuvre d'art totale', le *Gesamtkunstwerk*, qui est l'Œuvre absolument parlant — l'*organon* absolu de Schelling ou, comme le dira Nietzsche, l'*opus metaphysicum* —, se donne comme la *fin* même de l'art dans la forme de la réunion et de la synthèse (c'est le mot qu'utilise Wagner) de tous les arts particuliers.

> [The work of art, as Wagner understands and proposes it, represents a [...] challenge [...] to poetry, more narrowly defined, which it places in competition with music, reversing [...] the (logocentric) metaphysical hierarchy of the arts [...]. [T]his reversal also bears the stamp of dialectical operativity itself, as will be the case again in *The Birth of Tragedy*: what is already beginning to be translated as 'the total work of art', the *Gesamtkunstwerk* — which is the Work in absolute terms, the absolute *organon* of Schelling, or, as Nietzsche will say, the *opus metaphysicum* — posits itself as the very end of art in the form of the unification and synthesis (this is the word Wagner uses) of all the individual arts.][15]

Here Wagner's opera is not presented as one genre amongst others, but as a super-genre, one providing within itself hierarchies of the various arts (music, poetry, theatre), and ultimately itself *being* art. Indeed, a clue lies in the name that Lacoue-Labarthe insists on: what is at stake is *l'opéra* — the cognate of Latin *opus* i.e. the work in general — rather than a particular, musico-theatrical genre sometimes known as *le drame lyrique*.

Lacoue-Labarthe's account of this process is illuminating regarding his relationship to the distinct concepts of the 'theatre' and the 'stage', insofar as opera here plays the role of a dominating, system-building force. This is to say that in its totalizing, Wagnerian form it provides the ultimate expression of 'theatre' understood as a form dominated by the single horizon of the gaze. As such it comprises and represents its own 'theory' (understood in the proper sense, as a gaze or vision), just as Jena Romanticism presented literature and theory as interconnected: in Lacoue-Labarthe and Nancy's words, as '*la théorie elle-même comme littérature* ou, cela revient au même, la littérature se produisant en produisant sa propre théorie' (AL 22, emphasis original; '*theory itself as literature* or, in other words, literature producing itself as it produces its own theory', LA 12, emphasis original). For Lacoue-Labarthe there seems to be a distinct sense that opera is a system calling to be deconstructed, demanding that its systematizing urges be interrupted. This is one reason why it demands his attention: rather than establishing new philosophical constructions, he instead sees his task as that of responding to pre-existing constructions. This response can be called either deconstruction or mimesis; in any case, there are two further areas in which this response is elaborated — let us turn to the first of these.

'La Naissance (?) d'un opéra'

We have begun to see that similarly to tragedy, though in a different way, opera for Lacoue-Labarthe represents a site of conflict that one can choose, with varying consequences, to attempt to resolve or to leave to the interplay of conflicting elements. In other words, opera raises the question of whether it is to be read via speculative philosophy, or via an alternative, more open mode of thought. The text in question, dated October 1964–September 1966 and found in a folder also containing texts later published in *L'Allégorie'*, develops these questions in notable ways.[16] It consists of five handwritten prose pages, after which come several pages of fragments, including the quotation from the *Requiem* mass 'Liber scriptus proferetur | in quo totum continentur,' ['a book will be brought forth, | in which all will be written'] — notable lines given Lacoue-Labarthe's characterization of much opera as a totalizing, metaphysical art. After what is surely the most significant, early part of this prose section, it goes on to detail his ideas for the staging of a minimalist opera. We can note in passing that this text instructs us about his will to shun conventional elegance: 'le meilleur éclairage sera le plus cru, le plus violent — le plus éblouissant' ['the best lighting will be the harshest, the most violent — the most dazzling']. At the same time, however, sobriety and classicism were privileged: the soloists' costumes were not to contain any 'accoutrements ridicules destinés à faire époque' ('ridiculous accoutrements liable to date'). In a key passage, his thinking on opera as a conflicted or divided art-form is developed here when we read that:

> L'opéra [...] est un genre impur, divisé. En disposant ainsi les choses, il s'agira de rendre sensible, de manifester [...] cette impureté même, de sorte que l'écart du chant et du texte, la différence même de la représentation éclatent et soient infiniment vertigineux.

> [Opera [...] is an impure, divided genre. In setting things up in this way, it will be a question of making palpable, of showing [...] this impurity itself, in such a way that the gap between the song and the text, the very difference of representation shine forth and be infinitely vertiginous.]

The notion of vertiginous or dizzying 'difference' here establishes Lacoue-Labarthe either as a very early reader of Derrida (this was written in 1964–66 and the latter's articles had begun to appear in 1963), or as someone as it were organically making use of a term which would go on to become famous when written performatively as *la différance*.

In any case, it is the early part of 'La Naissance (?) d'un opéra' which seems to be most important in terms of how opera, this divided or 'impure' genre, is presented as emerging or being born (notably the text's title inserts a question mark after the term 'naissance', and the question mark is itself placed between parentheses: these are early indications of Lacoue-Labarthe's hesitations regarding metaphors of birth which we saw in chapter 1). Let us read this part of the text at some length:

> J'avais rêvé de quelque chose comme un *opéra naturel*. Je devrais mieux dire: un opéra originaire. On m'avait dit une fois que les Grecs faisaient donner leurs tragédies à l'aube. J'imaginais que la lumière descendait sur le versant des montagnes et que les voix s'élevaient de la nuit des vallées, seules, venues de nulle bouche, expirées par nul corps — les voix d'aucun personnage mais de la nuit même quand elle se retirait, comme la rumeur que fait l'obscurité à la venue du jour, ce chant visible, mais peut-être jamais entendu, toujours s'effaçant, de l'herbe et des ronces. Puis, lorsque la lumière parvenait au théâtre, surgissaient des personnages immobiles adossés à la pierre. La clarté illuminait peu à peu l'horreur: les monstres se dressaient dans l'aube, meurtres et blessures, des fautes impensables s'exposaient et se jouaient au grand jour. Etrange dévoilement des hommes. Car ce sont eux qui chantaient lorsque le bruit du monde s'était apaisé et que la lumière avait tout obscurci, sauf leur regard qui vacillait à l'abri des masques. Il y avait alors un grand mutisme des choses: c'est pourquoi se disaient les souffrances et la mort, l'effondrement, la joie terrible de ceux qu'une insupportable connaissance entrevue, infiniment approchée, infiniment déçue — qu'un insupportable défaut de connaissance contraignaient à parler. [...] J'ai cru cet éblouissement, cette souffrance l'origine du chant; qu'un émoi comme celui du ciel au plus fort de l'été, l'infini tremblement qui secoue la lumière et d'où paraissent les choses, traversaient les hommes et les brisaient — et que de là venait notre chant. J'ai cru qu'à la jonction des choses, entre l'ombre et la lumière où s'ébauche le vent, dans l'incendie verbal de la lumière, dans ce qui sépare le corps de lui-même où s'ébauche le souffle, dans la différence des regards et le jeu de la discorde, c'est là qu'il y avait chant (emphasis original).

> [I had dreamed of something like a *natural opera*. I should sooner say: an originary opera. Someone once told me that the Greeks would stage their tragedies at dawn. I imagined the light descending over the mountainsides and voices arising from the night of the valleys, alone, coming from no mouth, breathed out by no body — the voices of no character, but of night itself as it withdrew, like the murmuring that the darkness makes at daybreak, this song which was visible, but which had perhaps never been heard, always effacing itself, of grass and brambles. Then, when the light would reach the theatre, there would appear immobile characters, backed up against the rock. Little by little, clarity illuminated horror: monsters appeared in the dawn, murders and woundings, unthinkable sins were shown forth and were acted out in the broad daylight. A strange unveiling of men. For it is they who would sing when the noise of the world had grown quiet and the light had obscured everything, except their gaze which wavered behind their masks. Then there would be a great muteness of things: this is why the sufferings of death would be enunciated, and the collapse, the terrible joy of an unbearable knowledge that had been glimpsed, infinitely approached, infinitely found to disappoint — all of which was forced to speak by an unbearable lack of knowledge. [...] I thought that this dazzling, this suffering were the origin of song; that an overwhelming sentiment [*émoi*] like that of the height of the summer, the infinite trembling which shakes the light and from which things emerge, would traverse men and shatter them — and that from this came our song. I thought that at the joining of things, between shadow and the light where wind takes shape, in the verbal fire of light, in what separates the body from itself and where breath takes shape, in

the difference of gazes and the play of discord, that was where there was song
(emphasis original).]

This narrative depicts a theatre over which dawn is breaking, but does so in a
highly allegorical rather than realist perspective. Although the scene described
is notionally located in ancient Greece, in truth its interest for Lacoue-Labarthe
lies in the wider significance of this particular time and context. For just as above
we saw him describe 'l'affrontement à la contradiction' (IM 210; ['confronting
contradiction']) as the *general* condition for the *essence* of knowledge, here further
instances of contradiction are illustrated as part of the allegory. This can be seen in
the various descriptions of struggle or antagonism between light ('light', 'clarity',
'dawn') and various types of darkness both literal and metaphorical ('night itself',
'horror', 'murders and woundings'). What the struggle between these two elements
gives rise to as dawn breaks over the theatre is 'chant' or song: 'I thought that at the
joining of things, between shadow and light [...] that was where there was song.'
Whereas elsewhere Lacoue-Labarthe describes conflict as giving rise to knowledge,
here song plays an analogous role. In fact, the two are not fundamentally distinct:
this song is surely to be taken to be opera — the passage opens with the term, after
all.

The verbal tense 'I had dreamed' places Lacoue-Labarthe's vision of this scenario
firmly in the past, as something since abandoned. And indeed, the passage quoted
is preceded by the words, '[j]'avais, au commencement, projeté tout autre chose'
('[at the beginning, I had planned something quite different']): the dream or vision
recounted is thus always already demarcated as an abortive version. In order to see
the new state of affairs, i.e. the new vision which has replaced this initial one of a
'natural opera' taking place in a Greek theatre at dawn, it is necessary to continue
reading the text from the point at which we broke off:

> Mais non. Rien de visible à l'origine du chant, je dois le dire encore, rien
> d'audible même. S'il y a bien une brûlure, on ne supporterait pas de s'y brûler.
> S'il y a une séparation, elle est antérieure à tout. [...] Parfois, [...] n'importe où,
> n'importe quand, dans une ville par exemple où l'on habite depuis longtemps,
> qu'on a pris l'habitude de ne plus voir, d'où l'on dirait presque que toute lumière
> est absente; l'événement survient; il y a que l'on se perd, on disparaît à soi, on
> ne se reconnaît plus; on est pris de vertige, le corps étrangement s'exalte. Cela
> chante. On ne sait pourquoi; on ne peut même pas savoir d'où cela vient. Le
> chant est sans origine.

> [But no. There is nothing visible about the origin of song, and I must even say,
> nothing audible either. If a burning goes on, we could not bear to burn within
> it. If there is a separation, it is anterior to everything. [...] Sometimes, [...] no
> matter where, no matter when, for instance in a town in which one has lived
> for a long time, which one has grown used to no longer really seeing, from
> which one could almost say that all light is lacking; the event arrives; and there
> is this — that one loses oneself, one disappears [*disparaît*] to oneself, one no
> longer recognizes oneself; one is overcome with dizziness, the body in strange
> exaltation. There is singing. One doesn't know why; one cannot even discover
> where it is coming from. Song is without origin.]

This passage is the highly allegorical beginning of a meditation on a different type of poetry or song, one that stems not from the dialectic of light and dark, but instead taking place in the town where one lives. We have therefore lost the setting for song that is properly speaking dramatic, theatrical, or spectacular; but this does not mean that some version of song is not retained: we are still told that 'there is singing'. This singing that does somehow, irreducibly take place despite being stripped of all external characteristics — above all its evocative setting in the Greek dawn — is now presented as being somehow unapproachable, interruptive of any approach we might make towards it. Instead, it comes towards us: 'the event arrives; and there is this — that one loses oneself, one disappears [*disparaît*] to oneself, one no longer recognizes oneself; one is overcome with dizziness'). It is notable here that whilst we are in an arena to which Lacoue-Labarthe will also respond discursively or critically, 'La Naissance (?) d'un opéra' shows many narrative or even poetic characteristics, with its description of context — 'for instance in a town in which one has lived for a long time' — and its seemingly autobiographical or autothanatographical (*disparaître* sometimes means to die) tone. These characteristics are shared with many of Lacoue-Labarthe's poems, later published in *L'Allégorie*' and *Phrase*, although this assimilation to the genre of poetry does not sit easily, given that his literary writing speaks first and foremost of the difficulties and constraints of writing.

Beyond the circumstances in which it arises or 'survient', the text tells us more about the nature and implications of the 'chant' in question. This can be seen here:

> J'ai supposé longtemps quelque chant unique que chaque voix reprendrait jusqu'à mourir, ne l'épuisant jamais (et morte à l'avance d'en provenir), comme on a supposé déjà souvent une infinie parole dont toutes nos paroles seraient la résonance, ou un livre absolu dont tous les livres seraient des fragments. J'ai donc longtemps rêvé d'un grand opéra antérieur: les choses faisaient un universel théâtre, un dieu nous chantait, nous étions les signes d'une partition pour nous d'ailleurs indéchiffrable — séparés, nos corps (jusque d'eux-mêmes), brisées, nos voix le sont.

> [I supposed for a long time that some single voice existed, that each voice would take up unto death, never exhausting it (and being always already dead, because it came from it), just as previously people have often imagined that there is an infinite speech to which all of our words would provide the echo, or an absolute book of which all books would be fragments. I therefore dreamt for a long time of a great, anterior opera: things made up a universal theatre, a god sang to us, we were the signs of a musical score which we could not interpret — our bodies were separated (even from themselves) and our voices were broken.]

This is important as it aligns the 'chant' in question with a tendency that Lacoue-Labarthe will later go on to study: namely the mythology of oneness, which finds expression in the notion of a universal or total artwork: 'an absolute book of which all books would be fragments'. This notion will prove central for the Jena Romantics (as studied in *L'Absolu littéraire*) as for Wagner (see *Musica ficta*); and the mention of the term 'book' also brings to mind Blanchot's *Livre à venir* (1959; *The Book to Come*), which Lacoue-Labarthe was certain to have read. The presence of this mythology of unification in the text in question confirms that the thinker's interest lies not in an empirical study of theatre — in either its early Greek or operatic guises — but in a highly allegorical understanding of knowledge or thought in general terms. However, it is intriguing that whilst establishing himself within such horizons, Lacoue-Labarthe does not resort to philosophical investigation properly speaking, i.e. the mode of discourse that we might assume to be most universal (although he certainly did not). Instead he remains with narrative or allegory; and indeed further commits himself to it by concentrating on the figure of a female singer charged with singing the universal and impossible song evoked above. This can be seen in a description of how he came to suspect the existence of such an always already anterior song. He writes:

> C'est pourquoi j'ai cru bon de faire apparaître la cantatrice — une cantatrice, qui aurait chanté cet opéra unique dont j'ai parlé, dans cette confusion des langues qui parfois nous émerveille, en qui se serait joué ce grand combat du chant comme un événement mythologique analogue à quelque guerre de Troie, etc...

> [This is why I thought it a good idea to have the singer appear — a singer who would have sung this single opera I have spoken of, in this confusion of tongues which sometimes makes us marvel, and in whom would be played out this great struggle, like a mythological event analogous to some Trojan war, etc...]

It is worth bearing in mind that this is the text of a writer in his mid-twenties who had published very little, if anything at all. It is true that the trope of realization or revelation can appear naïve and mystifying, and there is of course wild over-ambition in the presentation of the 'song' in question as analogous to the Trojan war in its status as the foundational myth for Greek literature. It is nonetheless important in confirming the importance of the mythic or allegoric mode of writing for Lacoue-Labarthe at this stage. And as if in echo to this early text, the final one published in his lifetime is a collection of fragments or poems, many of which date from the 1960s. And to this collection the title *L'Allégorie'* is given, being taken from one of the collected texts, which recounts the tale of the singer evoked in 'La Naissance (?) d'un opéra'. There was therefore a desire late in the thinker's career to return to this scenario of a song or opera whose allegorical status gives it wide-reaching implications. Let us therefore now pursue those implications further by turning to that text.

L'Allégorie'

In 2006 a volume of fragmented texts was published, standing at a remove from Lacoue-Labarthe's writing on philosophy. From the outset, the texts in question engage in a reflection on the status of literature as an alternative discourse to philosophy, for instance in presenting themselves as an allegory, a term that can be read etymologically as meaning 'speaking otherwise' (the prefix 'allo-' denoting alterity). On this reading, literature would be a speaking otherwise, that which is not philosophy but comes to address similar questions of representation, language, and form. But as elsewhere in Lacoue-Labarthe's work, he does not identify himself directly or straightforwardly as a writer of literature; the inverted commas placed around the term 'allegory' ensure that its presence in his discourse is placed under erasure, called into question. In the same vein, at no point is the work identified as poetry, although as a collection of short, non-prose texts, it brings the term to mind.

In addition to the texts published in *Le Nouveau commerce* at the turn of the 1970s, those included in the 2006 volume draw on a considerable archive of unpublished, associated texts — particularly in relation to the one which we shall now look at, named (like the collection) 'L'"Allégorie"'. This text recounts the tale of an opera singer, and the music she is described as singing is represented only by extended ellipses, single lines of dots stretching across the page. However, an earlier, unpublished version tells us that these fragments were originally conceived as being taken from a range of operas and pieces of music: *Tristan and Isolda*, *Don Giovanni*, the *Requiem* mass, and musical versions of Nietzsche's *Thus Spake Zarathustra* and the book of *Lamentations*.[17] These pieces are invested with considerable philosophical and metaphysical weight: Lacoue-Labarthe describes the *Requiem* as 'le chant métaphysique par excellence' ['the metaphysical song par excellence'], just as he had repeatedly quoted Nietzsche's view of *Tristan and Isolda* as 'the real *opus metaphysicum* of all art'.[18] This weight is a clue suggesting that his interest lies not so much in opera as a particular art-form, but as having wider implications for our thinking of art and representation in general. Indeed, we shall go on to see that in his eyes opera informs us more generally about the processes and status of art, particularly in its relation to metaphysical transcendence.

It is in this light that Lacoue-Labarthe uses the trope of opera to aid his reflection on writing, which is to say that he uses it as another way of writing about writing, i.e. as an *allegory* of writing. This is shown by the straightforward but far-reaching statement, found in his notes on the figure of the opera singer, that 'la cantatrice n'est rien d'autre que l'allégorie de l'écrivain | (ou: le chant n'est rien d'autre que l'allégorie de l'écriture)' ['the singer is nothing other than the allegory of the writer | (or: the song is nothing other than the allegory of writing)'].[19] The singer in question is sketched out by the pages of 'L'"Allégorie"' and recites operas by Wagner, Mozart, et al., which of course are some of the major reference points in Western art. The motif of culmination or completion of this tradition is therefore present in Lacoue-Labarthe's mind, as it is when he speaks of the Western metaphysical tradition as a single entity (however forbidding such an approach might be). And similarly to his discussions of philosophy in other parts of his work, noting the existence of such a unitary tradition goes hand in hand with diagnosing its closure, and consequent attempts to deconstruct it. In the current case of opera, this motif of closure is present via his narrative of the singer's physical difficulties and proximity to death. The account of the singer's experience of a literally existential drama locates Lacoue-Labarthe's field of exploration not as the tradition of opera in and of itself, but instead as the conflicts that it makes apparent. These conflicts are those crystallized by the question of the physical stage: that between the song as art-form and the singer, and the underlying tension between a metaphysical essence (located in music or song) and its more contingent worldly or physical expression. This conflict is the paramount factor in the attention Lacoue-Labarthe pays to music or song, as it finds expression in his writing on the stage, but also in his investigation into whether poetry can act in a similar way to song, or whether it instead arises when song asphyxiates or expires. The equivalence in his mind between song and poetry is made clear by a reference to an earlier project which states that 'il s'agissait d'effacer à tout jamais la tentation du chant (de la poésie)' ['the aim was to erase absolutely forever the temptation of song (of poetry)]'.[20] Shortly we shall see how placing this conflict centrally in this way is crucial to understanding the short text 'L'"Allégorie"' in all its importance for the collection of the same name, and Lacoue-Labarthe's general thinking of non-philosophical writing, or at least writing that seeks to comment *on* philosophy without adhering to it.

First, however, one of his unpublished texts associated with this project demands our attention, insofar as it provides some background to the figure of the dying singer, she whom in 'L'"Allégorie"' we witness undergoing some sort of physical attack, ultimately singing 'son propre déchirement et sa fin toujours proche [...] entre le souffle et son manque' (ALEG 31; ['her own being torn apart and her own end which is always near [...] between breath and its absence']). The closing line of the same text then tells us that she 'ne cesse de disparaître' (ALEG 31; ['unceasingly disappears/dies']). Now, the unpublished text in question presents, alongside earlier and more extensive versions of the published material, a series of biographical notes relating to an opera singer.[21] We are told that the singer discussed in this way, a Jew who had fled central Europe, toured extensively, and looked up to the major Norwegian soprano Kirsten Flagstad (1895–1962). The text alludes to Lacoue-Labarthe's hesitations as to whether such biographical elements should be included: 'elle ne portait pas encore de nom. Parfois, seulement, une initiale. Dans une première version, elle n'avait non plus de biographie (fictive ou réelle); dans une seconde, elle était née à Vienne en 1930' ['as yet she bore no name. Sometimes an initial, but nothing more. In a first version, she had no biography (fictitious or real) either; in a second version, she had been born in Vienna in 1930']. But most importantly of all, the narrative describes the critical illness of this singer, which seems to have occurred at the music festival in Donaueschingen in October 1964 (other texts in Lacoue-Labarthe's same folder on this figure of a dying singer are dated October 1964-September 1965). We are told that she died in the American hospital in Stuttgart four days after the attack, which is described as follows:

> On vit son corps s'affaisser lourdement [...], sa tête heurter le sol avec violence. On entendit une sorte de rumeur venue de la salle invisible, quelques cris, couvrir l'orchestre qui continuait à jouer. L'image se brisait en lacis et l'on voyait son visage parcouru d'ombres tremblantes, strié de lignes multiples et mouvantes de lumière vive, se décomposer lentement, comme éclaté. Mais ses lèvres bougeaient encore, la déformation de l'image, sans doute, lui faisait un rictus rappelant l'ébauche ou la fin d'un rire. On la vit fermer les yeux, tourner plusieurs fois la tête de gauche à droite, très vite, ouvrir la bouche comme si l'air lui avait soudain manqué, elle avait tenté de reprendre sa respiration, de conjurer par ses mouvements l'étouffement dont elle était menacée — elle avait encore refusé l'horreur de perdre souffle...

> [Her body was seen heavily slumping [...], her head violently hitting the ground. A sort of murmur was heard from the invisible auditorium, some cries, dominating the orchestra which had continued to play. The image was

breaking up and trembling shadows could be seen traversing her face, which was striated with multiple, mobile lines of bright light, and which was slowly collapsing, as if it had imploded. But her lips were still moving, the distortion of the image doubtless creating the rictus recalling the beginnings or the end of a smile. She was seen closing her eyes, repeatedly and very quickly shaking her head from left to right, opening her mouth as if she had suddenly found herself short of air; she had tried to start breathing again, to exorcise by her movements the suffocation that threatened her — she had once again refused the horror of ceasing to breathe...]

With considerable pathos, Lacoue-Labarthe takes us through the consequences of the physiological events unfolding (the references to the distortion of the image suggest that the event is being witnessed on a video screen). It is notable that this is not simply a case of the physical coming to dominate the metaphysical, in some demonstration of the limitations on human beings' attempts to create or perform art (in this case by singing). Instead, a real struggle against the attack is depicted: the show, as it were, had to go on. But at the same time, this is an early instance of Lacoue-Labarthe's tendency to address the metaphysical aspect of song almost exclusively in terms of its interaction with the physical world. His interest seems to lie not in some metaphysical essence in and of itself, but rather in the fact that the latter exists as that which is always just out of reach, that which can never be fully present in any stable or definitive way. In short, this passage seizes this singer's demise as a contemporary event to make its point regarding Western opera and indeed song in general: the point being that the latter is always already dying or expiring, it always already has difficulties with breathing (or literally, in-spiration), perhaps because it exists precisely in order to address this breakdown in inspiration.

Having looked at the explicitly contemporary background to the attack the singer suffers in the published version of 'L'"Allégorie"', we can now move on to that text itself. Beyond the excisions of lines from notable operas — and the gathering of those based on the *Lamentations* as a 'Prétexte' preceding the main section — the text mixes together two main elements. The first is the description of the singer on stage suffering some sort of attack, perhaps a stroke or heart attack. The second element appears to be wholly unconnected to the first: it consists in descriptions of a mountain or wilderness landscape and a failed expedition that takes place there, where the unnamed protagonists lose their way and remain stuck on the hillside overnight: 'des branches cingleraient le visage, on s'écorcherait aux ronces; bientôt, il faudrait avancer en tâtonnant et les paumes des mains se déchireraient aux pierres' (ALEG 30–31; ['branches would be scratching at our faces; soon, we would have to grope our way forwards, and the palms of our hands would be torn by the rocks']). The emphasis here is on an inhabitable hostility; the non-human environment is unwelcoming and even does violence to the earth itself: we read of 'des mousses qui se confondent avec les pierres où elles s'accrochent et qui finissent par recouvrir presque entièrement le sol qu'elles asphyxient' (ALEG 27; ['moss which blends into the rock on which it grows, ending up almost completely covering the ground, asphyxiating it']).[22] However, despite the apparent lack of relation it seems that there is a connection between the operatic and mountain elements, and indeed this connection is crucial in demonstrating what lies behind Lacoue-Labarthe's interest in opera and song: namely both the attraction and the impossibility of metaphysics.

This is to say that the stubbornly physical aspects of the landscape described serve to throw into greater relief the non-physical song that in the text emerges alongside it; similarly, the physical suffering undergone by the singer is not recounted for mawkish or pathetic (in the proper sense) reasons, but to underline how her physical body struggles to continue singing, i.e. producing music, which after all is a physically impalpable art-form. Throughout the text, the narrating voice switches unexpectedly between the two registers, between descriptions of landscape and the sketch of the dying singer. For instance, the first example of such switching is found in the opening of the main section:

> Souvent —, le soir, on entend un chant très pur et l'on pense à la mort d'une cantatrice, car cette voix qui chante expire avec la provenance de la nuit: c'est la fin de l'été, dans un pays de montagne. L'air est vif et sec. Au tiers de la pente, on domine une très vaste plaine qui repose, visible jusqu'à ses confins, dans la clarté du soir. (ALEG 24)

> [Often — in the evening, you hear a very pure song and you think of the death of a singer, because this singing voice is expiring with the coming of night: it is the end of summer, in a mountain landscape. The air is lively and dry. A third of the way up the incline, you are looking down into an extremely wide plain which is at rest, seeing even its far side, in the clarity of evening.]

The link between the two registers or aspects of the text begins to become explicit via an insistence on certain shared characteristics. For instance, in discussing the intermingling of voices accompanying the lead singer, the text evokes the impenetrable thickness of wild grassland:

> ... ici — du bruissement confus de la lumière parmi l'herbe couchée —, de l'ample et bas murmure du chœur s'élèvent une à une, se mêlent puis se taisent et reprennent successivement des voix d'hommes et de femmes [...], qui chantent une souffrance ou célèbrent une mort... Mais l'herbe est impénétrable (ALEG 27).

> [... here — from the muddled rustling of the light amidst the flattened grass —, from the wide, low murmur of the chorus, one by one, men's and women's voices rise, mix together, alternately ceasing and then continuing [...], singing of suffering or to mark a death... But the grass is impenetrable.]

The same connection, between the intermingling of light amongst the grass and that of choral voices, is made when it comes to the soloist. She is described as moving through the grass and emerging from it (in other words, her voice emerges from those of the accompanying singers):

> [la cantatrice] porte une robe noire somptueuse.......... d'entre les herbes, elle apparaît et s'avance, — dans le désordre de l'herbe. Elle marche vers la lumière qui la divise et couche derrière elle son ombre sur le sol: ainsi provient-elle des ténèbres et quand elle est passée, une trace profonde est marquée dans l'herbe.......... (ALEG 28)

> [[the singer] is wearing a sumptuous black dress.......... from amongst the grasses, she appears and moves forward, — in the disorder of the grass. She walks

> towards the light which splits her in two and lays her shadow down behind her
> on the ground: she thus comes from the shadows and when she has passed by,
> a deep track is left in the grass...........]

It is notable that we are far from a bucolic natural landscape: the grass represents disorder, that which is untameable and resistant; accordingly, it seems that similar qualities can be attributed to the music from and against which the solo singer emerges. Performing music — which Lacoue-Labarthe intends to stand for writing in its general relation to the metaphysical — is less an affair of romantic inspiration and enthusiasm than it is an ordeal. This can be confirmed by returning to the motif of the singer's suffering and death, which is the main focus of the final parts of the text.

In the latter, we read that three singers are standing near the front of the stage, and that the main soloist steps forward from this line. Suddenly, an event — seemingly a physiological attack of some kind, though it is left unspecified — occurs. It is described as follows:

> son visage se tord affreusement, son corps s'agite, elle tend les mains devant son visage. Ses yeux s'agrandissent comme sous l'effet de la peur. On dirait qu'elle va mourir, qu'elle succombe dans un dernier tremblement [...].
>
>   C'est à peine si maintenant elle trouve la force d'un dernier chant pour célébrer toutes les voix qui ont agité l'obscurité de son corps.......... (sa passion.......... cette lente et désespérante dépossession, cet effondrement vertigineux au centre même où se faisait le chant) (ALEG 29–30).

> [her face contracts horrifically, her body convulses, she holds out her hands in front of her face. Her eyes grow wide as if she were afraid. It looks as if she is about to die, as though she is giving in to a final trembling [...].
>
>   She barely manages to find the strength for a last song celebrating all the voices that have animated the darkness of her body.......... (her passion.......... this slow, despair-inducing dispossession, this vertiginous collapse of the very centre in which song was produced)].

Again, what is depicted here is not a simple surrender to the demands of one's body. A struggle is going on: the singer is only 'barely' able to find the strength to sing, but find it she does. In this existential drama which is understood by the audience as having reached a critical moment — 'it looks as if she is about to die' — she does not abandon what seemed to be only a role, a fiction being acted out: the importance she places on song is clear from the way this struggle is carried on in the face of adversity. Something of this importance comes through in the narrator's description of the song as having touched upon 'the darkness of her body': this is to say that without this song, her body would only have been darkness, something without illumination, inhumane and brutish. After a last return to the imagery of the mountainside, in which the unnamed ramblers are also shown in severe difficulty, we come to the final passage. This does not present the obvious or expected conclusion of the singer dying. Instead, Lacoue-Labarthe leaves the text at a point of oscillation or in-betweenness, as can be seen here:

> elle ne cesse de réapparaître, la même voix ne cesse de chanter, quoi qu'il arrive, même si, murmure à peine audible, elle ne chante que son propre déchirement et sa fin toujours proche, puisqu'on sait, dans le mouvement que font les

lèvres pour s'ouvrir, entre le souffle et son manque.......... le vertige est infini, précisément.......... Elle ne cesse de disparaître (ALEG 31).

[she reappears endlessly, the same voice sings endlessly, no matter what, even if this barely audible murmur only sings its own tearing-apart and its own nearing end, because it is known that, in the opening movement of the lips, between breath and its absence.......... the vertigo is infinite, precisely.......... She disappears [*disparaît*] endlessly.]

At this point of crisis, mid-way through the attack that the singer suffers on stage before an audience, everything seems to have slowed down and become dissociated. No one side seems to gain the upper hand in the struggle between the song (representing the metaphysical), which wants to carry on, and the singer's body (representing the physical), which is threatened with imminent expiration, in all senses of the term (the French *disparaître* means both to disappear and to die). Lacoue-Labarthe's choice of phrasing is deliberate in preventing any ultimate distinction between the two processes: 'she reappears endlessly' and 'she disappears endlessly'.

In truth, however, this apparently ambiguous conclusion can convey several key aspects of the argument being made via what we must remember is an 'allegory' — the inverted commas are Lacoue-Labarthe's — for the writer and writing: 'la cantatrice n'est rien d'autre que l'allégorie de l'écrivain (ou: le chant n'est rien d'autre que l'allégorie de l'écriture)' ['the singer is nothing other than the allegory of the writer | (or: the song is nothing other than the allegory of writing)']. First of all, although he extensively probes the attraction and the impact of the metaphysical, he does not do so in order to seek its rehabilitation. There is no sense that he wishes the singer could simply sing the allegorical song — indeed, there is no representation of that song except in its limit-state. Translated into philosophical language, this is tantamount to saying that metaphysics calls to be deconstructed. Second, though by the same token, what is represented here is a struggle rather than an outright victory for what lies outside or is opposed to 'song'. In other words, Lacoue-Labarthe is not celebrating any clear-cut victory over metaphysics or the inauguration of any alternative, non-philosophical language. This we can translate as deconstruction (with which he identifies) being something other than a simply oppositional approach, but instead one that works in and through the existence of previous critical languages and bodies of knowledge. Lacoue-Labarthe, despite spending a surprising amount of energy exploring a transcendent metaphysical impulse surely foreign to many accounts of deconstructive thought, in fact adapts the latter in a bold and refreshing way. And he does so through his attention to opera as an allegory for writing. The necessary counterpart to these investigations, giving us a greater sense of the weight that writing bore in his mind, is to be found in the work by which he approaches poetic or literary writing.

Notes to Chapter 4c

1. In *Scène* suivi de *Dialogue sur le dialogue*, pp. 14–15.
2. *Einstein on the Beach* was first performed at the Avignon festival in 1976, and has been reprised beginning in 2012 in numerous locations.

3. Ibid., p. 15.
4. It is sometimes argued that metaphysics is a misleading term, referring not to that which lies beyond (meta-) the physical, but simply referring to the title of the *Metaphysics*, the work following the *Physics* in Aristotle's writings. Nonetheless, Lacoue-Labarthe did often understand metaphysics as the meta-physical and I therefore use the term in that sense.
5. In *Scène* suivi de *Dialogue sur le dialogue*, p. 15 (emphasis original).
6. Ibid., p. 15.
7. In Lacoue-Labarthe and Steiner, 'Correspondance ouverte', pp. 18–19.
8. Unless stated otherwise, all material quoted here and below is from the archive at IMEC in LAC 11.7; emphasis original.
9. In 'Richard Wagner in Bayreuth', in *The Untimely Meditations (Thoughts out of Season parts I and II)*, trans. by Anthony M. Ludovici and Adrian Collins (New York: Digireads, 2009), pp. 54–94 (p. 79).
10. Interestingly, a note in *Le Mythe nazi* elevates the work on Wagner's reception to a status equivalent to *La Fiction du politique*, both stemming from his and Nancy's work on the political; p. 17.
11. Lacoue-Labarthe states that Nietzsche is *le grand absent* from this survey of reactions to the German composer, although in fact the thinker features heavily in the Heidegger chapter; in 'Nietzsche contre Wagner: Chronique d'une rupture annoncée' ['How a Rupture was Announced'], in *Le Nouvel Observateur*, 1545 (16–22 June 1994), p. 126.
12. In *Musica ficta*, p. 12 (emphasis original); *Musica Ficta*, p. xv.
13. In *Le Mythe nazi*, p. 48.
14. In *Musica ficta*, pp. 37–38 (emphases original); *Musica Ficta*, pp. 6–7 (emphases original).
15. In *Musica ficta*, pp. 38–39 (emphases original); *Musica Ficta*, p. 7 (emphases original).
16. In a dossier with the code LIV 1966 F (not presently held at IMEC); this reference applies to all quotations in the remainder of this chapter, unless indicated otherwise.
17. In the archival dossier LIV 1966 F.
18. The statement on the *Requiem* is found in 'Lettre (c'est une lettre)' ['Letter (This is a Letter)'], in Bénézet, Blanchot, Lacoue-Labarthe et al., *Misère de la littérature* ([*Poverty of Literature*]; Paris: Bourgois, 1978), pp. 55–72 (p. 67).
19. In the archival dossier, not currently held at IMEC, NOT 1964 A.
20. In 'Naissance (?) d'un opéra', in LIV 1966 F.
21. Ibid.
22. In similar vein, Lacoue-Labarthe coins the term 'dépaysagement', bringing together *dépaysement* ['disorientation'] and *paysage* ['landscape'], in an article introducing photographs of deserts by Thibaut Cuisset, *Le Dehors absolu* [*The Absolute Outside*]; 'Le Dépaysagement', in *Écrits sur l'art*, pp. 249–55.

CHAPTER 5

Phrase

We have seen how a thinking and practice of the stage lead Lacoue-Labarthe both to relate to and distance himself from various philosophical and metaphysical traditions, and how that line of enquiry is not alone in inflecting his reflections on philosophy carried out in proximity to Nancy and Derrida. For his work is influenced considerably, albeit in an often subterranean way, by the idea and the practice of writing.

It is necessary to choose our words carefully here. For to state that this interest of Lacoue-Labarthe's can be defined as 'literature' risks returning to the dualism between literature and philosophy that we saw him deconstruct via a thinking of *l'écriture*. Indeed, his use of 'l'écriture' to refer to a radically destabilizing, non-locatable principle suggests that there will be no easy habitation of a given written form at any point in his career. For instance, the term 'fiction' is altogether too associated with *la fiction du politique*, a communitarian identification with a central narrative, figure or figurality. As for another possible term, 'poetry', he has written that 'j'exècre ce qu'on range de manière emphatique sous le nom de "poésie"' (PH 19; ['I loathe what is emphatically classed under the name of "poetry"']). Many well-trodden avenues for exploring singular or fragmented modes of expression are therefore closed off to us. Faced with such a situation, it seems best to adopt a double strategy — on the one hand, looking at Lacoue-Labarthe's reasons for not adopting terms such as 'literature', 'fiction', or 'poetry', whilst on the other, addressing his practice of writing via a term he used for a late collection of texts, *Phrase*. The omission of the article here — he does not write *la phrase* —, serves to signal that this term is no longer entirely a common noun, compatible with and able to circulate within mainstream conceptual discourse. Instead of acting as a common noun (*nom commun*), it acts as a proper name (*nom propre*), thereby interrupting — if this is possible within language — the generalizing processes of comprehension and proposing instead a stubborn, fragmented singularity. Such is the motif informing Lacoue-Labarthe's relation to writing and the cause of his unwillingness to adopt pre-existing conceptions of it.

In a similar vein, the writers admired by Lacoue-Labarthe are those for whom literature is not a straightforward practice, but a site of ambiguity or question. He corresponded with Maurice Blanchot and with Roger Laporte, as well as often writing on them, as he also did on Paul Celan, Friedrich Hölderlin, and others. What is more, in his work the line between criticism and practice is thoroughly blurred; the dream of being a writer inflects Lacoue-Labarthe's narrative of his own work in important ways. For instance, he wrote that '[i]l a fallu m'admettre après coup — la loi de ce retard est effrayante — né pour la littérature. "Écrivain" était un mot magique. Un livre, la chose au monde la plus bouleversante' ['I had to admit, after the fact — the law of this delay is terrifying — that I was born for literature. "Writer" was a magical word. A book was the most overwhelming thing in the world'].[1] The strength of this impulse or attraction affected Lacoue-Labarthe's thinking despite or owing to the fact that his literary ambitions were to remain fragmentary. Nancy, for his part, writes that the idea of Lacoue-Labarthe as a writer informed the pair's relationship at an early stage: 'Philippe fut pour moi sinon tout de suite, du moins très vite et de manière soulignée, la figure de l'écrivain' ['Philippe for me, if not straight away then very quickly, was the figure of the writer'].[2] And beyond this, in the 1970s Lacoue-Labarthe collaborated with Mathieu Bénézet (and others, including Nancy) on a series of projects that were more oriented toward writing than the work around *L'Absolu littéraire* and shortly afterwards on the political.[3] Nonetheless, these various involvements in group activity — to which can be added the theatre collaborations with Michel Deutsch and the grouping around Nancy, Derrida, Kofman, et al. — shared a similar aim. Speaking of *Première livraison*, a journal co-edited with Bénézet, Lacoue-Labarthe later stated that '1976 était encore une époque où nous cherchions à nous déprendre des mouvements d'avant-garde, *Tel Quel* et tous ses succédanés — tout ce qui avait occupé la scène pendant les dix ou quinze dernières années' ['1976 was still an era when we were trying to free ourselves of the avant-garde movements, *Tel Quel* and all the imitations of it — everything that had occupied centre stage for the previous ten or fifteen years'].[4] In other words, the aim was to question theoretical self-reflexivity taken as a touchstone or fixed value, instead exploring the limits and blind-spots of such a mode of thinking.

The hypothesis that Lacoue-Labarthe's texts and writerly practices address a *phrase* therefore poses the following question: given the tendency for deconstruction to be oriented towards singularity rather than conceptual generality, might Lacoue-Labarthe go further than either Derrida or Nancy in his dedication to the singularity of writing? But a problem arises insofar as in his remarks on the topic this dedication is often couched in terms of an overarching dedication to writing (e.g. 'I was born for literature'): might this approach, almost metaphysical in its single-mindedness, by that same token fundamentally distort the very singularity addressed by the first hypothesis? These hypotheses inform this chapter, which is divided into two sections. First, we look at Lacoue-Labarthe's reading of Celan in *La Poésie comme expérience*, which develops the notions of caesura and interruption previously explored in relation to Hölderlin. The second section then explores Lacoue-Labarthe's own writing via various aspects of the poetic collection *Phrase* (2000), notably its dialogue with Blanchot in texts that would only be united posthumously as *Agonie terminée, agonie interminable* (2011).

La Poésie comme expérience

The title of Lacoue-Labarthe's 1986 book on Paul Celan echoes that of John Dewey's *Art as Experience*, but whilst it performs a similar move away from the view of writing or poetry as an artefact or final product, here unlike in Dewey there is no compensatory privileging of art or poetry as an ongoing process.[5] Instead, Lacoue-Labarthe tells us that to live one's experience as poetry means to live it as the fragmentation or interruption of wider narratives. Figuring prominently among these narratives is that of art as the expression of some universal human spirit; thus poetry is able to interrupt art, rather than being part of it. Indeed, as Lacoue-Labarthe writes in a ventriloquization of Celan's thought — but which can also be taken to be close to his own position — 'la poésie est l'interruption de l'art' ['poetry is the interruption of art'].[6] In short, his horizons on this point are radically wide, and he suggests that even as broad a notion as art is too limiting when it comes to measuring all the implications of the interruption that Celan addresses. This is the light in which Lacoue-Labarthe draws out of Celan an interrogation of various motifs in his own thinking: on the one hand Heidegger's silence regarding the concentration camps, and on the other the thesis (as expounded in 1987's *Fiction du politique*) that '[d]ans l'apocalypse d'Auschwitz ce n'est ni plus ni moins que l'Occident, en son essence, qui s'est révélé' (FP 59; ['In the Auschwitz apocalypse, it was nothing more or less than the West, in its essence, that revealed itself'; HAP 35, trans. mod.]). As in other parts of his oeuvre, the emphasis placed here upon interruption is so strong that he is able to use the non-deconstructive term 'essence'; here we have a thinker striking out on his own rather than remaining within the horizons of his deconstructive associates.

The first part of *La Poésie comme expérience* is spent looking at two Celan poems, 'Tübingen, Jännar' ['Tübingen, January'] and 'Todtnauberg' ['Todtnauberg']. The titles alone make clear the interest in the relation between place and thought, both in the case of Hölderlin, who spent thirty-six years of his life in the infamous tower in Tübingen, and in that of Celan who visited Heidegger at his mountain hut in Todtnauberg. In both cases, Celan's visit to the place in question is a matter for discussion (Lacoue-Labarthe himself in turn visited both Tübingen and Todtnauberg). The discussion begins by reproducing both poems in German, later quoting the two existing French translations of each poem (PE 19–22; PE2 9–12), and finally providing his own translations (PE 28–29, 52–53; PE2 16–17, 34–35). Although he states that his ultimate aim is not a study in comparative translation, the scholarly approach adopted is illuminating in this domain, and can be read in parallel with his translations of Hölderlin (see chapter 4b). Again, his avowed preference is for a literalist rather than naturalizing approach; indeed, André du Bouchet, one of the translators quoted, is criticized for his use of canonical French poetic language to translate the German: 'le style, "mallarméen" si l'on veut, des traductions d'André du Bouchet, leur afféterie ou leur préciosité, ne rendent pas justice à la dureté lapidaire, à l'abrupt de la langue maniée par Celan' (PE 22; ['the "Mallarmean" style of André du Bouchet's translations, their effete or precious quality, does not do justice to the lapidary hardness, the abruptness of language as handled by Celan'; PE2 12]). In Lacoue-Labarthe's reading, fragmentation is therefore privileged over fluidity, and an approach closely following every contour is preferred to one soaring free of the original. This approach may or may not be valid for translations into French from a variety of languages; but the fact is that Lacoue-Labarthe's attention is given overwhelmingly to German texts — the concrete abruptness of translation style he proposes corresponds to his vision of poets such as Celan bringing out concrete abruptness as an essential quality of the German language. As we read,

> Prosodie et syntaxe, chez Celan, surtout vers la fin, font violence à la langue: elles la hachent, la désarticulent, l'abrègent (c'est-à-dire la coupent). Il y a là quelque chose d'assurément comparable à ce qui se passe dans les dernières esquisses, 'parataxiques' comme dit Adorno, de Hölderlin: condensation et juxtaposition, étranglement de la langue (PE 22–23).

> [Especially in his late work, prosody and syntax do violence to language: they chop, dislocate, truncate or cut it. Something in this certainly bears comparison to what occurs in Hölderlin's last, 'paratactic' efforts, as Adorno calls them: condensation and juxtaposition, a strangling of language (PE2 13).]

These qualities, which Lacoue-Labarthe sees in both Celan and Hölderlin (the comparison is explicit here), would appear to be simply aesthetic ones, ways of reiterating and altering a metrical or prosodic tradition: in this view, their sole function would be to disarticulate and interrupt classical, literary German. But it soon becomes clear that in Lacoue-Labarthe's mind, these qualities of poetic language in fact represent something like a machine for thinking, which can be set to work on issues lying outside of what is formally metrical or literary. In other words, the poetic capacity for interruption serves to disarticulate a wider range of discourses of totality and continuity. This is the case in the analysis of 'Todtnauberg', which was written following Celan's visit to Heidegger in his hut in the Black Forest located in the hamlet named in the poem's title. It addresses the poet's desire that the philosopher express some remorse for his involvement with Nazism, mentioning — with disarming simplicity, given the issue at hand — his addition to the hut's visitor's book:

> là, dans le livre
> [...]
> la ligne écrite sur
> un espoir, aujourd'hui,
> dans le mot
> à venir
> d'un penseur (PE 52, trans. Lacoue-Labarthe).

> [there, in the book
> [...]
> the line written in
> a hope, today,
> for the word
> to come
> of a thinker; PE2 52, trans. mod.]

That no such word — for instance of apology or even recognition — was offered by Heidegger at the time or subsequently confirms the unfulfilled, interrupted status of Celan's wish.

Let us look now at the other poem discussed by Lacoue-Labarthe, 'Tübingen, Jännar' (the second part of the title is an archaic spelling of January). It relates or stems from Celan's visit to Tübingen to see the tower by the Neckar river in which, following Hölderlin's return from Bordeaux and his declaration that 'Apollo has struck me', he spent 36 years in what is known as his madness.[7] However, it is important for Lacoue-Labarthe's argument that whilst relating to this visit to Tübingen, Celan's poem does not simply recount or represent it. He writes that '[l]e poème n'est pas né dans l'instant de la visite à la *Hölderlinturm*. Il n'est proprement né dans aucun instant' ['[t]he poem was not born in the moment of the *Hölderlinturm* visit. Properly speaking, it was not born in any moment'], before continuing to argue that one reason for approaching the poem in this way is that 'un vertige, un éblouissement, ne fait jamais aucun instant, par définition' (PE 35; ['dizziness or bedazzlement by definition never constitutes a moment', PE2 21]). Thus the vertigo that is recounted in the poem is one that takes us away from the unfolding of personal experience, from circumscription or rootedness in any particular time or place (for instance Tübingen in January). This can be seen in the reading that Lacoue-Labarthe constructs from his translation of the poem's opening: the German describes the reaction to seeing Hölderlin's tower as follows: 'Zur Blindheit über-| redete Augen' (PE 13; ['Eyes talked into | blindness']).[8] The translation given by the French thinker is: 'Sous un flot d'éloquence | aveuglés, les yeux' (PE 28; ['Beneath a flow of eloquence | blinded, the eyes', PE2 16]). Now, his declarations on his approach to translation are not wholly followed through insofar as this is not exactly a literal translation, and is certainly less so than the Martine Broda version Lacoue-Labarthe had previously quoted ('[d]es yeux sous les paroles | Aveuglés,' PE 20; ['Eyes under words | blinded']). But if he abandons his declared, literalist approach in this way, it is because employing the natural-sounding French idiom 'un flot d'éloquence' presents another advantage. Namely, this is that a tighter link is drawn between the Neckar flowing beneath Hölderlin's tower, and the river or flow of words addressed by Celan in the poem's opening. We can see this when Lacoue-Labarthe writes:

> ce qui provoque le vertige et rappelle les eaux du Neckar, ce ne sont pas les eaux du Neckar, c'est un autre fleuve: c'est le fleuve hölderlinien lui-même. Ce qu'il faut entendre doublement: le fleuve, ou les fleuves, que chante Hölderlin (le Rhin, l'Ister, la source du Danube, etc.), et la poésie de Hölderlin comme fleuve. Ou, ainsi que nous disons, comme 'flot d'éloquence' (PE 35).

> [what brings on the dizziness and recalls the waters of the Neckar is not those waters, but another river: the Hölderlinian river itself. A double meaning here: first the river, or rivers, that Hölderlin sings (the Rhine, the Ister, the source of the Danube, etc.), and then the river of Hölderlin's poetry. Or, as I have said, the 'flood of eloquence' (PE2 21).]

In other words, the waters of the Neckar are evoked by Celan's poem, and all the more so in what Lacoue-Labarthe presents as his more explicit or interpretative

French translation of it, opening with the words '[s]ous un flot d'éloquence'. But paradoxically, they are evoked merely in order for the poem to distance itself from any standard representation or narrative of the town as Celan saw it on his visit there. This is to say that rather than poetry presenting an account of lived experience, we are always already within poetry, witnessing poetic language commenting reflexively on itself (and past versions of itself, in this case Hölderlin's production). The 'flood' at first seems to refer to the real river, but because it is a 'flood of eloquence' we realise that it is a metaphorical or poetic river — indeed, the river of poetic metaphor itself.

However, for Lacoue-Labarthe, unlike for contemporaries such as *Tel Quel*, to comment on this reflexivity of poetic discourse is not necessarily to endorse it. Indeed, the argument that he constructs out of his translation does not maintain that such a practice of thinking poetry, of poetry concerned with the legacy and the possibility of poetry itself, is necessarily anything to be celebrated. In his words, the poem 'n'est pas [...] une célébration de Hölderlin (il dirait plutôt l'être-floué par Hölderlin). [...]. Le poème dit la "noyade" dans la poésie de Hölderlin' (PE 37; '[is not] a celebration of Hölderlin (it comes closer to saying how Hölderlin swindles us). [...]. The poem speaks the experience of "drowning" in Hölderlin's verse'; PE2 22, trans. mod.]). Hölderlin's poetry certainly pays extensive attention to rivers, even before his confinement above the waters of the Neckar — see amongst others his poems 'The River Main', 'The Neckar', 'The Fettered River', 'The Rhine', 'Remembrance' (on the Garonne at Bordeaux; Lacoue-Labarthe translated the poem), and 'The Ister' (a name for the Danube and also the title of the film featuring Lacoue-Labarthe discussing Hölderlin).[9] But in Lacoue-Labarthe's reading, this feature is altered and distorted by Celan to the point where the force of the rivers evoked threatens to drown anyone attempting to write poetry — the 'flot' of his French translation easily merges into 'l'être-floué', being swindled. Poetry, then, represents a language that it is impossible to speak, one representing a danger of drowning to those who would enter it. This understanding has much in common with *Phrase* where, as we shall see, Lacoue-Labarthe replaces the Romantic approach to poetry as inspiration with a thinking of asphyxiation.

Beyond the two poems 'Tübingen, Jännar' and 'Todtnauberg', his reading of Celan also takes in *Der Meridian* (1961), 'pratiquement le seul document de sa poétique' (PE 9; ['practically the only document of his poetics']), and explores the collection *Atemwende*, whose title he translates as *Tournant du souffle* (*The Turning-Point of Breath*). These aspects of his reading redouble the gesture relating to the overwhelming, stultifying force of Hölderlin's poetry which led it to be conceived of as a river. In these further sections of *La Poésie comme expérience*, such qualities are attributed to art as a whole — and notably, poetry is not taken as a representative of that art, i.e. one of the many forms contributing to it, but instead as a method of resisting it. In Lacoue-Labarthe's words, '["Le Méridien" dit] [n]on pas exactement que l'art est étranger à la poésie mais bien, oui, que la poésie est l'interruption de l'art. Quelque chose, si l'on veut, comme le "souffle coupé" de l'art (je pense au motif de l'*Atemwende*, du "tournant du souffle", qui fait là chez Celan sa première apparition)' (PE 65; ['["The Meridian" says] [n]ot, exactly, that art is a stranger to poetry, but that yes, poetry is the interruption of art. Something, if you will, that "takes art's breath away" (I am thinking of the motif of the *Atemwende*, of the "turn-of-breath", which makes its first appearance in Celan here)'; PE2 44, trans. mod.]). In other words, Celan's poetics as expressed in this work raises the possibility of an interruption of art, which we can read as an interruption of art conceived as a possibility, i.e. as something which it is possible to create and to react to. The art that is interrupted in this way is therefore a possible language, a well-functioning system enabling the transfer and general circulation of sense. In place of this model, poetry acts as a reminder of what happens when language breaks down, when fragmentation replaces fluidity or circulation. In Lacoue-Labarthe's words,

> L'interruption du langage, le suspens du langage, la césure (la 'suspension anti-rythmique', disait Hölderlin), c'est donc cela, la poésie: 'le souffle et la parole coupés', le 'tournant' du souffle, le 'tournant à la fin de l'inspiration'. La poésie advient là où cède, contre toute attente, le langage (PE 74).

> [The interruption of language, the suspension of language, the caesura ('counter-rhythmic rupture', said Hölderlin) — that is poetry, then. 'Robbed of breath and speech', the 'turn' of breath, the 'turn at the end of inspiration'. Poetry occurs where language, contrary to all expectations, gives way (PE2 49).]

This is to say that when language gives way, perhaps doing so unexpectedly, poetry remains as a fragment, speaking in and as interruption. Beyond this, it is notable that here and throughout this reading of Celan, the language is that of an end to inspiration. This should be understood both in the Romantic sense of an effusion, the poet's overwhelming sense of creative possibility, and in the more literal sense of a breathing-in. This second sense of inspiration, breathing, is of course necessary for life; but Lacoue-Labarthe insists upon distancing his reading from this understanding precisely in order to avoid the assumption that poetry creates a liveable atmosphere.

Instead, it might be that which is impossible; or rather, it might speak to us of the moments in Western history that are impossibly horrifying, exceeding our capacity to understand them (not least the atrocities of Nazism for which Heidegger failed to apologise, even after the opportunity provided by Celan's visit to Todtnauberg). This is the reading presented by Lacoue-Labarthe in an interview:

> [Heidegger] ne pouvait pas percevoir ce que j'essaie d'appeler césure. [...] Moi, je maintiendrais cela en pensant cette histoire de souffle, du suspens du souffle. Il y a un recueil de Celan qui s'appelle *Atemwende, Tournant du souffle*, ça pourrait s'interpréter un petit peu de la même manière. [...] L'esprit a toujours été défini à partir du souffle [...] en tous les cas *pneuma, spiritus, anima, animus*, etc., tout ça a à voir avec le souffle. Je dirais qu'après cette césure on a du mal à reprendre notre souffle. Nous sommes non pas asphyxiés (parce que ce serait l'oubli), mais après tout on respire peu — même si on respire encore. Disons que l'humanité, ou en tout cas l'humanité européenne — c'est large, très large — a des difficultés pulmonaires. Je dirais qu'il y a une sorte d'emphysème historiale.[10]

> [[Heidegger] was not able to see what I am trying to call caesura [...]. Personally, it is the idea of breath, of the suspension of breath, which would allow me to think in this way. There is a collection by Celan named *Atemwende*, which one could interpret as *The Turning-Point of Breath* [...]. Spirit has always been defined

beginning from breath [...] in any case *pneuma, spiritus, anima, animus*, etc., all that is related to breath. I would say that after this caesura we are struggling to get our breath back. We are not asphyxiated (because this would be sheer oblivion), but ultimately we are barely able to breathe — even if we are still breathing. Let us say that humanity, or at least European humanity — it is broad, very broad — has pulmonary difficulties. I would say that there is a sort of historial emphysema.]

The concreteness of the medical terms on which this passage closes suggests, despite the emphasis on the end of inspiration and the breathlessness or impossibility it leads to, that some role might remain for a fragmented, residual treatment of inspiration and its absence. If we collectively suffer from 'historial emphysema', then the situation can at least be noted and described. In order to continue our exploration of Lacoue-Labarthe's approach to this marginal, uncertain possibility — rather than to locate and exposit texts unambiguously affirming that poetry can be identified with some metaphorical sense of asphyxiation — let us turn to the aspects of his work that most closely resemble a practice of writing.

Phrase

In *Le Chant des muses: petite conférence sur la musique* (2005), a text stemming from Lacoue-Labarthe's intervention before an audience of children, he makes a revealing statement. It reads as follows:

> La science moderne du langage montre que ce qui est premier, dans le langage, ce ne sont pas les mots (isolés, pris un à un [...]), mais les *phrases*: une certaine organisation, un ordre ou une 'structure' sonore préalable, dans laquelle, ensuite, on fait entrer les mots: structure de la demande (ou de la question), de la plainte, de la satisfaction, de l'exigence, etc. L'enfant, tout petit, avant de savoir ou d'articuler un seul mot, 'gazouille'. Cela semble insignifiant. Mais en étudiant ce 'gazouillis' de près, on voit que l'enfant apprend à *phraser* (une fois de plus un mot grec, on va finir par en prendre l'habitude, qui signifie 'parler': les Grecs avaient beaucoup de mots pour désigner la parole).[11]

> [Modern linguistics shows that what is primordial, in language, is not words (isolated, taken individually [...]), but *phrases*: a given way of organizing, a pre-existing order or 'structure' of sounds, into which words can subsequently be placed: for instance the structures of requests (or questions), complaints, satisfaction, orders given, etc. When they are still very small, children 'gurgle', before knowing or articulating any single word. This seems insignificant. But by closely studying this 'gurgling', we see that the child is learning to *phrase* (another Greek word, you will get used to it, which means 'to speak': the Greeks had many words for speech).]

Several points stand out here: first, in presenting the discoveries of '[m]odern linguistics', Lacoue-Labarthe is in fact reiterating a principle of deconstructive reading: that discourses cannot be reduced to abstract terms or concepts, but instead rely on subtleties of emphasis and repetition. Second, this layer in language lying beyond the conceptual means that it functions in relation to itself as well as to an exterior body of references. In this sense, language shares functions with music —

and indeed, the notion of a phrase or phrasing is ambiguous, potentially referring to music just as much as to language or literature. And third, the statement that 'the Greeks had many words for referring to speech' sets up an implicit distinction between *phrase* and the more common Greek term for language (but not for that alone): *logos*. To follow these three points through, by giving the title *Phrase* to his collection of texts published a few years previously to *Le Chant des muses*, Lacoue-Labarthe is therefore setting it up as follows: first as needing to be read not simply on the basis of concepts but deconstructively, second as problematizing the distinction between poetry and music (with all the latter's metaphysical significance in his mind), and finally he is setting up *Phrase* as lying outside the realm of *logos* (understood as language, order, reasoning).

It is not simply the collection's title that suggests the importance of *phrase* as a motif, but the titles given to each of the work's twenty-one sections. Each is numbered sequentially as 'Phrase I', 'Phrase II', etc., and the vast majority also bear a subtitle. One such subtitle features twice: it is '[c]larification', reminding us that whilst Lacoue-Labarthe's writing here stands outside philosophical language, it is no less oriented towards clarity or clarification. Each of the twenty-one sections is dated, and the fact that these dates range from 1976 to 2000 means that no one period in Lacoue-Labarthe's production is particularly privileged. This collection therefore provides no sense of an early poetic vocation being abandoned, in the way sometimes suggested by Lacoue-Labarthe's own comments on his possible status as a writer: it was merely kept under wraps before publication late on in his career. Another notable element is that in an interview, Lacoue-Labarthe stated of *Phrase* that 'quand j'ai pris la décision de le publier, je le dis une fois pour qu'on ne parle plus, j'étais dans une clinique psychiatrique' ['when I took the decision to publish it, I say this once in order to avoid endless speculation, I was in a psychiatric clinic'].[12] Placed under a sign involving illness, the collection is hereby set in a category apart from much of the rest of Lacoue-Labarthe's writing, which provides no formal reference to its author beyond the ordinary ones (and at the end of 1975's 'Typographie' even gestures in the opposite direction, undermining even the apparently minimal biographical reference of the author's signature by placing the latter in inverted commas). And whilst the desire for clarification is not necessarily diminished by this meta-discursive comment, it can help to provide nuance. Indeed, 'Phrase XIX (Prose)' describes the psychiatric hospital in which Lacoue-Labarthe finds himself: 'La clinique où je suis est propre, nette, blanche' (PH 114; ['The clinic I am in is clean, tidy, white']). More importantly — and perhaps problematically — it discusses his relationship with the other patients:

> Ceux-là, si proches, sont déjà
> morts. Leur élocution à peine audible
> est la véridiction. C'est pour apprendre ce balbutiement
> que j'ai choisi de venir ici, contre moi,
> au bord de la menace et de la destruction,
> dans cette infâme solitude, entre les tables
> de la cafétéria, les arbres du parc,
> non pour me ressaisir ou renoncer à l'éloquence,
> mais pour essayer de dire au plus près

> ce à quoi je dois renoncer:
> cette falsification amère, ce discours
> évasif, ces restes (cet excédant) de 'poésie'
> qui ont détérioré notre plus juste prose (PH 114).

> [These ones, so close, are already
> dead. Their barely audible elocution
> is veridiction. Learning this stammering
> is why I chose to come here, against myself,
> on the brink of threat and destruction,
> in this squalid solitude, between the tables
> in the cafeteria, the trees in the park,
> not to get a grip on myself or to renounce eloquence,
> but to try to say most precisely
> what I must renounce:
> this bitter falsification, this discourse
> of evasion, these remnants (this irritation) of 'poetry'
> which have worsened our most just prose.]

Although on the face of things there is certainly a danger of insincerity in the gesture whereby 'I chose to come here', in fact this is only one factor amongst others in Lacoue-Labarthe's thinking, for example the compulsion to undergo this experience, his own very real incapacity during this period to function in the wider world, and respect for the other patients. The latter is clearly present in the term 'veridiction'. Just as *Phrase* does not represent a wilfully obscurantist approach or any shying away from 'clarification' but rather a more direct relationship to it, so it locates in the patients' 'stammering' nothing less than a 'véridiction': *veri-diction* or the saying of truth. This is what Lacoue-Labarthe's collection addresses, clearly setting aside what it names 'these remnants [...] of 'poetry' | which have worsened our most just prose'. *Phrase* therefore puts forward a broad range of discourses and ambitions, rather than simply being the literary counterpart to Lacoue-Labarthe's main body of work *on* philosophy (which nonetheless does not designate itself *as* philosophy, preferring 'thought' or 'deconstruction'). The breadth of this range becomes particularly apparent in two salient sections, 'Phrase II (Clarification)' ['Phrase II (Clarification)'] and 'Phrase V (L'Émoi)' ['Phrase V (Commotion)'] — let us look first at the latter.

'Phrase V (L'Émoi)'

The first of the twenty-one 'Phrase' sections we shall look at was initially published in an issue of *Digraphe* entitled 'Littérature, encore' ['Literature, Again'], and consists of six pages (which represent a drastic compression of the fifty or so pages of the text's first version).[13] Besides the subtitle of '[l]'émoi', it is inscribed under the words '[i]n der lydischen Tonart,' ['[i]n the Lydian Mode'], a technical musical reference, which elsewhere in *Phrase* Lacoue-Labarthe glosses as follows: 'la lydienne, mixte ou soutenue, accompagne des chants de déploration, élégies ou thrènes, c'est un mode de l'expression réprouvable de la douleur' (PH 90; ['the Lydian mode, mixed or elevated, accompanies songs of lament, elegies or threnodies; it is a mode of the rebuke-worthy expression of pain']). The use of this musical term suggests that for the thinker there are porous boundaries between music and the type of fragmentary language explored in *Phrase*. Beyond this, the text shares some characteristics with those already seen regarding 'Phrase II (Clarification)', insofar as some sort of event or happening is described, and the notion of inspiration — or literally, breath — is invoked as this description takes place. This event, then, is presented as

> un trajet précis que j'identifierais volontiers, vaille que vaille, au passage, entre nuque et larynx, de la pensée à l'énonciation: à ce moment insaisissable et vraisemblablement inexistant, soustrait au temps, où, du côté de l'arrière-gorge, la *pensée*, donc (quel autre mot utiliser?), prend comme une sorte d'intangible consistance — je dirai approximativement: *prend souffle* — et vient se confondre avec l'expiration où il me semble qu'elle ne se perd pas mais s'altère simplement et, s'altérant, s'articule ou se module en un vague chant atone, de tout façon peu mélodique, 'pauvre' (sinon parfaitement nul), mais scandé plus ou moins selon le rythme de la respiration (PH 45–46, emphases original).

> [a precise journey which I would willingly identify, whatever the cost, to the passage, between the neck and the larynx, of thought to enunciation: I would identify it with this ungraspable and probably non-existent moment, withdrawn from time, when from the back of the throat, *thought* (what other word to use?) takes on a sort of intangible consistency — I shall say roughly: *takes its first breath* — and comes to intermingle with expiration in which it seems not to get lost but simply to change, and in changing, articulates or modulates itself into a vague atonal, unmelodious, 'plain' song (if not one that is utterly null), but one more or less conforming to breathing's rhythm).]

Whilst what is being described here is the enunciation or expression of thought — thus confirming once again that Lacoue-Labarthe's perspective is comparative rather than exclusively literary — this is carried out in the physiological terms we might expect from a technical description of singing (neck, larynx, throat). As in 'Phrase II (Clarification)', the reader is presented with a relationship to the human body that is much less pronounced in Lacoue-Labarthe's writing on philosophy. But this area of his work informs the others insofar as this ability to address the body focuses the attention on the interaction between the physical and the metaphysical — as in *L'Allégorie'* — not in order to identify or render present the latter (thus forming a metaphysics of presence, rejected by Heidegger and Derrida), but to approach it as an imperative or demand.

In addition to the paratextual elements mentioned above, this text is dedicated to Blanchot — an element key to understanding its genesis, as well as its relation to a wider swathe of Lacoue-Labarthe's thinking. We can begin to see this via its description of an event, similar to those recounted earlier in the same text and in 'Phrase II (Clarification)', and again presented initially in terms of external circumstances:

> Ayant traversé le gravier qui borde la maison (même bruit de tempête non survenue), j'ai marché jusque vers le fond du jardin et je me suis arrêté près du tas de terre et de cendre [...], peut-être pour regarder, par-dessus la clôture, les vagues collines, la plaine. Ce n'était pas encore l'hiver mais il faisait froid, très froid [...]. Il ne s'est évidemment rien passé, mais je savais que cela m'était déjà arrivé: je le savais, l'ignorant: je reconnaissais cette nouveauté absolue, ce ruissellement, cette fatigue.

Non, je n'étais pas interdit, mais d'une indifférence sans limite: je pouvais mourir. (PH 48)

[Having crossed the gravel which surrounds the house (to the same sound of a storm not yet come), I walked towards the bottom of the garden and stopped by the pile of earth and ashes [...], perhaps to look, beyond the fence, at the vague hills, the plain. It was not yet winter but it was cold, very cold [...]. Obviously, nothing happened, but I knew that it had already happened to me: I knew this even without knowing it: I recognized this absolute newness, this flowing stream, this fatigue.

No, I was not lost for words, but of an indifference without limits: now I could die.]

This text presents us with problems — although it retains the structure of an event, a moment of realization or even revelation, it is simultaneously a non-event. Although nothing less than an 'absolute newness' can now be discussed, at the same time '[o]viously, nothing happened'. Even the speaking voice relates to this event or non-event in an unstable manner, stating that 'I knew this even without knowing it'. But rather than seeing this situation as a simple paradox, we can recognize certain characteristic patterns of deconstructive thought at work here: granted, the event does not happen in that given moment, but this is because it has always already happened. The event itself is withdrawn, but it nonetheless informs and inflects the voice speaking in Lacoue-Labarthe's text.

The relation to Blanchot is important for any reading of 'Phrase V (L'Émoi)'. In order to see precisely why, we need to go back to 1976, when Lacoue-Labarthe was editing together with Bénézet an issue of *Première livraison*. They asked authors for a text of a single page, and Blanchot was duly invited to contribute. The set-up of the review was thus fragmentary and experimental, as Lacoue-Labarthe later described: 'Nous avions déjà l'idée de disposer la revue *Première Livraison* de cette manière: six fois par an les abonnés de la revue recevraient un feuillet plié et à la fin de l'année nous ferions faire une couverture indiquant le nom des auteurs' ['We already had the idea of setting out *Première Livraison* as follows: six times per year the journal's subscribers would receive a folded sheet and at the end of the year we would have produced a cover indicating the name of the authors'].[14] Some authors responded to this formal constraint by writing short texts, others by providing a page of prose cut arbitrarily from a longer piece of work. As for Blanchot, less than two weeks following the request from Lacoue-Labarthe and Bénézet, he sent in the following text:

Une scène primitive
Vous qui vivez plus tard, proches d'un cœur qui ne bat plus, supposez, supposez-le: l'enfant — a-t-il sept ans, huit ans peut-être ? — debout, écartant le rideau et, à travers la vitre, regardant. Ce qu'il voit, le jardin, des arbres d'hiver, le mur d'une maison; tandis qu'il voit, sans doute à la manière d'un enfant, son espace de jeu, il se lasse et lentement regarde en haut vers le ciel ordinaire, avec les nuages, la lumière grise, le jour terne et sans lointain. Ce qui se passe ensuite: le ciel, le *même* ciel, soudain ouvert, noir absolument et vide absolument, révélant (comme par la vitre brisée) une telle absence que tout s'y est depuis toujours et à jamais perdu, au point que s'y affirme et s'y dissipe le

savoir vertigineux que rien est ce qu'il y a, et d'abord rien au-delà. L'inattendu de cette scène primitive (son trait interminable), c'est le sentiment de bonheur qui aussitôt submerge l'enfant, la joie ravageante dont il ne pourra témoigner que par les larmes, un ruissellement sans fin de larmes. On croit à un chagrin d'enfant, on cherche à le consoler. Il ne dit rien. Il vivra désormais dans le secret. Il ne pleurera plus.

[*A Primal Scene*
You who live later, close to a heart that beats no more, suppose, suppose this: the child — is he seven years old, or eight perhaps? — standing by the window, drawing the curtain and, through the pane, looking. What he sees: the garden, the wintry trees, the wall of a house. Though he sees, no doubt in a child's way, his play space, he grows weary and slowly looks up toward the ordinary sky, with clouds, grey light — pallid daylight without depth. What happens then: the sky, the same sky, suddenly open, absolutely black and absolutely empty, revealing (as though the pane had been broken) such an absence that all has since always forevermore been lost therein — so lost that therein is affirmed and dissolved the vertiginous knowledge that nothing is what there is, and first of all nothing beyond. The unexpected aspect of this primal scene (its interminable feature) is the feeling of happiness that straightaway submerges the child, the ravaging joy to which he can bear witness only by tears, an endless flood of tears. He is thought to be suffering from a childish sorrow; attempts are made to console him. He says nothing. He will live henceforth in the secret. He will weep no more.][15]

Lacoue-Labarthe described his surprise on receiving this text which, in his words in a letter to Laporte, 'm'a laissé muet, interdit' (ATAI 20; ['left me dumb, speechless']). And indeed, it represented a considerable departure for Blanchot, a writer known for his meditations on writing as passage from *Je* to *Il*, on notions of impersonality and neutrality. In this light, Lacoue-Labarthe's surprise was due to the fact that, as he puts it, 'à cette date, à ma connaissance du moins, ce texte était le seul texte de Blanchot qu'on pût dire autobiographique, presque sur le mode de la confession' (ATAI 24; ['at that time, to my knowledge at least, this text was Blanchot's only text that could be called autobiographical, one written almost in a confessional mode']). The third-person presentation of the infant's discovery or revelation is taken to be only a thin veil — and this has recently been confirmed with the discovery, though not yet the publication — of a 1966 letter to Laporte in which Blanchot recounts the episode in explicitly autobiographical terms.

Lacoue-Labarthe's reaction was therefore one of astonishment as a reader; and together with his reaction to Blanchot's *L'Instant de ma mort* (1994; [*The Instant of My Death*]), a short work with a similar relation to autobiography or autothanatography, it would feed into the project for a work named *Agonie terminée, agonie intermimable* that was announced but not completed in his lifetime, and published posthumously in 2011. Before this book project, however, his reaction also extended into his practice as a writer. For the text of 'Phrase V (L'Émoi)', which is dated Summer 1976-Summer 1981 (and a version of which was published in the journal *Digraphe* in 1978), articulates a reading of Blanchot's text. Indeed, in Lacoue-Labarthe's words on his text in a letter to Laporte, '[u]ne fois achevé, je me suis toutefois rendu compte que cela constituait d'une certaine manière une espèce de "réponse" au texte de Blanchot paru dans *Première livraison*. Bizarre' (ATAI 21; ['Once I had finished it, I realized that this somehow constituted a sort of "response" to Blanchot's text in *Première Livraison*. Bizarre']). And indeed, the text in question demonstrates a notable relationship to Blanchot's 'scène primitive', from the circumstances described (looking at the winter sky from a garden) to the opening which features two interlocutors discussing the designation 'scene': '– Et ce n'était pas une scène? | — Non. Je ne crois pas du moins' (PH 43; ['"And it was not a scene?" | '"No. I do not believe so, anyway"']). More importantly, there is the oscillation or alternation between the status of what is described in the text as an event and a non-event, similarly to how Blanchot's text presents a revelation, but one where what is revealing is a void or 'absence'. Such are some of the effects on Lacoue-Labarthe's practice as a writer of what he later described as 'l'un des plus beaux poèmes en prose de ce siècle' ('one of the most beautiful prose poems of this century').[16]

The strand of dialogue between Lacoue-Labarthe and Blanchot does not stop there, however. For following the publication of a version of 'Phrase V (L'Émoi)' by the former in 1978, Blanchot collected his 1976 text in *L'Écriture du désastre* (1980; *The Writing of the Disaster*). Some relatively minor changes are made to this second version; but one major change is present, namely a change in its status. From the thinly veiled autobiographical text that it had initially been, 'La scène primitive' now featured within the fragmentary framework of Blanchot's new work. In addition to this, and perhaps as a symptom of it, it bore a new title: no longer 'La scène primitive', but '(Une scène primitive)?'. The addition of parentheses and a question mark, as well as the change from definite to indefinite article, ask more pressing epistemological questions regarding the status of the events narrated: they are no longer so easily placed with the autobiographical frame that Lacoue-Labarthe suspected existed (and which has since been confirmed thanks to Blanchot's letter, which I have seen although it has not been published). Further still, many other fragments in *L'Écriture du désastre* are placed in some relation to this text — from the two subsequent versions of it (bearing the same title) to the discussions of relevant theories from the psychoanalysis of infancy (understood etymologically as an *in-fans*, a being without language).[17] Now, to follow the dialogue between the two writers, it seems possible that these added qualifications and relativizations are themselves a response to Lacoue-Labarthe's response to the initial version, published in 1978. For his re-writing of Blanchot's 'scène primitive' had ended with the words 'now I *was able* to die' (my emphasis) — surely anathema to the older writer who had so often insisted that *le mourir* (dying) lies outside the power or possibilities of the subject. On this view, Blanchot's 1980 revision of his text represents an admonishment to Lacoue-Labarthe (albeit one for following the avenue of directness and possibility that the 1976 text had opened up: this criticism is at some level a self-criticism). Whatever the truth concerning whether Blanchot had read Lacoue-Labarthe's response or not, the former's alteration of his text means that its unusual, confessional quality is diminished as it is incorporated into a wider fragmentary format. And although Lacoue-Labarthe recognizes the radical potential of the latter, he also has doubts about it:

Blanchot, tout en le maintenant (presque) intégralement, détruit au moins partiellement ce texte, le 'déconstruit' si l'on veut [...], voire le conteste et l'annule dans sa visée et sa portée initiales, ou dans un certain effet qu'il peut — ou qu'il a pu — produire. Au risque évidemment, bien qu'en la matière il soit le premier averti, d'une opération de type dialectique (ATAI 138).

[Blanchot, even in (almost) completely reproducing his text, destroys it at least in part, 'deconstructs' it if you will [...], even contests and annuls its initial aims and field of reference, or a certain effect that it could — or had already been able to — produce. At the risk, obviously, even though on this topic he is as forewarned as anyone, of engaging in an operation of a dialectical type.]

Between the first and second versions of the text, then, between ['l]a scène primitive' and '([u]ne scène primitive?)', something has changed. Owing to this change, there is a risk that the new fragmentary format — because of its negation of the text's initial, autobiographical qualities and the incorporation of them into a larger totality (albeit a fragmentary one) — in fact carries out an 'operation of a dialectical type'. Lacoue-Labarthe's language is revelatory here, inasfar as it seems to be one of disappointment: the opening glimpsed in the 1976 text has been closed down again, its autobiographical-autothanatographical power diminished, a 'destruction' or 'annulment' has taken place. And it is worth pursuing his line of thinking here because it shows that, whilst strongly marked by Blanchot, he also provides a rigorous reading showing that fragmentation is a form and a possibility pertaining to modernist writing, rather than to the more radical interruption of all tradition that Blanchot and others were presenting it as during this period.

This thought informs another important element of Lacoue-Labarthe's reaction to Blanchot and his writerly practice. Lacoue-Labarthe responded to *L'Écriture du désastre* in a text written in collaboration with Nancy, 'Noli me frangere' (1981; ['Do Not Fragment Me']).[18] It is a playful text, divided between co-authored fragments (part I), a dialogue between two anonymous voices (part II), and finally a more formal *Gespräch* featuring 'Lothario' and 'Ludovico' as interlocutors. But in fact this playfulness has a message — or rather, it *is* the message. By giving the final interlocutors these faintly ridiculous names, Lacoue-Labarthe and Nancy underline how far the form of the dialogue and of the fragmentary text are associated with Jena Romanticism (*L'Absolu littéraire* had been published only three years previously, containing a translation of Schlegel's 'Entretien sur la poésie' ['Dialogue on Poetry'] which features Ludoviko and Lothario as interlocutors). In other words, fragmentary writing and thinking has a strong historical connection to the period of speculative or dialectical thought. And indeed, this connection to dialectics can also be seen if we note that a fragmentary text, rather than being defined positively, on its own terms, is in the first instance one that is not whole or unitary; on this view, fragmentation is a negative gesture. Léonid Kharmalov and Aristide Bianchi, the editors of Lacoue-Labarthe's posthumous book on Blanchot, *Agonie terminée, agonie interminable*, adopt this argument in setting up how for Lacoue-Labarthe fragmentation is not always necessarily a radical mode of writing:

Si *L'Absolu littéraire* rapporterait le projet moderne de la littérature à son origine dans le projet romantique du roman et du fragment, il marquait en même temps, inversement, une clôture radicale de la possibilité de ces deux formes. Comme toute fin, celle-ci ne signifiait pas qu'il n'était pas possible d'écrire en fragments, mais qu'on ne pouvait confier le renoncement à l'absolu, le désœuvrement, à la négativité de la forme fragmentaire (ATAI 26).

[Whilst *The Literary Absolute* linked the modern project of literature to its origin in the Romantic project of the novel and the fragment, at the same time — but inversely — it marked a radical closure of the possibility of these two forms. Like all endings, this did not mean that it was not possible to write in fragments, but that fragmentary form could not be entrusted with worklessness or with renouncing the absolute.]

Let us now see briefly how this doubt or scepticism regarding fragmentation is presented by 'Noli me frangere'. The expression used for the article's title of course means something like 'do not break me, do not fragment me'; and it re-iterates and alters Christ's statement to Mary Magdalen when she attempted to touch his body in order to overcome her incredulity at the resurrection — that statement being *noli me tangere*, do not touch me (*John* 20:11–18). Lacoue-Labarthe and Nancy interpret this latter statement as follows: 'Ne me touche pas [...] parce que tu ne saurais pas ce que tu touches, et parce que tu croirais le savoir. Tu ne peux rien savoir ni rien vouloir de ce qu'on nomme un corps glorieux' ['Do not touch me [...] because you would not know what you would be touching, and because you would think you did. You cannot know anything about, or wish for anything in relation to, what is called a body in glory'].[19] But of course, their reading has rather different stakes from those of the Biblical setting. Whilst some sort of resurrection is still what is being discussed, in their case this is not a resurrection of Christ's body, but of dialectical discourse in its capacity to reinvent itself, i.e. to find its bearings itself amidst alterity and to overcome death. Instead of Christ stating 'noli me tangere', the two thinkers therefore confront us with a figure of dialectical discourse itself stating 'noli me frangere'. In their words, 'la dialectique — le discours — est indestructible. *Noli me frangere*, ordonne-t-elle en tout texte, et dans le texte fragmentaire aussi, et dans le discours en fragments sur le fragment' ['dialectics — discourse — is indestructible. *Noli me frangere*, it orders in all texts, and even in fragmentary texts, as well as in the fragmented text on fragments'].[20] In other words, this reaction to *L'Écriture du désastre* argues that despite the clear differences of degree between fragmentary and unitary writing, the same 'operation' — a word closely associated with their thinking of Romanticism — is carried on in both forms.

In terms of Lacoue-Labarthe's thinking, and particularly his thinking of writing as a separate strand from his main work on philosophy (which nonetheless takes pains not to identify itself as philosophy), this scepticism regarding fragmentation is at once important and inhibiting. It is important because it allows him to move out from under the shadow of Blanchot, a writer of whom he said that 'il fut, plus que d'autres, avec plus de passion et d'acharnement, plus de fièvre et d'obstination, plus de hauteur et d'abnégation, la Littérature elle-même' (ATAI 127–28; ['he was, more than others, with greater passion and stubbornness, greater fever and obstinacy, greater hauteur and self-denial, Literature itself']). But it is also inhibiting insofar as even the radical form of fragmentary writing is rendered unavailable. In the simplest terms, this is a factor in why so many of Lacoue-Labarthe's writing projects were unfinished or unpublished. But beyond this, it suggests that he had taken the lesson of Hölderlin's caesura to heart: that any interruption worthy of the name must be one opening onto nothing, without solution or resolution.

'Phrase II (Clarification)'

Another of the sections of *Phrase* is important for situating Lacoue-Labarthe's view of writing in relation to his thinking of philosophy. The series of texts in question is around six pages long and divided into four parts, alternating between free verse and prose; it bears the date of 20 January 1979, and is followed by a five-page post-scriptum dated June 1979. The latter states that the questions driving the texts as a whole are: 'pourquoi y a-t-il "phrase"? Et d'où vient-elle? Qu'est-ce qui attire, ou dicte, la "phrase"? Qui la donne?' (PH 19; ['why is there "phrase"? And where does it come from? What attracts, or dictates, the "phrase"? Who gives it?']). This is to say that the texts are set up not as examples of the *phrase* in question, but rather as a way of questioning our relationship to it, a primordial phrase that somehow is always already there. And indeed, such a questioning is the main concern early on in these texts — it proceeds by negation, bringing up several ways in which the notion of *phrase* cannot be understood. For instance, we read about something which is 'vide de sens, privé la plupart du temps de contenu, | à peine organisé en mots, | une phrase' (PH 11; ['emptied of meaning, most of the time of content, | barely organized into words, | a phrase']). Shortly afterwards we are told regarding this *phrase* that 'je n'ai pas le sentiment de l'avoir recueillie. | Jamais tout à fait. Je ne pense pas non plus | la produire' (PH 11; ['I do not feel that I have grasped it. | Never in its entirety. I do not think either that | I produce it']). And then on the following page:

> Je crois donc plutôt qu'elle, la phrase, cherche encore à se former
> et que jamais, en somme, elle n'a abouti. Jamais
> en tout cas je ne l'ai entendue. Au contraire je
> soupçonne que si parfois il m'arrive d'entendre — des paroles,
> une diction, de la musique —, c'est à cause
> de cette phrase en attente, indéfiniment,
> de sa chute et de sa fermeture (PH 12).

> [Therefore I sooner believe that it, the phrase, is trying to take shape
> and that ultimately, it has never reached completion. Never
> in any case have I heard it. On the contrary I
> suspect that if I sometimes happen to hear — words,
> a diction, music —, it is due
> to this phrase waiting, indefinitely,
> to fall and to close.]

The suggestion here is that *phrase* is not a positive entity that can be heard, but instead something that from its position of withdrawal or unavailability, allows a certain act of hearing to take place — i.e. a hearing of 'words, | a diction, music'. In this view, it would be something like a predisposition, an opening thanks to which and without which no appreciation of words or music could take place. Although withdrawn and *en attente*, it has a definite role, namely to cast positive art-forms into starker relief.

This relief and the differentiations and distinctions the *phrase* makes possible, then, are an important part of 'Phrase II', this series of texts which after all are subtitled '[c]larification'. For whilst the identity of the phrase may seem frustratingly mysterious, we come across several other significant, more concrete assertions. For instance, on several occasions an epistemological relationship to death is established; the realization of death's certainty — and perhaps also its imminence — is dramatized by the setting described. The first of these occasions is found here:

> [À] ces moments d'oubli terrifiant où la moindre lumière d'hiver sur un mur, l'herbe pauvre d'un jardin, l'eau d'une rivière, est, en hiatus, le signe pur que je vais mourir, je pourrais dire [...]: j'aurai été une phrase.
> Ou plutôt: il y aura eu phrase, *cette* phrase — qui m'aura hanté, que je n'aurai jamais prononcée (PH 12, emphasis original).

> [At these moments of terrifying oblivion where the slightest winter slight on a wall, the poor grass in a garden, the water in a brook represent, in hiatus, the pure sign that I shall die, I could say [...]: I will have been a phrase.
> Or rather: there will have been phrase, *this* phrase — which will have haunted me, which I will never have uttered].

With these lines we understand slightly better what *phrase* might be, or at least when it might arise or have arisen: in moments when an exterior stimulus, found in a physical aspect of one's surroundings, provides a reminder of mortality: namely a reminder that one will *have been*, been not this or that particular thing, but simply been. But the indirect aspects are still present: this phrase arises only retrospectively, never *being* but only ever *having been* ['I will have been a phrase', 'there will have been phrase']. What is more, although it arises — or will have arisen — from a stimulus external to the speaking subject, it is not something that the latter can straightforwardly thematize or speak, but instead that he/she 'will never have uttered'. The relation with mortality arises again when the text discusses a mode of pure address, a sort of prayer addressed to no-one — or without destination —, and which seems to be synonymous with the *phrase*. We read that 'la pure adresse [...] délivre. Quelqu'un sait très bien de quoi je veux parler: joie inouïe du deuil: je vais mourir, je vais mourir. C'est d'une clarté sans égal' (PH 16; ['pure address [...] provides deliverance. Someone knows full well what I am speaking about: the unheard-of joy of mourning: I am going to die, I am going to die. It is of a clarity without equal']). Here the realization of one's mortality, and the fact of repeating it to oneself, leads to the language of 'clarification'. And the latter is couched in strikingly forceful terms: this is not one realization amongst others, nor a moment of clarity caught up in a dialectic of light and dark, or of knowledge and ignorance. Instead it is a 'clarity without equal': we are outside the dialectical domain where everything can be balanced against an opposing force. It is as if Lacoue-Labarthe's work can only express such directness and force in the fragmented arena of this collection, rather than in a more philosophical language carrying within it a philosophical bias. Whilst philosophy would like to paint other discourses as deficient in clarity, here it is precisely an excess of clarity that takes us beyond philosophical confines.

'Phrase II' understands its task as a 'clarification' in yet another way. For over the six pages of its main text, we find five definitions of literature, which are the most direct anywhere in Lacoue-Labarthe's oeuvre. It is simplest to quote them in sequence (the underlinings of 'littérature' are all from the original):

> Phrase: ce qui se prononce en moi — loin, ailleurs, presque dehors — depuis très longtemps,
> depuis, je crois, que m'a été donnée la possibilité d'oublier,
> je l'appelle *littérature*. (PH 11)
>
> [Phrase: what has been being uttered within me — though far away, elsewhere, almost externally — for a very long time,
> since, I believe, that the possibility of forgetting was given to me,
> I have called it *literature*.]
>
> Cette prononciation avortée, cette hantise, je l'appelle décidément *littérature* (PH 12).
>
> [This aborted uttering, this haunting, I decidedly call it *literature*.]
>
> J'appelle [...] *littérature* cette paraphrase infinie (PH 14).
>
> [I call [...] this infinite paraphrase *literature*.]
>
> Dans cette mesure, dans cette simple mesure, la phase — la *littérature* — est orale (PH 17).
>
> [To this extent, to this simple extent, phrase — *literature* — is oral.]
>
> Je pense à la naissance toujours innée (dégénérée)
> de la *littérature*: la diction des enfants,
> la prosodie plus vieille que notre mémoire
> des légendes (PH 17).
>
> [I think of the always innate (degenerate) birth
> of *literature*: the diction of children,
> the prosody older than our memory
> of legends.]

Although there is here an undeniable will to definition, demonstrating that Lacoue-Labarthe was influenced in his approach by a certain understanding of the metaphysical, we must be careful to draw out the nuance with which it is presented. For the definitions or descriptions given of literature largely go against what we might take to be a straightforwardly essentializing approach. For instance, literature is distinguished from a positive, knowable object and instead said to be a 'aborted uttering'; and it is presented as being found not in any directly comprehensible expression, but in an 'infinite paraphrase'. After all, that we should be infinitely paraphrasing, reiterating and reformulating our discourses in an approach to clarity but without such clarity ever becoming definitively fixed or present, seems close to a working definition of deconstruction.

We could perhaps see this as an imperative, a demand made upon this subject or upon writing in general, and consisting in the verb *phraser* (meaning to dictate, articulate, or sometimes simply 'faire des phrases') in the second-person singular imperative: *phrase*. Such, perhaps, is the imperative to which the texts in question attempt to respond: at once to write and to be a writer, these demands that drove much of Lacoue-Labarthe's thinking to the point of never being fully realizable. The resulting texts, which often draw on readings of Celan and Blanchot, are fragmented, pursuing a thinking of interruption or caesura (the term he draws from Hölderlin). But despite this — or because of it — they are highly communicative, allowing an often striking directness which suggests that philosophy does not have a monopoly over clarity. 'Il faut la clarté' (IM 230), the phrase he had uttered in dialogue with Derrida, is felt here in its status as a *demand*, a necessity strongly felt and pushing Lacoue-Labarthe's writing into areas unimaginable to the calculating reason of philosophical tradition.

Notes to Chapter 5

1. In 'La Fiction du biographique', p. 197.
2. In 'Un commencement', p. 135.
3. These collaborations were: the editing of the journal *Première livraison*, a book series of the same name with Christian Bourgois's publishing house, two collective volumes, *Misère de la littérature* (1978) and '*Haine de la poésie*' (['*Hatred of Poetry*']; Paris: Bourgeois, 1979) — to which a dialogue between Lacoue-Labarthe and Bénézet provided an introduction —, and 'Précis', Lacoue-Labarthe's review of Bénézet's work *Dits et récits du mortel: Ménipée*.
4. In interview with Pascal Possoz, unpublished (early 2000s).
5. John Dewey, *Art as Experience* (London: Allen & Unwin, 1934).
6. In *La Poésie comme expérience* (Paris: Bourgois, 1986), p. 65, henceforth abbreviated to PE; *Poetry as Experience*, trans. by Andrea Tarnowski (Stanford: Stanford University Press, 1999), p. 44, henceforth abbreviated to PE2.
7. In *Essays and Letters*, p. 213. Lacoue-Labarthe's own voyage to Tübingen, in the company of Roger Laporte, is alluded to in *La Poésie comme expérience*, pp. 145–46. Laporte's account of the excursion is his 'Souvenir de Tübingen' ['Memory of Tübingen'], in *Entre deux mondes* ([*Between Two Worlds*]; Montpellier: Gris banal, 1988), pp. 39–46.
8. In *Poems of Paul Celan*, trans. by Michael Hamburger (London: Anvil, 1988), p. 177.
9. See Hölderlin, *Selected Poems and Fragments*, trans. by Michael Hamburger (London: Penguin, 1998). For the translation of 'Andenken' ['Remembrance'], see *Lignes*, 22 (May 2007), 248–51.
10. In *The Ister*.
11. In *Le Chant des muses* ([*The Song of the Muses*]; Paris: Bayard, 2005), pp. 26–27 (emphasis original).
12. In *Poème de Philippe Lacoue-Labarthe*. Mehdi Belhaj Kacem, having saluted the collection *Phrase* as 'le plus grand poème de notre temps' ['the greatest poem of our time'], comments on its relation to mental illness: 'Sa [Lacoue-Labarthe] pensée et sa poésie ne découlent pas de sa pathologie, c'est sa pathologie qui aura découlé du fait qu'il lui incombait d'écrire, un jour ou l'autre, ce poème' ['[h]is [Lacoue-Labarthe's] thought and poetry do not flow from his pathology, it is his pathology which will have flowed from the fact that it befitted him to write, some day, this poem'], in *Inesthétique & mimésis: Badiou, Lacoue-Labarthe et la question de l'art* ([*Inæsthetics & Mimesis : Badiou, Lacoue-Labarthe and the Question of Art*]; Paris: Lignes, 2010), pp. 134–35. This comment identifies *Phrase* as the poem that it was somehow Lacoue-Labarthe's destiny to write; we might object that it was precisely the lack of any single, identifiable work-as-destiny that provoked his troubles.
13. See Léonid Kharmalov and Aristide Bianchi's account in 'Présentation', in *Agonie terminée, agonie interminable*, pp. 9–53 (pp. 20–21).
14. In interview with Pascal Possoz, early 2000s.
15. In *Première livraison*, 4 (February-March 1976), 1 (emphasis original); after Ann Smock's translation in Blanchot, *The Writing of the Disaster* (London: University of Nebraska Press), p. 72.
16. In Possoz interview.

17. In *L'Écriture du désastre* (Paris: Gallimard, 1980), pp. 110–17, 176–79, 191–96.
18. 'Noli me frangere', (1982) in *Europe*, 973 (May 2010), 32–42.
19. Ibid., p. 33.
20. Ibid.

CONCLUSION

Mimesis

Each of the chapters of this study has addressed questions that might have been explored at much greater length. Nonetheless, doing so would have obscured the sheer variety and energy of Lacoue-Labarthe's writing, and thereby obscured his clarity. The writing in question is full of significant turning-points, autobiographical or autothanatographical texts, and references to its own status, not least in the repeated attempts to take a distance from philosophy. The latter point is surely crucial, underlining as it does that no single language or system is able to convey the multiplicity we find throughout his work. In this spirit, it is difficult to focus on a centre or reduce things down to a conceptual core. Nonetheless, if the itinerary of Lacoue-Labarthe's work is so tortuous (and his biography so tortured), it is because setting aside philosophy does not dispense us from the rigours of thought. He does not go in for insouciant eclecticism, as can be seen in this reflection on deconstruction:

> Déconstruire [...] n'est pas [...], de l'extérieur, avec un autre langage, abattre l'édifice pour reconstruire autre chose: nous n'avons plus, personne n'a plus, d'extériorité ni d'autre langage [...]. Il s'agit donc d'habiter l'édifice, puisqu'il n'y a nulle autre part où habiter. Mais il s'agit d'habiter l'édifice, pour, de l'intérieur — un peu comme la taupe de Marx —, le miner ou, la comparaison serait peut-être plus juste, le laminer jusqu'à ce que l'une ou l'autre de ses parois devienne suffisamment diaphane pour laisser deviner la fragile image d'un dehors.[1]

> [To deconstruct [...] is not [...], from the outside, using another language, knocking down the building in order to build something new: we no longer have, no-one any longer has, either exteriority or any other language [...]. Therefore we must inhabit the building, as there is nowhere else to live. But we must inhabit the building in order — a little like Marx's mole — to undermine it or, perhaps it is a better comparison, to erode it until one or another of its walls become diaphanous enough to allow the fragile image of an outside to be glimpsed.]

Here the tradition of deconstruction is married to Lacoue-Labarthe's striving for clarification: we are said to be already within 'the building' — recalling Heidegger's famous statement that 'language is the house of Being' — which is to say always already situated in a way lying outside our powers of decision.[2] But rather than simply walking out of the door, thus leaving the edifice untouched and free to be inhabited by others after us, the necessary thing to do is said to be to wear away the building's walls until the distinction between it and the outside begins to break down. A fragile image is then said to appear — and we can note that it appears as if automatically, in any case not as something designed or decided by conscious endeavour. Thus by working towards such diaphanous clarity, and admitting that we do so beginning from a position of darkness, it becomes possible to glimpse something that lies beyond the rationalistic calculations often implied by the term.

Such might be a way to characterize Lacoue-Labarthe's relationship with philosophy, which we have seen to be extremely fraught — particularly but not exclusively in his condemnations of Heidegger (see chapter 2). Whilst he is sometimes seen as a philosopher, for instance by John Martis, the difficulty of this relationship surely requires that we see him as someone who wrote *on* philosophy, but not from within that discipline or discourse. My approach of looking at his multiple shifts between timely and untimely modes of writing speaks to this same marginal or undecided position: Lacoue-Labarthe never fully subscribed to the theoretical movements that were timely for his generation, but neither did he appeal to the untimely understood as ahistorical, unchanging values. What we can do — and I hope to have done — is to track how this tension pushes him into strikingly different domains of activity. And what we can say is that across these domains, whilst there is no single term that would sit at the apex of his thinking, one term with its associated nexus of reflections has shown itself to be particularly important. Namely, Lacoue-Labarthe's thought returns again and again to the notion of mimesis: in Jean-Luc Nancy's words, it was his 'maître-concept ou son leitmotiv obsédant' (AN 110; ['his master-concept or the leitmotiv that obsessed him']). Given this, let us as a final exercise explore how the major concerns of this varied oeuvre are assembled and dispersed, iterated and relayed, by this mimesis.

Whilst *diegesis* is a mode whereby the speaking subject engages in direct narration, *mimesis* by contrast is when this narration is indirect, the subject instead making use of characters, masks, or voices that are not his or her own. We have seen Lacoue-Labarthe questioning in the cases of Nietzsche and Zarathustra, Plato and Socrates, whether the underlying subject can still be said to be unchanged if it must rely on such external figures to dissimulate its presence: his thinking here was much stimulated by Derrida's *écriture*. But the relevance of the distinction between *diegesis* and *mimesis* reaches more widely: for if there *were* to be a direct speaking in the case of Lacoue-Labarthe's work, it would be from the position of a philosopher. That was his profession, as it was that of his timely companions Derrida and Nancy who both have more direct — although of course not straightforward — relations to it. However, whilst familiar with this discourse, Lacoue-Labarthe saw it as impossible to inhabit: instead he sought to point out its problems. This allowed him to characterize in a clear and provocative way Western philosophy as a single, continuous system, beginning with Plato, reaching its culmination with the speculative thought of Hegel and the Romantics, and still exercising its influence on Heidegger. Indeed, he even diagnosed *Tel Quel*'s programmatic avant-gardism and interest in self-reflexivity as just another expression of this metaphysical system: this led him to reject the modern subject's desire to speak freely and directly, and instead to seek out impossible, fragmented, or untimely modes of expression. In this sense, he could be called mimetic because he rejects what Nancy calls 'la protension vers l'avenir qui implique une volonté d'autoproduction, ou d'autoengendrement, dont le ressort inavoué est un refus, ou plutôt une dénégation de la mimesis originaire' (AN 110; ['the protension towards the future which involves a will to self-production, or to self-generation, which unavowedly refuses or denies originary mimesis']). The 'will to self-generation' mentioned here, i.e. the will to establish modern philosophical systems, believes naïvely in the ability to speak diegetically or directly, and remains ignorant of the claim that mimesis has upon us, i.e. the claim that we might be responding to, or imitating, patterns and traditions that are always already within us.

Understood in this way, mimesis poses the question of *imitatio*: the Latin translation of the Greek term connoting an entire tradition of European literary production. We can ask whether in rejecting modernity Lacoue-Labarthe is proposing an anti-modern classicism, a stiffly conservative rewriting of previous authors and previous forms (the Petrarchan sonnet being a prime example of *imitatio* in practice).[3] This is perhaps true to some degree — Nancy has spoken of this tendency in Lacoue-Labarthe, both in the anecdotal form of a young writer wishing for complete detachment from the world, and in the more precise account of their joint translation practice: there is something classicizing about Lacoue-Labarthe's role in finding the *mot juste* in French (although if this was a tendency, he nonetheless struggled against it: see the comment on translating Hölderlin: 'Le français n'est pas capable d'une telle brutalité, la mélodie racinienne l'emporte toujours. J'avais fait de mon mieux pour la casser' ['French is not capable of such brutality, Racinian melodiousness always wins out. I did my best to smash it']).[4] These are two ways in which the influence of mimesis understood as *imitatio* can be found in Lacoue-Labarthe's work, with its implications of an evacuation or self-effacement of the individual subject (although the subject returns at a collective level, in the conformism of the classical). There is further evidence that this type of thinking is present for Lacoue-Labarthe: for instance, he regularly quotes a Thomas Mann phrase on '"la vie dans le mythe"' ['"life in myth"'] which refers to a method of bricolage of quotations and examples, and the title of an abortive book project, *L'Exemple* (*The Example*), speaks to this question. The early article 'Typographie' and the two *Typographies* volumes reference this same thinking, playing as they do on the notion of publishers' type-setting and that of types or typologies: in each case reproduction or imitation is at stake.[5]

However, in truth Lacoue-Labarthe's interest in mimesis cannot be explained wholly as an *imitatio* with all its conservative implications. This much can be seen in the various ways in which he characterizes mimesis not as reassuringly conservative but instead as radically destabilizing and interruptive. For him, moving beyond *diegesis* and the subject's direct control over discourse is no glib postmodernism, but a challenging and painful experience. The symptoms of mimesis are being out of control, aping previous models and patterns without realizing it, with the initiative ceded to words (as Mallarmé put it). In this vein, Lacoue-Labarthe characterizes mimesis as 'irrécupérable' ['irrecuperable'] and variously as a 'déclinaison, instabilité, "désinstallation"' ['declination, instability, "disinstallation"'].[6] He states that it refers to a situation where the subject is no longer merely speaking through a mask or character, but has completely disappeared, eerily leaving the mask speaking alone. This disappearance of the subject is recounted in relation to the myth of the encounter between Ulysses and Polyphemus in which the former tricks the cyclops by telling him that his name is *outis*, meaning no-one. Lacoue-Labarthe recounts the myth as follows:

> On voit la 'scène': l'œil unique et puissant, mais désormais aveugle, de la métaphysique [...], incapable de 'théoriser', au moment où il lui échappe, le ci-devant sujet qu'il avait cru fixer, en pleine lumière, comme l'être lui-même. Au lieu de quoi et faute de quoi: théâtre d'ombres, faux-semblants et présences fantomatiques, jeux de langage: la mimèsis déchaînée — c'est-à-dire que nulle scène (nul théâtre) n'est plus à même de contenir.[7]

> [You can picture the 'scene': the single powerful but now blinded eye of metaphysics [...] is unable to 'theorize' the subject in front of it, which it had thought it had pinned down, in broad daylight, just as it pins down Being itself. Instead of and without this happening, we get: a theatre of shadows, misrepresentations, phantomatic presences, and plays on words: mimesis unchained — which is to say, something that no stage (no theatre) is able to contain any longer.]

In other words, the ignorance and confusion of Polyphemus are attributed to the shortcomings of his vision — his 'theorizing', as Lacoue-Labarthe states Hellenistically — and described as giving rise to mimesis, indeed as 'unchaining' it. Mimesis therefore speaks to a savage and benighted condition, rather than the calm classicism with which it might be associated when translated as *imitatio*. The Ulysses episode is also crucial in that Lacoue-Labarthe suggests that the response 'no-one' is not merely a trick played by the hero, but in fact goes to the heart of his being: 'a-t-on remarqué [...] que lorsqu'Ulysse répond "Personne" (en grec: *outis* ou bien *oudeis*), c'est son propre nom (Odysseus) qu'il déforme à peine? La ruse [...] comporte le risque, au défaut (ou au plus juste) de la prononciation, de l'aveu du vrai nom' ['has it been noticed [...] that when Ulysses responds "No-one" (in Greek: *outis* or *oudeis*), he is only slightly altering his own name (Odysseus)? The trick he plays [...] runs the risk, if pronounced wrong (or right), of revealing his true name'].[8] The thinker's interest here is in Ulysses as an empty figure, with no inner essence or particularity: he is a subject who is no-one, and whom Lacoue-Labarthe takes to have become emblematic for that very reason. With the response he provides to Polyphemus, his external mask no longer has positive characteristics, as did the mask of Zarathustra for Nietzsche, for instance; instead its emptiness strangely reflects the emptiness within.[9] In short, mimesis is the condition we enter into when we heed this emptiness or neutrality — when we acknowledge what Derrida's essay for Lacoue-Labarthe named 'la désistance du sujet'.

Mimesis thus speaks to an emptiness, barrenness or absence of the subject, and one that cannot simply be remedied by returning to *imitatio*, where the greater subject based in tradition comes to fill the gap. This is to say that instead of a model where absence is relayed or relieved — *relevé* or *aufgehoben* — by presence, we have the strange situation of absence meeting absence. There might be mimesis, but this is not mimesis *of* any particular model or tradition. Lacoue-Labarthe formulates this on several occasions as a 'mimesis sans modèle' ['mimesis without model'], for instance here in an autobiographical text on his activities with the stage:

> Représenter: imiter, ou plutôt: mimer (mot qui est une pure énigme: nul ne sait d'où il vient). On peut très bien *mimer sans modèle*: la simple distance à soi y suffit. C'est ce qui produit dans l'exercice le plus 'élémentaire' qui soit, celui de la parole.
>
> L'acteur est un mime en ce sens: c'est un porte-parole. Pour dire les choses plus justement: il (nous) représente que nous sommes tous de tels porte-parole, des mimes. Le théâtre n'est pas la mimesis, mais le révélateur de la mimesis (AN 196, emphasis added).

> [To represent: to imitate, or rather: to mime (a word that is a pure enigma: no-one knows where it comes from). It is wholly possible to *mime without a model*: you just have to be distant from yourself. This is what happens in the most 'elementary' exercise there is, that of speaking.
>
> The actor is a mime in this sense: he is a *porte-parole*. To say it in a better way: he represents (to us) the fact that we all are this kind of *porte-paroles* or mimes. Theatre is not mimesis, but that which reveals mimesis.][10]

It seems clear that whilst addressing stage-practice, the reflection here is much broader, addressing that which 'we all are'; and whilst the idea that we act out roles in society is perhaps not new, this passage with its image of an actor simply acting without script, instructions, or 'destination' (to recall a term used by Lacoue-Labarthe), inventing roles and characters as s/he goes, depicts a situation of childish madness.[11]

And if this 'mimesis without model' provides a scene closer to the centre of Lacoue-Labarthe's thinking than many others — despite understandable hesitations regarding the existence of such a centre in the first place —, we can also find repeated evidence of its presence throughout his written work. For instance, it is surely significant that the tradition he drew on most often was not French but German: a real tradition, but one displaced, absent, safely across the border (even from Strasbourg). Elsewhere, whilst the ferment of avant-gardism in the 1970s had its attractions for him and Nancy in their experimental community, he also signalled his distance from its totemic textuality: 'on ne peut pas "en venir" au texte: car le texte est précisément sans rivage' (SP 27; ['one cannot "come to" the text, for the text is precisely without a shore', SP2 12]). And similarly, whilst he had an interest in the stage, it was not such a strong presence as to allow him to depart the deconstructive circles he moved in: he wrote that 'le théâtre est un art trop brutal, trop impitoyable. Il ne souffre aucune "approche"' ['theatre is too brutal, too pitiless an art. It allows of no "approach"'].[12] These are just a few instances where models that others may have taken to be available, discourses they may have taken to be welcoming — whether innovative or traditional —, were approached by Lacoue-Labarthe in the mode of impossibility. Writing understood as mimesis, then, would be a mask neither referring back to the subject wearing it, nor — as it were — forward to whatever it might otherwise have represented or imitated. It could be seen as an absence (of subject) responding to an absence (of model). But as absence leads to absence in Lacoue-Labarthe's thinking, it has an extraordinary capacity to churn up, pull apart and elucidate a wide range of questions.

⋆   ⋆   ⋆   ⋆   ⋆

Lacoue-Labarthe's thinking of mimesis, in short, reaches far beyond our usual definitions of imitations and models, originals and copies. He pushes his explorations in this area to the point of suggesting that writing is a 'mimesis without model', which is to say that it can be a sheer appearance, coming into being without needing to refer to any previous reality. Several conclusions proceed from this point: not least that Lacoue-Labarthe's 'mimesis' is not at all to be understood as cognate with representationalist or realist approaches to literature. Beyond this, we can recall his frequent autobio(thanato)graphical texts: writing for him was not a job, a discourse or a discipline, but an allegory for the very fact of existence itself. 'Il a fallu m'admetttre [...] né pour la littérature' ['I had to admit [...] that I was born for literature'], he wrote, making in this crucial statement an exception to his reticence for metaphors of birth.[13] This line of thinking, according to which 'writing' in the broadest of senses does not refer back to any model but is a precarious act of sheer invention, certainly stems from the in-depth readings of Heidegger that he pursued in dialogue with Jean-Luc Nancy. The latter's thinking of a commonality which is without characteristics as such, but irreducible because it simply exists, and of our bodies as an originary spacing from and exposure to one another, surely draw on this same sense of existing without any previous model.

The two thinkers' dialogues on the notion of the stage as such an originary or irreducible space — rather than theatre, with its connotations of vision — speak to their investigations in this area. In his solo work, Lacoue-Labarthe pushed this notion of the stage much further than Nancy, in his work on Hölderlin, but notably also around opera and the allegorical figure of the *cantatrice*. It is surely no coincidence that his depictions of the latter should place her under mortal threat, undergoing a medical emergency where her very existence is called into question. As he wrote, 'elle ne cesse de réapparaître [...] elle ne cesse de disparaître' (ALEG 31; ['she reappears endlessly [...] she disappears endlessly']). The significance of this double statement relates to all that the *cantatrice* represents, as an allegory of the writer in Lacoue-Labarthe's words, and therefore ultimately as an autobiographical rendering of himself, given his self-identification with literature. And the significance in question is that we never simply *are*, but are always both coming into presence and departing from it. The latter point is underlined by the fact that in French, *disparaître* means both 'to disappear' and 'to die': the allegorical '*cantatrice*' is therefore always in the process of dying.

We could say the same of Lacoue-Labarthe, not least because his life was so fully dedicated to writing. But his relationship to death was by no means a purely allegorical one: his alcoholism and his heavy smoking habit — his reflections on asphyxiation and emphysema are not without referents — saw to that. Shortly before his death at age 66, he was in fact pronounced dead in May and then December 2006, as he recounts in a single page written in January 2007, fittingly entitled 'Postface'.[14] Weighing his words for obvious reasons, Lacoue-Labarthe nonetheless finds time to give one quotation — the notion of reading, quoting, working through others' texts persists till the end — which is taken from Baudelaire's 'À une passante' ['To a Passer-by']. In its setting it reads as follows: 'Tel fut l'envers de la disparition. Un effacement de la condition de l'exister — cette pure impossibilité. En somme, furtivement, l'impossible me fut possible ("... [u]n éclair, puis la nuit...")' ['Such was the reverse side of death. An effacement of the condition of existing — this pure impossibility. In sum, furtively, the impossible was possible for me ("... [a] flash, then night...")']. Referring in Baudelaire to the vision of a captivating female passer-by, in this instance the quotation is used to refer to the medical death which Lacoue-Labarthe had overcome. Now, an *éclair* is a flash of light — for Lacoue-Labarthe to speak of death in these terms, rather than with the usual language of obscurity or extinction of lights, is important: it seems to confirm that the process of clarification that his work undertook was not to be thought of in terms of completion. Clarity was not something to be definitively arrived at on the page, but rather a flash produced by the extinction of human consciousness, and lasting only an instant.

Notes to the Conclusion

1. In 'La Philosophie fantôme', pp. 213–14.
2. In 'Letter on Humanism', in *Martin Heidegger: Basic Writings* (London: Routledge, 1993), pp. 213–66 (p. 217).
3. Regarding the two terms, there is an interesting remark in the discussion featuring the six contributors, of whom Lacoue-Labarthe was one, to the volume *Mimesis: des articulations*. Sarah Kofman comments that 'Si nous avons gardé le terme grec, "Mimesis", ce n'est pas [...] pour marquer une référence à un sens originaire, propre, vrai, par rapport auquel toute traduction serait trahison, sens dérivé et déformé' ['Whilst we have kept the Greek term, "Mimesis", it is not [...] in order to refer to an originary, proper, true meaning, in relation to which all translation would be treason, derivative and denatured meaning'], in Agacinski et al., 'Six philosophes occupés à déplacer le philosophique à propos de la "mimesis"' ['Six Philosophers Trying to Displace the Philosophical on the Issue of Mimesis'], in *La Quinzaine littéraire*, 231 (16–30 april 1976), 19–22 (p. 20).
4. In '"Réfléchis!": un hommage', p. 86 (emphasis original).
5. In *Heidegger: la politique du poème* (Paris: Galilée, 2002), p. 101; *Heidegger and the Politics of Poetry*, trans. by Jeff Fort (Urbana and Chicago, University of Illinois, 2007), p. 73, trans. mod; see Lacoue-Labarthe's archive at IMEC, reference LAC 2.2 and LAC 19.1.
6. In 'Typographie', in *Mimesis des articulations*, pp. 167–270 (pp. 250, 210); in *Typography: Mimesis, Philosophy, Politics*, pp. 120, 82.
7. In *La Réponse d'Ulysse et autres textes sur l'Occident* ([*The Response of Ulysses and Other Texts on the Occident*]; Paris: Lignes/IMEC, 2012), p. 7.
8. Ibid., p. 9.
9. Ulysses is not the only example Lacoue-Labarthe gives: his essay 'Diderot: Le paradoxe et la mimesis' ['Diderot: Paradox and Mimesis'] explored the view of the *philosophe* that it was inner emptiness that made the actor able to play numerous external roles; see *L'Imitation des modernes*, pp. 15–38 and *Typography*, pp. 248–66.
10. Emphasis added. *Porte-parole* is the French term for a spokesperson, but it also means literally a 'word carrier'.
11. Nancy repeatedly takes up the formulation 'mimesis sans modèle' in his writing on Lacoue-Labarthe following the latter's death, for instance here: 'la mimèsis sans modèle, [qui] supprim[e] toute figure ou archifigure pouvant occuper la place du modèle, c'est-à-dire du sujet, c'est-à-dire, aussi, la place du nom' ['mimesis without model, [which] remove[s] all figures or archifigures able to occupy the place of model, which is to say that of the subject, which is to say, also, that of the name'], in 'Philippe', p. 425.

12. In 'La Fiction du biographique', p. 203.
13. In 'La Fiction du biographique', p. 197.
14. In *Préface à 'La Disparition'*, pp. 45–46. 'La Disparition' is a text written by Lacoue-Labarthe in 1965–66, and published in 2009 for the first time.

PRIMARY BIBLIOGRAPHY

1. Solo works and collaborations with others than Jean-Luc Nancy

1a. Books

LACOUE-LABARTHE, PHILIPPE, *Le Sujet de la philosophie (Typographies I)* (Paris: Aubier-Flammarion, 1979).

——*L'Imitation des modernes (Typographies II)* (Paris: Galilée, 1986).

——*La Poésie comme expérience* (Paris: Bourgois, 1986).

——*La Fiction du politique: Heidegger, l'art et la politique* (Paris: Bourgois, 1987).

——and MICHEL DEUTSCH, *Sit venia verbo* (Paris: Bourgois, 1988).

——*Musica ficta: Figures de Wagner* (Paris: Bourgois, 1991).

——*Pasolini, une improvisation: d'une sainteté* (1995; Bordeaux: William Blake, 2004).

——*Métaphrasis* suivi de *Le théâtre de Hölderlin* (Paris: PUF, 1998).

——*Phrase* (Paris, Bourgois, 2000).

——*Poétique de l'histoire* (Paris: Galilée, 2002).

——*Heidegger: la politique du poème* (Paris: Galilée, 2002).

——*Le Chant des muses* (Paris: Bayard, 2005).

——*L''Allégorie'* (Paris: Galilée, 2006).

——*La Vraie semblance* (Paris: Galilée, 2008).

——*Écrits sur l'art* (Genève: Réel, 2009).

——*Préface à 'La Disparition'* (Paris: Bourgois, 2009).

——*Agonie terminée, agonie interminable: sur Maurice Blanchot* (Paris: Galilée, 2011).

——*La Réponse d'Ulysse et autres textes sur l'Occident* (Paris: Lignes/IMEC, 2012).

——with JACQUES DERRIDA and HANS-GEORG GADAMER, *La Conférence de Heidelberg (1988): Heidegger, portée philosophique et politique de sa pensée*, ed. by Mireille Calle-Gruber (Paris: Lignes/IMEC, 2014).

——*Écrits sur la musique* (Paris: Bourgois, forthcoming).

1b. Articles

——'Biographie', *Le Nouveau commerce*, 13 (Spring 1969), 93–100.

——'L'"Allégorie"', *Le Nouveau commerce*, 18–19 (Spring 1971), 8–18.

——'La Dissimulation', in *Nietzsche, aujourd'hui,* vol. 2: *Passion* (Paris: U.G.E., 1973), pp. 9–36.

——et al., '[Discussion]', in *Nietzsche, aujourd'hui*: vol. 2: *Passion* (Paris: U.G.E., 1973), pp. 36–58.

——'Note sur Freud et la représentation', *Digraphe*, 3 (Autumn 1974), 70–81.

——'Présentation', *Poétique*, 21 (1975), 1–2.

——'L'Imprésentable', *Poétique*, 21 (1975), 53–95.

——'Typographie', in Derrida, Lacoue-Labarthe, Nancy et al., *Mimesis des articulations* (Paris: Flammarion, 1975), pp. 167–270.

——'Précis: Compte-rendu de Mathieu Bénézet, *Dits et récits du mortel: Ménipée*', *Critique*, 357 (February 1977), 146–53.

——'[À ce qu'il me semble...]', in François Laruelle, *Le Déclin de l'écriture* (Paris: Aubier-Flammarion, 1977), pp. 267–68.

——'De l'Impossibilité de connaître Heidegger en français', *La Quinzaine littéraire*, 264 (1–15 October 1977), 18–20.

——and MATHIEU BÉNÉZET, MAURICE BLANCHOT, MICHEL DEUTSCH et al., 'Avant-propos', in Bénézet, Blanchot, Lacoue-Labarthe et al., *Misère de la littérature* (Paris: Bourgois, 1978), p. 7.

——'Lettre (c'est une lettre)', in Bénézet, Blanchot, Lacoue-Labarthe et al., *Misère de la littérature* (Paris: Bourgois, 1978), pp. 55–72.

——'Tradition et vérité: à partir de la philosophie' (1979), *Europe*, 873 (May 2010), 61–71.

——and BÉNÉZET, 'L'Intimation', in Bénézet, Lacoue-Labarthe, Nancy et al., *'Haine de la poésie'* (Paris: Bourgois, 1979), pp. 9–21.

——and BÉNÉZET, 'Addendum', in Bénézet, Lacoue-Labarthe, Nancy et al., *'Haine de la poésie'* (Paris: Bourgois, 1979), 163–66.

——'Le Baudelaire de Benjamin: l'Utopie du livre' (1983), *L'Animal*, 19–20 (Winter 2008), 217–19.

——'Bye bye farewell' (1983), *L'Animal*, 19–20 (Winter 2008), 191–98.

——'Introduction', in Friedrich Hölderlin, *Hymnes, élégies et autres poèmes*, trans. by Armel Guerne (Paris: Flammarion, 1983), pp. 7–20.

——'Détroits' (1985), *L'Animal*, 19–20 (Winter 2008), 123–38.

——'Logos et technè' (1985) *L'Animal*, 19–20 (Winter 2008), 227–28.

——'Où en étions-nous?', in Jacques Derrida, Vincent Descombes, G. Kortian et al., *La Faculté de juger* (Paris: Minuit, 1985), pp. 165–93.

——'Avant-propos', in Walter Benjamin, *Le Concept de critique esthétique dans le romantisme allemand*, trans. by Lacoue-Labarthe and Anne-Marie Lang (1986; Paris: Flammarion, 2008), pp. 7–25.

——'L'Ampleur du désastre', *Libération* (12 March 1987), 31.

——and PATRICK HUTCHINSON, 'Entretien sur Hölderlin' (1987), *Europe*, 873 (May 2010), 43–60.

——'La Fiction du biographique' (1987), *Lignes*, 22 (May 2007), 195–204.

——and MAURICE ATTIAS, JACQUES DERRIDA, VÉRONIQUE HOTTE et al., 'De l'Écrit à la parole: table ronde' (1988), <http://hors-sol.net/revue/100111/> [consulted 19 February 2010].

——'La Vérité sublime' in Jean-François Courtine, Lacoue-Labarthe, Nancy et al., *Du sublime* (Paris, Belin, 1988), pp. 123–88.

——'Avant-propos', in Roger Laporte, *Lettre à personne* (Paris: Plon, 1989), pp. 11–18.

——and GEORGE STEINER, 'Correspondance ouverte', *Journal de l'amicale de philosophie (Strasbourg)*, 3 (January 1989), 6–19.

——and ALAIN BADIOU, JACQUES RANCIÈRE, and JEAN-FRANÇOIS LYOTARD, 'Liminaire sur l'ouvrage d'Alain Badiou, *L'Être et l'événement*', *Le Cahier (Collège international de philosophie)*, 8 (October 1989), 201–68.

——'Le Règne', *La Nouvelle barre du jour*, 216–17 (1989), 83–107.

——'De l'Éthique: à propos d'Antigone', in *Lacan avec les philosophes* (Paris: Albin Michel, 1991), pp. 20–36.

——'La Philosophie fantôme' (1991), *Lignes*, 22 (May 2007), 205–14.

——'Au Nom de l'Europe' (1992), *L'Animal*, 19–20 (Winter 2008),

——'L'Avortement de la littérature', *Du Féminin* (Grenoble: Le griffon d'argile and Presses Universitaires de Grenoble, 1992), pp. 3–19.

——'Une Figure pour (l')Europe ?', in *Géophilosophie de l'Europe: Penser l'Europe à ses frontières* (La Tour d'Aigues: Aube, 1993), pp. 74–76.

——et al., '[Discussion]', *Géophilosophie de l'Europe* (1993), pp. 77–85.

——'Préface', in Jean-Marie Pontévia, *La Peinture, masque et miroir*, 2nd ed. (1984; Bordeaux: William Blake & Co., 1993), pp. vii–xvii.

——'Nietzsche contre Wagner: Chronique d'une rupture annoncée', *Le Nouvel observateur*, 1545 (16–22 June 1994), 126.

——'Remarque sur Adorno et le jazz (d'un désart obscur)' (1994), *L'Animal*, 19–20 (Winter 2008), 203–09.

——'Dankrede' (1995), *Lignes*, 22 (May 2007), 215–23.

——'Éloge' (1995), *L'Animal*, 19–20 (Winter 2008), 241–42.

——'La Forme toute oublieuse de la fidélité' (1995), *L'Animal*, 19–20 (Winter 2008), 165–69.

——'Y a-t-il aujourd'hui une nouvelle problématique identitaire ?', *Transeuropéennes*, 6–7 (Winter 1995–96), 16–20.

——'L'Horreur occidentale' (1996), *Lignes*, 22 (May 2007), 224–34.

——'Les Intellectuels. Tentative de définition par eux-mêmes, enquête' (1997), *Lignes*, 22 (May 2007), 235–41.

——'Nous sommes dans l'urgence', *Lignes*, 31 (1997).

——'Syberberg: de l'Allemagne après Hitler' (1997), *L'Animal*, 19–20 (Winter 2008), 221–24.

——'Le Cinéma comme relais de l'idée nationale' (1998), *L'Animal*, 19–20 (Winter 2008), 225–26.

——'La Leçon de Burckhardt', in Jakob Burckhardt, *Leçons sur l'art occidental*, trans. by Bernard Kreiss (Paris: Hazan, 1998), pp. 5–13.

——'La Naissance est la mort' (1998), *Lignes*, 22 (May 2007), 242–46.

——'La Tragédie de Sophocle' and 'La "version" de Hölderlin', in leaflet accompanying production of *Œdipe le tyran* (1998), unpublished.

——'Traduction et histoire' (1999), *L'Animal*, 19–20 (Winter 2008), 141–48.

——'Entretien du 22 juin 2000', in Dominique Janicaud, *Heidegger en France, vol. 2: entretiens* (Paris: Hachette, 2001), pp. 198–209.

——Interview with Pascal Possoz, unpublished (early 2000s).

——'L'Antithèse ironique', *Lignes*, 7 (February 2002), 308–19.

——'Avant-propos', in Roger Laporte, *Le Cahier posthume* (Paris: Léo Scheer, 2002), pp. 7–19.

——'Un'Impressione d'*atelier*', interview with Federico Nicolao (2000), <http://chorusday.blogspot.co.uk/2008_04_01_archive.html> [consulted 8 April 2014]

——'De la Clarté' (2002), *L'Animal*, 19–20 (Winter 2008), 233–36.

——'Katharsis et Mathèsis' (2002), *Europe*, 873 (May 2010), 72–94.

——'Peut-on montrer la philosophie ?' (2003), <http://tinyurl.com/n9b9n27> [consulted 25 March 2011].

——'"Réfléchis !" (un hommage)' (2003), in Jean-Christophe Bailly, *La Véridiction (sur Phlippe Lacoue-Labarthe)* (Paris: Bourgois, 2011), pp. 81–90.

——'De Hölderlin à Marx: mythe, imitation, tragédie: Entretien réalisé par Bruno Duarte', *Labyrinthe*, 22 (2005), 121–33.

——'Le Dépaysagement', in Thibaut Cuisset, *Le Dehors absolu* (Trézélan: Filigraines, 2005), pp. 7–11.

——'Hommage', *Rue Descartes*, 48 (2005), 74–78.

——and MICHEL DEUTSCH, 'Pièces', in Euripide, *Les Phéniciennnes*, trans. by Lacoue-Labarthe and Claire Nancy (Paris: Belin, 2007), pp. 5–11.

1c. Translations

——(and ANNE-MARIE LANG), BENJAMIN, WALTER, *Le Concept de critique esthétique dans le romantisme allemand* (Paris: Aubier-Flammarion, 1986)

——(and FEDERICO NICOLAO), CAPRONI, GIORGIO, *Cartes postales d'un voyage en Pologne* (Bordeaux: William Blake & Co., 2004)

——(and CLAIRE NANCY), EURIPIDES, *Les Phéniciennes* (Paris: Belin, 2007)

——(and Ana Domenech), Foix, Josep Vicenc, *Gertrudis* suivi de *KRTU* (Paris: Bourgois, 1987)

——(and Roger Munier), Heidegger, Martin, 'Le Défaut de noms sacrés', *Contre toute attente*, 2–3 (Spring-Summer 1981)

——(and Ana Samardzija), Heidegger, Martin, *La Pauvreté* (Strasbourg: Presses Universitaires de Strasbourg, 2004)

——Hölderlin, Friedrich, *Antigone de Sophocle* (1978; Paris: Bourgois, 1998).

——Hölderlin, 'Deux poèmes de la "folie" [La Vue, Vue]' (1980), *L'Animal*, 19–20 (Winter 2008), 139–40.

——Hölderlin, 'Pain et vin', *Digraphe*, 22–23 (March 1980).

——Hölderlin, *Œdipe le tyran de Sophocle* (Paris: Bourgois, 1998).

——Hölderlin, 'Andenken: Je pense à vous (Don d'un poème)', *Lignes*, 22 (May 2007), 248–51.

——Nietzsche, Friedrich, *La Naissance de la tragédie* (1977; Paris: Gallimard, folio/essais, 1992).

——(and Claire Nancy), Pindar, 'Sixth Nemean (Extract)', *Lignes*, 22 (May 2007), 247.

2. Collaborations with Jean-Luc Nancy

2a. Books

Lacoue-Labarthe, Philippe and Nancy, Jean-Luc, *Le Titre de la lettre: Une lecture de Lacan* (1973; Paris: Galilée, 1990).

——(eds.), *Littérature et philosophie mêlées*, *Poétique*, 21 (1975).

——*L'Absolu littéraire: Théorie de la littérature du romantisme allemand* (Paris: Le Seuil, 1978).

——*La Panique politique* suivi de *Le Peuple juif ne rêve pas* (1979, 1980; Paris: Bourgois, 2013).

——(eds.), *Les Fins de l'homme: à partir du travail de Jacques Derrida* (1980; Paris: Hermann, 2013).

——*Le Mythe nazi* (1980; La Tour d'Aigues, 2005).

——(eds.), *Rejouer le politique* (Paris: Galilée, 1981).

——(eds.), *Le Retrait du politique* (Paris: Galilée, 1983).

——*Scène* suivi de *Dialogue sur le dialogue* (1992, 2005; Paris: Bourgois, 2013).

2b. Articles

——'Présentation', *Poétique*, 5 (1971), 99–103.

——'Le Dialogue des genres', *Poétique*, 21 (1975), 148–57.

——with Sylviane Agacinski, Jacques Derrida et al, 'Six philosophes occupés à déplacer le philosophique à propos de la "mimesis"', *La Quinzaine littéraire*, 231 (16–30 april 1976), 19–22.

——'Philippe Lacoue-Labarthe, *Le Sujet de la philosophie*', interview conducted by Jean-Luc Nancy, *L'Actualité littéraire*, 18 (April 1979), 13.

——'Ouverture' in Étienne Balibar, Lacoue-Labarthe, Nancy et al., *Rejouer le politique* (Paris: Galilée, 1981), pp. 11–28.

——with Alain David and Philippe Jandin, 'Entretien', *Exercices de la patience*, 3–4 (Spring 1982), 219–31.

——'Noli me frangere' (1982), *Europe*, 973 (May 2010), 32–42.

——'Le "Retrait" du politique', in Denis Kambouchner, Lacoue-Labarthe, Nancy et al., *Le Retrait du politique* (Paris: Galilée, 1983), pp. 183–200.

——'Chers amis: a Letter on the Closure of the Political' (1984), in *Retreating the Political*, trans. and intro. by Simon Sparks (London: Routledge, 1997), pp. 143–47.

——'Monogrammes X' (1992), *L'Animal*, 19–20 (Winter 2008), 229–32.

——'Derrida à Strasbourg', in Derrida, Lacoue-Labarthe, Nancy et al., *Penser à Strasbourg* (Paris/Strasbourg: Galilée/Ville de Strasbourg, 2004), pp. 11–20.

——and JACQUES DERRIDA, 'Dialogue', *Rue Descartes*, 52 (May 2006), 86–99.

2c. Translations

——BENJAMIN, WALTER, 'Sur la *Trauerspiel* et la tragédie', *Furor (esthétique et rhétorique)*, 7 (1982), pp. 3–14.

——BENJAMIN, 'Métaphysique de la jeunesse (dialogue)' (1985), *L'Animal*, 19–20 (Winter 2008), 211–15.

——FREUD, SIGMUND, 'Personnages psychopathiques sur la scène', *Digraphe*, 3 (Autumn 1974)

——NIETZSCHE, FRIEDRICH, *Rhétorique et langage* (1971; Chatou: Transparence, 2008).

——NIETZSCHE, FRIEDRICH, 'Fragments posthumes 1874–1876', in *Œuvres philosophiques complètes*, vol. 2 (Paris: Gallimard, 1988).

——(and ANNE-MARIE LANG), texts by FRIEDRICH SCHLEGEL, A. W. SCHLEGEL, SCHELLING, NOVALIS, and of collective or uncertain authorship, in *L'Absolu littéraire* (Paris: Seuil, 1978), passim.

SECONDARY BIBLIOGRAPHY

1. Collective Volumes / Journal Issues

CHOULET, PHILIPPE and EMMANUEL LAUGIER, eds, *Cahier Philippe Lacoue-Labarthe* in *L'Animal*, 19–20 (Winter 2008), 93–273.

LAWTOO, NIDESH, ed., *Conrad's 'Heart of Darkness' and Contemporary Thought: Revisiting the Horror with Lacoue-Labarthe* (London: Bloomsbury, 2012).

ROGOCINSKI, JACOB, ed., *Philippe Lacoue-Labarthe: la Césure et l'impossible* (Paris: Lignes, 2010).

VARIOUS, *Philippe Lacoue-Labarthe* issue of *Lignes*, 22 (May 2007).

VARIOUS, *Philippe Lacoue-Labarthe* issue of *Europe*, 973 (May 2010).

2. Films

BARISON, DAVID and DANIEL ROSS, *The Ister*, featuring Lacoue-Labarthe, Jean-Luc Nancy, Bernard Stiegler and Hans-Jürgen Syberberg (Australia, 2004).

BAUDILLON, CHRISTINE and FRANÇOIS LAGARDE, 'Entretiens de l'île Saint-Pierre', featuring Lacoue-Labarthe and Jean-Christophe Bailly, in *Proëme de Philippe Lacoue-Labarthe* (Montpellier: Hors œil, 2011).

—— *Philippe Lacoue-Labarthe: Altus* (Montpellier: Hors œil, forthcoming)

BAUDRILLON, CHRISTINE and LACOUE-LABARTHE, PHILIPPE, 'Andenken' in *Proëme de Philippe Lacoue-Labarthe* (Montpellier: Hors œil, 2011).

DEUTSCH, MICHEL, *Voyage à Tübingen: un Portrait de Philippe Lacoue-Labarthe* (2009), <http://www.filmsdocumentaires.com/films/434-philippe-lacoue-labarthe> on [consulted 2 November 2010].

3. Internet Resources

Recording of a memorial conference for Lacoue-Labarthe at Columbia University, NYC on 23 March 2007, available at <https://slought.org/resources/philippe_lacoue_labarthe>.

4. Articles and Books on Lacoue-Labarthe

N.B. I have not given individual details of the numerous interventions contained in the collective journal issues or volumes listed above, except in the case of Jean-Luc Nancy (see section 5), given his exceptional importance for Lacoue-Labarthe's work, and other articles directly quoted.

AESCHIMANN, ERIC, 'Jean-Luc Nancy, philosopher à Strasbourg', *Libération*, 2 July 2011.

BAILLY, JEAN-CHRISTOPHE, 'Préface: l'Étrange émotion', in Lacoue-Labarthe, *Ecrits sur l'art* ([Dijon]: Presses du réel, 2009).

—— *La Véridiction (sur Philippe Lacoue-Labarthe)* (Paris: Bourgois, 2011).

BARNARD, PHILIPPE and CHERYL LESTER, 'Introduction', in Lacoue-Labarthe and Nancy, *The Literary Absolute: the Theory of Literature in German Romanticism* (Albany: SUNY Press, 1988).

BELHAJ KACEM, MEHDI, *Inesthétique et mimésis: Badiou, Lacoue-Labarthe et la question de l'art* (Paris: Lignes, 2010).

BERNSTEIN, SUSAN, 'Re-re-re-reading Jena', *Modern Language Notes*, 110: 4 (1995), 834–55.

BIANCHI, LÉONID and ARISTIDE KHARMALOV, 'Présentation', in Lacoue-Labarthe, *Agonie terminée, agonie interminable: sur Maurice Blanchot* (Paris: Galilée, 2011), pp. 9–53.

——'Les Écrits sur l'Occident de Philippe Lacoue-Labarthe', in *La Réponse d'Ulysse et autres textes sur l'Occident* (Paris: Lignes/IMEC, 2012), pp. 145–83.

BRAUN, LUCIEN, 'Rapport de pré-soutenance [Philippe Lacoue-Labarthe]', unpublished (1987).

CONLEY, VERA ANDERMATT, 'Philippe Lacoue-Labarthe', in *The Columbia History of Twentieth-Century French Thought* (New York: Columbia U. P., 2006), pp. 570–71.

CRITCHLEY, SIMON, 'Re-tracing the Political: Politics and Community in the Work of Philippe Lacoue-Labarthe and Jean-Luc Nancy', in *The Political Subject of Violence*, ed. by David Campbell and Michael Dillon (Manchester: Manchester U. P., 1993), pp. 73–93.

DREYFUS, ALAIN, 'Compte-rendu d'*Antigone* au festival d'Avignon', in *Libération* (13 July 1998).

FRASER, NANCY, 'The French Derrideans: Politicizing Deconstruction or Deconstructing the Political?', in *New German Critique*, 33 (Autumn 1984), 127–54.

FYNSK, CHRISTOPHER, 'Obituary: Philippe Lacoue-Labarthe, 1940–2007', *Radical Philosophy*, 144 (July-August 2007).

GASCHÉ, RODOLPHE, 'Situationniste pour une part?', *Lignes*, 22 (May 2007), 120–29.

GOURGOURIS, STATHIS, *Does Literature Think?: Literature as Theory for an Antimythical Era* (Stanford: Stanford U. P., 2003), pp. 34–39.

GOUX, JEAN-JOSEPH, 'Politics and Modern Art: Heidegger's Dilemma: Review of *La Fiction du politique* by Philippe Lacoue-Labarthe and *Le Nazisme et la culture* by Lionel Richard', trans. by Michele Sharp, *Diacritics*, 19: 3–4 (Autumn-Winter 1989), 10–24.

GUERLAC, SUZANNE, 'Review of Gusdorf, *Fondements du savoir romantique* and Lacoue-Labarthe and Nancy, *L'Absolu littéraire*', *Modern Language Notes*, 100:4 (September 1985), 887–94.

HIRT, ANDRÉ, *Un Homme littéral: Philippe Lacoue-Labarthe* (Paris: Kimé, 2009).

HOOSELMA, DANIEL J., 'The Echo of an Impossible Future in *The Literary Absolute*', *Modern Language Notes*, 119:4 (September 2004), 845–68.

JAMES, IAN, 'On Interrupted Myth' in *Journal of Cultural Research*, 4:9 (October 2005), 331–49.

——*The Fragmentary Demand: an Introduction to the Philosophy of Jean-Luc Nancy* (Stanford: Stanford U. P., 2006).

JAY, MARTIN, 'Mimesis and Mimetology: Adorno and Lacoue-Labarthe', *The Semblance of Subjectivity: Essays in Adorno's Aesthetic Theory*, ed. by Tom Huhn and Lambert Zuidervaart (London: MIT Press, 1997), pp. 29–54.

LAPORTE, ROGER, '[J'ai longtemps cherché en vain...]', *Avant-guerre*, 2 (1st quarter 1981), 72.

——'Souvenir de Tübingen', in *Entre deux mondes* (Montpellier: Gris banal, 1988), pp. 39–46.

LYOTARD, JEAN-FRANÇOIS, 'Rapport de lecture en vue de la soutenance sur travaux par Philippe Lacoue-Labarthe d'une thèse de doctorat ès-lectures', unpublished (1986).

MARTIS, JOHN, *Philippe Lacoue-Labarthe: Representation and the Loss of the Subject* (New York: Fordham University Press, 2005).

MAY, TODD, 'The Community's Absence in Lyotard, Nancy, and Lacoue-Labarthe', *Philosophy Today*, 37:3 (1993), 275–84.

MCKEANE, JOHN and HANNES OPELZ, *Blanchot Romantique* (Oxford: Peter Lang, 2010).

MEITINGER, SERGE, 'Idéalisme et poétique', *Romantisme: Revue du Dix-Neuvième Siècle*, 14.45 (1984), 3–24.

NEWMARK, KEVIN, 'L'Absolu littéraire: Friedrich Schlegel and the Myth of Irony', Modern Language Notes, 107 (1992), 905–30.

OPELZ, HANNES, 'L'Espoir d'une communauté: Philippe Lacoue-Labarthe, Agonie terminée, agonie interminable' in Cahiers Maurice Blanchot, 2 (Winter 2013-14), 138–56.

PEETERS, BENOÎT, Derrida (Paris: Flammarion, 2010).

REDFIELD, MARC, 'Romanticism, Bildung, and The Literary Absolute', in Lessons of Romanticism: a Critical Companion, ed. by Thomas Pfau and Robert E. Gleckner (London: Duke U. P., 1998), pp. 41–54.

RONELL, AVITAL, 'The Differends of Man', Finitude's Score: Essays for the End of the Millennium (London: University of Nebraska Press, 1994), pp. 255–68.

ROSS, ALISON, 'Lacoue-Labarthe: Aesthetic Presentation and the Figuring of the Political', in The Aesthetic paths of philosophy: Presentation in Kant, Heidegger, Lacoue-Labarthe and Nancy (Stanford: Stanford U. P., 2007), pp. 109–33.

SCHAEFER, MARTIN JOERG, Schmerz zum Mitsein: zur Relektüre Celans und Heideggers durch Philippe Lacoue-Labarthe und Jean-Luc Nancy (Würzberg: Königshausen & Neumann, 2003).

SCHUFREIDER, GREGORY, 'Sticking Heidegger with a Stela: Lacoue-Labarthe, Art and Politics', in French Interpretations of Heidegger: an Exceptional Reception, ed. by David Pettigrew and François Raffoul (Albany: SUNY Press, 2008).

SPARKS, SIMON, 'Editor's Introduction: Politica Ficta', in Retreating the Political (London: Routledge, 1997), pp. xiv-xxviii.

STONE, DAN, 'Review of Retreating the Political (1997)', French Studies, 53:3 (July 1999), 370.

TREZISE, THOMAS, 'Foreword', in Lacoue-Labarthe, The Subject of Philosophy, trans. by Trezise et al. (London: University of Minnesota Press, 1993), pp. xiii-xx.

XIROS COOPER, JOHN, 'Philippe Lacoue-Labarthe, The Subject of Philosophy', Canadian Philosophical Reviews, 15:4 (1995), 262–63.

5. Works by Jacques Derrida and Jean-Luc Nancy

DERRIDA, JACQUES, 'Le Théâtre de la cruauté et la clôture de la représentation', in L'Écriture et la différence (Paris: Seuil, 1967), pp. 341–68.

——'Les Fins de l'homme', in Marges de la philosophie (Paris: Minuit, 1972).

——'La Double séance', in La Dissémination (Paris: Seuil, 1972), pp. 215–347.

——'Fors: les Mots anglés de Nicholas Abraham et Maria Torok', in Nicholas Abraham and Maria Torok, Le Verbier de l'homme aux loups (Paris: Aubier-Flammarion, 1976), pp. 7–73.

——'La Loi du genre' (1979), in Parages, rev. ed. (Paris: Galilée, 2003), pp. 231–66.

——La Carte postale: de Socrate à Freud et au-delà (Paris: Flammarion, 1980).

——'Ponctuations: le temps d'une thèse' (1980), in Du Droit à la philosophie (Paris: Galilée, 1990), pp. 439–60.

——'[Rapport de lecture relatif à la soutenance par Philippe Lacoue-Labarthe d'une thèse de doctorat]', unpublished (1986).

——'Désistance', in Psyché: Inventions de l'autre (Paris: Galilée, 1987), pp. 597–638.

——De l'Esprit: Heidegger et la question (Paris: Galilée, 1987).

——Spectres de Marx: l'État de la dette, le travail du deuil et la nouvelle Internationale (Paris: Galilée, 1993).

——'The Time is Out of Joint', in Anselm Haverkamp (ed.), Deconstruction is/in America. A New Sense of the Political (New York, New York U. P., 1995), pp. 14–40.

——Demeure (Paris: Galilée, 1998).

——'Le Lieu dit: Stasbourg', in Derrida, Lacoue-Labarthe, Nancy et al., Penser à Strasbourg (Paris/Strasbourg: Galilée/Ville de Strasbourg, 2004), pp. 31–59.

——'Ex Abrupto', in Avant-guerre, 2 (1st quarter 1981), 70.

——with GEOFFREY BENNINGTON, Derrida (1991; Paris: Seuil, 2008).

NANCY, JEAN-LUC, *La Remarque spéculative: un Bon mot de Hegel* (Paris: Aubier-Flammarion, 1973).

——'Logodædalus (Kant écrivain)', *Poétique*, 21 (1975), 24–52.

——*Le Discours de la syncope: I. Logodædalus* (Paris: Aubier-Flammarion, 1976).

——'[Le drame commençait...]', *Avant-guerre*, 2 (1st quarter 1981), 73–74.

——*La Communauté désœuvrée*, rev. ed. (1983; Paris: Bourgois, 1986).

——*L'Impératif catégorique* (Paris: Aubier-Flammarion, 1992),

——*La Création du monde ou la mondialisation* (Paris: Galilée, 2002).

——'Un Commencement', in Lacoue-Labarthe, *L'Allégorie'* (Paris: Galilée, 2006), pp. 123–66.

——'À Philippe Lacoue-Labarthe' (2007), <http://tinyurl.com/nclwkau> [consulted 10 December 2009].

——'Tu aimais les *Leçons des Ténèbres'*, *Lignes*, 22 (May 2007), 11–15.

——'Philippe Lacoue-Labarthe, la syncope reste ouverte' (December 2007), <http://tinyurl.com/pkwnskw> [consulted 3 August 2010].

——'D'une "mimesis sans modèle": entretien avec Philippe Choulet', *L'Animal*, 19–20 (Winter 2008), 107–14.

——'Philippe Lacoue-Labarthe à Strasbourg', *Europe*, 973 (May 2010), 11–16.

——'Récit, récitation, récitatif', *Europe*, 973 (May 2010), 203–17.

——'Philippe', in *Philippe Lacoue-Labarthe: la césure et l'impossible*, ed. by Jacob Rogocinski (Paris: Lignes, 2010), pp. 409–33.

——Participation in *Les Chants de Mandrin*, directed by Rabah Ameur-Zaïmeche (2011).

——'Corps, théâtre', in *Passions du corps dans les dramaturgies contemporaines*, ed. by Alexandra Poulain (Paris: Septentrion, 2011).

——*Maurice Blanchot: Passion politique* (Paris: Galilée, 2011).

——Correspondence with the author, October 2011-April 2014.

——Interviews with the author, 27 July and 19 September 2013.

6. Other Works

AGAMBEN, GIORGIO, 'Oedipus and the Sphinx', in *Stanzas: Word and Phantasm in Western Culture*, trans. by Roland L. Martinez (London: University of Minnesota Press, 1993), pp. 135–40.

BEISSNER, FRIEDRICH, *Hölderlins Übersetzungen aus dem Griechischen* (1933; Stuttgart: Metzler, 1961).

BÉNÉZET, MATHIEU, *Dits et récits du mortel: Ménipée* (Paris: Flammarion, 1977).

BERMAN, ANTOINE, *L'Épreuve de l'étranger: Culture et traduction dans l'Allemagne romantique, Herder, Goethe, Schlegel, Novalis, Humboldt, Schleiermacher, Hölderlin* (Paris: Gallimard, 1984).

BLANCHOT, MAURICE, *Le Ressassement éternel* (Paris: Minuit, 1951).

——*Le Dernier homme* (Paris: Gallimard, 1957).

——*L'Entretien infini* (Paris: Gallimard, 1969).

——*L'Écriture du désastre* (Paris: Gallimard, 1980).

——*Écrits politiques 1953–1993* (Paris: Gallimard, 2008).

BÜRGER, PETER, *Theory of the Avant-Garde* (1974), trans. by Michael Shaw (Manchester: Manchester University Press, 1984).

CELAN, PAUL, *Poems of Paul Celan*, trans. by Michael Hamburger (London: Anvil, 1988).

CRITCHLEY, SIMON, *Very Little... Almost Nothing: Death, Philosophy, Literature* (London: Routledge, 1997), pp. 85–131.

——'A Commentary Upon Derrida's Reading of Hegel in *Glas*', in *Hegel After Derrida* (London: Routledge, 1998), pp. 197–226.

DEWEY, JOHN, *Art as Experience* (London: Allen & Unwin, 1934).

FARIAS, VICTOR, *Heidegger and Nazism* (1987), trans. by Paul Burrell, Dominic di Bernardi, and Gabriel R. Ricci (Philadelphia: Temple U. P., 1989).

FERRY, LUC and ALAIN RENAULT, *La Pensée '68: Essai sur l'antihumanisme contemporain* (Paris: Gallimard, 1985).

——*Heidegger et les modernes* (Paris: Grasset, 1988).

FICHTE, JOHANN GOTTLIEB, *Sämmtliche Werke und Nachlass*, vol. III: *Grundlage der gesammten Wissenschaftlehre* (1794–1802) (Charlottesville: InteLex, 2001).

FOUCAULT, MICHEL, *Les Mots et les choses: une Archéologie du savoir* (Paris: Gallimard, Tel, 1966).

FREUD, SIGMUND, 'Analysis Terminable and Interminable' (1937), in *The Standard Edition of the Complete Psychological Works of Sigmund Freud*, vol. XXIII (London: Vintage, 2001), pp. 209–54.

GOETHE, JOHANN WOLFGANG, *Wilhelm Meisters Lehrjahre* (1795–96; Stuttgart: Reclam, 1982).

GOLDHILL, SIMON, *How to Stage Greek Tragedy Today* (London: University of Chicago Press, 2007).

GUNTHERT, ANDRÉ, *Le Voyage du T.N.S.: 1975–1983* (Paris: Solin, 1983).

HEGEL, G. W. F., *Hegel on Tragedy*, ed. by Anne and Henry Paolucci (Westport: Greenwood, 1978).

HEIDEGGER, MARTIN, 'Discours et proclamations' (1933–34), trans. by Jean-Pierre Faye in *Médiations: Revue des expressions contemporaines*, 3 (Autumn 1961), pp. 139–50.

——*An Introduction to Metaphysics* (1935–1953), trans. by Ralph Manheim (Garden City: Doubleday, 1961).

——'The Origin of the Work of Art' (1935–1937), in *Basic Writings*, ed. by David Farrell Krell, rev. ed. (London: Routledge, 1993), pp. 139–212.

——*Nietzsche*, vols. I–IV (1936–1941), trans. by David Farrell Krell (London: HarperCollins, 1991).

——'Overcoming Metaphysics' (1936–1946), in *The Heidegger Controversy: a Critical Reader*, ed. by Richard Wolin (London: MIT Press, 1991), pp. 67–90.

——'Letter on Humanism' (1946), in *Martin Heidegger: Basic Writings*, ed. by David Farrell Krell (London: Routledge, 1993), pp. 213–66.

——*Elucidations of Hölderlin's Poetry*, trans. by Keith Hoeller (Amherst: Humanity, 2000).

JANICAUD, DOMINIQUE, *Heidegger en France*, vol. I: *Récit* (Paris: Albin Michel, 2001).

——*Heidegger en France*, vol. II: *Entretiens* (Paris: Albin Michel, 2001).

HÖLDERLIN, FRIEDRICH, *Selected Poems and Fragments*, trans. by Michael Hamburger (London: Penguin, 1998).

——*Hölderlin's 'Sophocles': Oedipus and Antigone*, trans. by David Constantine (High Green: Bloodaxe, 2001).

——*Essays and Letters*, trans. by Jeremy Adler and Charlie Louth (London: Penguin, 2009).

JEAN PAUL, *Werke*, ed. by Norbert Miller, vol. V: *Vorschüle der Æsthetik* (Munich: Carl Hanser, 1971).

LOUTH, CHARLIE, *Hölderlin and the Dynamics of Translation* (Oxford: Legenda, 1998).

LYOTARD, JEAN-FRANÇOIS, *La Condition postmoderne: rapport sur le savoir* (Paris: Minuit, 1979).

McKEANE, JOHN, '*Périmer d'avance*: Blanchot, Derrida, and Influence', in *Questions of Influence in Modern French Literature*, ed. by Thomas Baldwin, James Fowler, and Ana de Medeiros (Basingstoke: Palgrave Macmillan, 2013), pp. 111–25.

MORIN, MARIE-ÈVE, *Jean-Luc Nancy* (London: Polity, 2012).

NIETZSCHE, FRIEDRICH, *The Birth of Tragedy out of the Spirit of Music* (1872), trans. by Shaun Whiteside (London: Penguin, 1993).

——*The Untimely Meditations: Thoughts Out of Season, Parts I and II* (1873–76) trans. by Anthony M. Ludovici (New York: DigiReads: 2009).

——*Thus Spoke Zarathustra* (1883–85) trans. by R. J. Hollingdale (Harmondsworth: Penguin, 1961).

OTT, HUGO, *Martin Heidegger: a Political Life* (1988), trans. by Allan Blunden (London: HarperCollins, 1993).

POTOLSKY, MATTHEW, *Mimesis* (Abingdon: Routledge, 2006).

RICHARDSON, WILLIAM J., *Heidegger: Through Phenomenology to Thought* (The Hague: Martinus Nijhoff, 1963).

RONELL, AVITAL, 'The Sacred Alien: Heidegger's Reading of Hölderlin's "Andenken"', in *The Überreader: Selected Works of Avital Ronell* (Champaign: University of Illinois Press, 2007), pp. 205–26.

SARTRE, JEAN-PAUL, *L'Être et le néant: Essai d'ontologie phénoménologique* (Paris: Gallimard, 1943).

——*L'Existentialisme est un humanisme* (Paris: Gallimard, 1945).

SCHELLING, F. W. J., *The Unconditional in Human Knowledge: Four Early Essays 1794–96*, trans. by Fritz Marti (Lewisburg: Bucknell U.P., 1980).

SCHLEGEL, FRIEDRICH, *Lucinde and the Fragments*, trans. by Peter Firchow (Minneapolis: University of Minnesota Press, 1971).

SOLLERS, PHILIPPE, 'De quelques contradictions', *Tel quel*, 38 (Summer 1969), i–ix (p. vii).

SOPHOCLES, *The Three Theban Plays*, trans. by Robert Fagles (Harmondsworth: Penguin, 1982).

STEINER, GEORGE, *Antigones: the Antigone Myth in Western Literature, Art, and Thought* (Oxford: Oxford U.P., 1986).

SZONDI, PETER, *Essay on the Tragic*, trans. by Paul Fleming (1961; Stanford: Stanford U. P., 2002).

SYBERBERG, HANS-JÜRGEN, *Our Hitler: a Film from Germany* (1977; Berlin: Film Galerie 451, 2004).

TODOROV, TZVETAN (ed.), *Théorie de la littérature* (Paris: Seuil, 1965).

——*La Notion de littérature et autres essais* (Paris: Seuil, 1987).

VARIOUS, 'De la Misère en milieu étudiant' (Strasbourg: A.F.G.E.S., 1966).

VARIOUS, *Théorie d'ensemble* (Paris: Seuil, 1968).

BIBLIOGRAPHY OF
TRANSLATIONS INTO ENGLISH

1. Books

LACOUE-LABARTHE, PHILIPPE and JEAN-LUC NANCY, *The Literary Absolute: the Theory of Literature in German Romanticism*, trans. by Philippe Barnard and Cheryl Lester (Albany: SUNY Press, 1988).

—— *Typography: Mimesis, Philosophy, Politics*, ed. by Christopher Fynsk (1989; Stanford: Stanford University Press, 1998).

—— *Heidegger, Art and Politics: the Fiction of the Political,* trans. by Chris Turner (Oxford: Blackwell, 1990).

—— WITH JEAN-LUC NANCY, 'The Nazi Myth', trans. by Brian Holmes in *Critical Inquiry*, 16:2 (Winter 1990), 291–312.

—— WITH JEAN-LUC NANCY, *The Title of the Letter: a Reading of Lacan*, trans. by David Pettigrew and François Raffoul (Albany: SUNY Press, 1992).

—— *The Subject of Philosophy*, trans. and intro. by Thomas Tresize (Minneapolis: University of Minnesota Press, 1993).

—— *Musica Ficta: Figures of Wagner*, trans. by Felicia McCarren (Stanford: Stanford University Press, 1994).

—— WITH JEAN-LUC NANCY, *Retreating the Political*, trans. and intro. by Simon Sparks (London: Routledge, 1997).

—— *Poetry as Experience*, trans. by Andrea Tarnowski (Stanford: Stanford University Press, 1999).

—— *Heidegger and the Politics of Poetry*, trans. by Jeff Fort (Urbana: University of Illinois Press, 2007).

2. Other Texts

—— 'Mimesis and Truth: Review of René Girard, *Système du délire* and *La violence et le sacré*, translator unknown in *Diacritics*, 8:1 (Spring 1978), 10–23.

—— 'Talks' (trans. of 'Différend dans le judicieux', 1982) by Christopher Fynsk in *Diacritics*, 14:3 (Fall 1984), 24–37.

—— 'Required Reading: Review of Victor Farias's *Heidegger et le nazisme*', trans. by Stuart Barnett and Lynn Festa, *Diacritics*, 19:3–4 (Autumn–Winter 1989), 38–48.

—— 'Neither an Accident nor a Mistake', trans. by Paula Wissing, *Critical Inquiry*, 15:2 (Winter 1989), 481–84.

—— 'Poetry as Experience', trans. by Roxanne Lapidus, *SubStance*, 18:3:60 (1989), 22–29.

—— 'The Jewish People Do Not Dream', trans. by Brian Holmes, *Stanford Literature Review*, 6: 1 (1989), pp. 191–209 and 8: 1–2 (1991), pp. 39–55.

—— 'Sublime Truth (Part 1)', trans. by David Kuctha, *Cultural Critique*, 18 (Spring 1991), 5–31.

—— 'Sublime Truth (Part 2)', trans. by David Kuctha, *Cultural Critique*, 20 (Winter 1991–92), 207–29.

—— 'Phrase VII', trans by Leslie Hill, in *On Jean-Luc Nancy: the Sense of Philosophy*, ed. by Darren Sheppard, Simon Sparks and Colin Thomas (London: Routledge, 1997)

——'Poetry's Courage', trans. by Simon Sparks, in *The Solid Letter: Readings of Friedrich Hölderlin*, ed. by Aris Fioretos (Stanford: Stanford University Press, 1999), pp. 74–93.

——'Fidelities', trans. by Michael Syrotinski, *OLR*, 22 (2000), 132–51.

——'Introduction to Walter Benjamin's *The Concept of Art Criticism in German Romanticism*', trans. by David Ferris, in *Walter Benjamin and Romanticism*, ed. by Beatrice Hanssen and Andrew Benjamin (London: Continuum, 2002), pp. 9–18.

——'The Contestation of Death', trans. by Philip Anderson, in *The Power of Contestation: Perspectives on Maurice Blanchot*, ed. by Kevin Hart and Geoffrey H. Hartman (London: The John Hopkins University Press, 2004), pp. 141–55.

——'The Horror of the West', trans. by Nidesh Lawtoo and Hannes Opelz in Lawtoo (ed.), *Conrad's 'Heart of Darkness' and Contemporary Thought: Revisiting the Horror with Lacoue-Labarthe* (London: Bloomsbury, 2012), pp. 111–22.

——and NANCY and DERRIDA, 'Discussion', in Derrida, *For Strasbourg*, trans. by Pascale-Anne Brault and Michael Naas (New York: Fordham U. P., 2014), pp. 17–30.

INDEX

Adorno, Theodor 114, 132
Agacinski, Sylviane 68
Anouilh, Jean 108
Aristotle 21, 82, 128
Artaud, Antonin 81
Aubenque, Pierre 35

Badiou, Alain 2
Bailly, Jean-Christophe 2, 49
Balibar, Etienne 33
Balzac, Honoré de 27
Barthes, Roland 12, 19
Baudelaire, Charles 4, 111, 114–16, 156–57
Belhaj Kacem, Mehdi 148
Bénézet, Mathieu 4, 12, 130, 140
Bennington, Geoffrey 59, 77
Bianchi, Aristide 143–44
Blanchot, Maurice 2, 6, 11, 22, 23, 28, 29, 50, 54, 64, 69, 76–77, 120, 129, 139–44, 148
Braun, Lucien 13, 29, 35, 50
Brecht, Bertold 81–82, 84, 98–99
Büchner, Georg 107

Celan, Paul 2, 4, 6, 106, 129, 131–36, 148
Cervantes, Miguel de 114–15

David, Alain 29
Derrida, Jacques 1, 2, 3, 6, 11, 12–13, 17–18, 19, 24, 28, 33, 34–35, 41, 47, 49–51, 53–61, 63–77, 81, 91–92, 106, 113, 117, 129–30, 139, 148, 152, 154
Deutsch, Michel 11, 51, 91, 93–94, 98–99
Dewey, John 131
Diderot, Denis 157

Euripides 83

Farias, Victor 34, 35, 38
Ferry, Luc 33, 46–47, 53
Fichte, Johann Gottlieb 22
Foucault, Michel 12, 69, 102
Freud, Sigmund 100, 108

Gadamer, Hans-Georg 50
Glass, Philip 109
Goethe, J. W. 22, 87–88, 114–15
Goldhill, Simon 100
Granel, Gérard 5, 35

Hegel, G. W. F. 4, 11, 14, 20, 25–26, 87, 96–97, 101–04, 106
Heidegger, Martin 2, 3, 4, 6, 11, 19, 29, 34–52, 53, 55, 57, 58, 64, 69–70, 73–74, 83, 87–88, 114, 131–33, 135, 139, 151–52, 156
Hölderlin, Friedrich 2, 3, 4, 6, 11, 23, 27–28, 35, 43–44, 52, 53, 83–84, 87–108, 109, 129–35, 148, 153, 156
Husserl, Edmund 37, 64

Jandin, Philippe 29
Jean Paul 30
Joyce, James 28

Kafka, Franza 111
Kant, Immanuel 20, 21
Kharmalov, Léonid 143–44
Kierkegaard, Søren 111
Kofman, Sarah 2, 11, 53–54, 56, 68, 130, 157

Lacan, Jacques 12, 53, 76, 107
Laporte, Roger 91, 129, 141–42, 148
Lévi-Strauss, Claude 19
Levinas, Emmanuel 12
Loos, Adolf 28
Lyotard, Jean-François 2, 27, 33, 35, 47, 50

Mallarmé, Stéphane 4, 76, 114, 131, 153
Mann, Thomas 153
Martis, John 4, 20–21, 152
Marx, Karl 39, 54
Montaigne, Michel de 27–28
Mozart, Wolfgang Amadeus 122

Nancy, Jean-Luc 1, 2, 3, 6, 11, 12–13, 14–29, 33–40, 43–44, 47–49, 53–58, 60, 65–66, 68–69, 82–85, 91, 107, 129–30, 143–44, 152–53, 155–57
Nietzsche, Friedrich 1, 4, 6, 14, 19, 20, 37, 41, 53, 57, 60–68, 75, 76, 83, 87, 98, 104, 106, 111–12, 116, 122, 128, 152, 154
Novalis 4, 17, 19

Parmenides 61–62
Pautrat, Bernard 68
Plato 15, 39, 58–59, 62, 65, 67–68, 71, 75, 84, 152
Proust, Marcel 28

Racine, Jean 27–28, 81, 153

Rancière, Jacques 33
Renault, Alain 46–47, 53
Romanticism 4, 5, 6, 11–13, 16–26, 48, 53, 111, 113–
    16, 120, 143, 152
Ronell, Avital 2
Rousseau, Jean-Jacques 27–28, 64, 111

Saïd, Suzanne 35
Sartre, Jean-Paul 50, 69–70, 77, 107
Schelling, F. W. J. 11, 19, 87, 96–97, 104, 116
Schiller, Friedrich 87–88, 101
Schlegel, August Wilhelm 17, 19, 25–26
Schlegel, Friedrich 4, 16–17, 19, 22, 143
Schleiermacher, F. D. E. 17
Shakespeare, William 114–15
Socrates 62, 65, 67, 69, 75, 152
Stiegler, Bernard 107
Strehler, Giorgio 84
Syberberg, Hans-Jürgen 35, 45, 107, 109

Steiner, George 35, 56, 90, 96
Situationism 11, 16, 29, 33
Sollers, Philippe 87
Sophocles 3, 6, 84, 87–97, 100, 103, 109, 114
Stendhal 27

Tel Quel 11–13, 18–19, 24, 55, 87, 130, 152
Todorov, Tzvetan 21
Tse-Tung, Mao 87

Vincent, Jean-Pierre 84
Voss, Johan Heinrich 87

Wagner, Richard 4, 13, 23, 109–12, 114–16, 120, 122
Wilson, Robert 84, 109

Zarathustra 65–68, 75, 152, 154
Zola, Emile 27